DUMBARTON OAKS
MEDIEVAL LIBRARY

Jan M. Ziolkowski, General Editor

ONE HUNDRED LATIN HYMNS

DOML 18

One Hundred Latin Hymns

Ambrose to Aquinas

Edited and Translated by

PETER G. WALSH

with CHRISTOPHER HUSCH

DUMBARTON OAKS
MEDIEVAL LIBRARY

HARVARD UNIVERSITY PRESS
CAMBRIDGE, MASSACHUSETTS
LONDON, ENGLAND
2012

Library of Congress Cataloging-in-Publication Data
One hundred Latin hymns : Ambrose to Aquinas / edited and translated
by Peter G. Walsh.
     p. cm. — (Dumbarton Oaks medieval library ; doml 18)
    English and Latin.
    Includes bibliographical references (p.) and indexes.
    ISBN 978-0-674-05773-9 (alk. paper)
    1. Hymns, Latin.   2. Hymns, Latin—Translations into English.
I. Walsh, Peter G.
  BV468.O5413 2012
  264'.23—dc23   2012015958

Contents

CONTENTS

Introduction

Hymns formed part of Christian community-worship from apostolic times. So, after the Last Supper, "When they had sung the hymn, they went out to the Mount of Olives."[1] Early examples of hymns deriving from Jewish practice are the Magnificat (the joyful song sung by the Virgin Mary at her Visitation to her cousin Elizabeth, Luke 1:46–55); the prophecy of Zechariah (Luke 1:57–59, also known as the Benedictus); the Sanctus (Isaiah 6:3, with the Benedictus adapted into the text used in the Catholic Order of Mass).[2] Saint Paul cites aretalogies, or biographies of great and divine figures, addressed to Christ at 1 Timothy 3:16 and 6:15–16. There is abundant evidence for hymn singing in Greek congregations during the first three centuries of our era, most famously in the Younger Pliny's letter to Trajan,[3] and also in the Greek Fathers. This long tradition of hymnody is asserted by Eusebius in the fourth century: "All the psalms and hymns," he says, "written from the beginning by faithful Christians sing of Christ as the Word of God, and address him as God."[4]

In the West, Tertullian's *Apology* provides early evidence of spontaneous singing ("Each, from what he knows of the Holy Scriptures, or from his own heart, is called before the rest to sing to God"), and Cyprian half a century later prescribes the singing of psalms ("Let a restrained banquet ring with psalms").[5] In fourth-century Gaul Hilary of Poitiers compiled a hymnbook *(Liber hymnorum)* after his return from exile in Asia in 360 CE, the three surviving fragments of which indicate that they were written in classical measures, their purpose being to combat the Arian heresy.[6] Following his conversion from Neoplatonism, Marius Victorinus composed three hymns on the Trinity written in psalmodic prose rather than in verses. Others at this period, such as Damasus (pope 366–384), wrote hymns in classical meters or in prose without regular accentual rhythm; Augustine, for example, composed his *Psalm against the Donatists* in sixteen-syllable lines as a development of such free prose.[7]

I

The great pioneer in Latin hymnody was Ambrose (ca. 334–397). His innovation was to compose for antiphonal singing, "according to the custom of the East,"[8] hymns of eight four-line stanzas in iambic dimeters, with little hiatus or elision, and without recurring rhyme. Their success was such that they were imitated continually by anonymous versifiers during the next millennium, so that it has proved difficult to distinguish those composed by Ambrose himself from those of his later imitators. Fontaine's authoritative edition[9] identifies hymns 1–14 in this collection as his. At least three of them are guaranteed by citations in Augustine, and the rest are either attested by other near contemporaries or closely echo sentiments expressed by Ambrose in his other writings. Hymns 1–4 are composed for singing at specific hours of the day, and others for feast days chronologically ordered.

Ambrose's letters document his unremitting polemic against the Arians at Milan,[10] and several hymns instruct his congregation on the orthodox doctrine of the Trinity, and especially on Christ's divinity, which was anathema to Arians (see hymns 2–3, 5, 7, 9). Other hymns glorify martyrs buried at Rome and at Milan; hymns 10–11, which venerate those associated with Milan, are likewise directed against Arians skeptical of claims made for the martyrs.

2

The *Te Deum* (hymn 15), which earlier tradition ascribed to Ambrose or Hilary or Augustine, was later attributed to Nicetas, the missionary bishop of Remesiana in modern Serbia, chiefly on the evidence of a dozen Irish manuscripts; but this identification is now challenged. Recent studies argue that the liturgical character of the hymn indicates that it derives from a Paschal Vigil. The petitions that form the second part of the hymn are a later addition. In the revised Breviary (1970, after the Second Vatican Council) the hymn is now inserted in the Office of Readings.[11]

3

The success of Ambrose's innovation was at once underlined by the adoption of it by the celebrated poet Prudentius from the province of Hispania (348–410). In his two books of hymns, the *Liber Cathemerinon* ("Hymns for Daily Use") and *Liber Peristephanon* ("Crowns of Glory," praises of martyrs in Hispania), Prudentius emulated Ambrose's use of the iambic dimeter in half of the hymns of the first, and in some of the hymns of the second, the rest being composed in other classical verse forms. The hymns were written for private recitation rather than for communal singing, being too long and literary for liturgical use. But sections of them were later incorporated into the old Spanish hymnary, and into the Mozarabic liturgy that flourished in Spain until the late eleventh century.[12]

The three hymns of Prudentius in this collection (16–18) are all from the *Liber Cathemerinon*. The first two were composed for reading at cock crow and in the morning office, and the third to celebrate the Christian burial of the dead.[13]

4

In Italy the Ambrosian legacy was embraced in the fifth century by Sedulius, author of the long poem *Carmen Paschale,* which in five books commemorates the marvels of the Old Testament and the miracles in the life of Christ from his conception to the Resurrection. Of the other poems of Sedulius that survive, the one included here (hymn 19) likewise presents the miracles of Christ's life to demonstrate that he is both God and man. It is written as an *abecedarius* or alphabetic poem of twenty-three stanzas, a form earlier used by Hilary and Augustine in imitation of the alphabetic psalms. The two hymns of Sedulius in the revised Breviary consist of selected stanzas from this, as cited in the prefatory comments on hymn 19 below.[14] The Ambrosian tradition was continued in the early sixth century by Ennodius (472–521), whose twelve extant hymns include the second fully Marian composition (preceded only by the Barcelona Hymn to the Virgin, which dates from the mid-fourth cen-

tury at the latest. See R. Roca-Puig, *Himne a la Verge Maria,
"Psalmus Responsorius": papir llatí del segle IV* [Barcelona,
1965]), as well as hymns celebrating specific religious festi-
vals. These works, however, are labored or primitive, and
none of them has been included here.

The greatest of the sixth-century hymn writers from Italy
was Venantius Fortunatus (ca. 535–610). He was born near
Ravenna, but after a pilgrimage to the shrine of Saint Mar-
tin at Tours to seek the cure of an eye ailment, he settled in
Merovingian Gaul and eventually became bishop of Poitiers. Of the seven hymns which are attributed to him in *AH*
50, four are certainly his. Two of them (20–21 in this collection), the trochaic *Pange, lingua* and the iambic *Vexilla regis,*
were composed as triumphal hymns to welcome at Poitiers a
relic of the True Cross. A third hymn, *Crux benedicta nitet*
(22), is composed in elegiac couplets. In these hymns the an-
tithetical teachings of Paul (the first versus the second
Adam, the tree of Eden versus the tree of Calvary, death versus resurrection) are presented with all their vigor of scriptural symbolism—the Cross as fruitful tree, Christ as the
hanging vine, the Victim as redeemer. The first two of the
three hymns make their way into the Breviary and play a
memorable part in the liturgy of Holy Week.[15]

5

The Old Hymnal, represented by hymns 23–35 in this collection, originated when Benedict in his Rule (ca. 540) made
hymns part of the daily Office. It consisted initially of fifteen hymns, one for each of the canonical hours (Nocturns,
Lauds, Prime, Terce, Sext, None, Vespers, and Compline),

one for each of the three feasts of Christmas, Epiphany, and Easter, and the rest in honor of saints and martyrs. The collection was reconstructed from the liturgy practiced at Milan and thereafter at Arles in the Rule established by Caesarius and continued by his successor, Aurelius. Benedict himself did not compose any of them. A manuscript now lost, which, it was claimed, was sent to Augustine of Canterbury by Gregory the Great, contained a hymnal closely resembling that of Benedict. The incipits of the fifteen hymns are recorded by Thomas of Elmham (late 14th/early 15th century); most (here hymns 1–6, 9, and 12) were composed by Ambrose. The venerable hymn *Mediae noctis tempus est* (28 in this volume) heads the list.[16]

Subsequently a new and more elaborate version of the Old Hymnal came into use in France and Germany. It is preserved in half a dozen manuscripts of the eighth and ninth centuries.[17] It offered a range of alternatives for each canonical hour, indicated in each case by the content. Most of the hymns assigned to the Old Hymnal in this collection belong to this expanded version.

6

The Old Hymnal remained in use on the continent of Europe until the Carolingian age, but in the course of the ninth and tenth centuries it fell out of use everywhere except at Milan, being replaced by the New Hymnal, which probably originated in France. In England it appears first at Durham in the mid-tenth century, and subsequently at Canterbury. It is represented in this collection by hymns 36–63, almost all of which are found in both the Durham hymnal and the

Canterbury hymnal, as the notes on each individual hymn indicate.[18]

7

In Ireland (where Christianity had spread from Gaul and Britain), evidence for the development of hymn writing comes from the Antiphonary of Bangor, compiled in northern Ireland in the seventh century, and also from the eleventh-century *Liber hymnorum*.[19] The earliest known Irish hymn, *Audite omnes amantes Deum,* a panegyric of Patrick ascribed to Secundinus (Sechnall), his fifth-century disciple, reflects features which become characteristic of Irish hymns generally. It is alphabetic, it is composed in the trochaic meter, and there is an abundance of alliteration and assonance. Irish hymnology is represented in this collection by *Altus Prosator* (hymn 64), which is persuasively if not certainly ascribed to Columba (ca. 521–597), founder of the monastery of Iona. This long hymn in praise of the Trinity recounts the history of the Creation from the birth of the angels, the fall of Lucifer, and the creation of the world to the Day of Judgment and the general resurrection. This hymn, like that of Secundinus, is an *abecedarius,* and is written in heavy iambic rhythm. It has regular rhyme and incorporates the arcane diction labeled "Hisperic" with its admixture of Hebraic and Greek words.[20]

The Anglo-Saxon hymnologists were greatly influenced by the Irish tradition. The most important among them are Æthelwald (a student of Aldhelm) and the Venerable Bede (ca. 673–735), who composed a *Liber hymnorum diverso metro sive rhythmo.*[21] His hymns are mostly in iambic trimeters, but

xiii

the best of them, the alphabetic *Alma Deus Trinitas*,[22] honoring Saint Etheldreda (Audrey), is in elegiac couplets and is epanalectic (that is, the first half of the hexameter is echoed in the second half of the pentameter, an Ovidian device also much affected by Carolingian poets). Another of Bede's compositions, *De die iudicii*, is in hexameters and exercised strong influence on the *Dies irae*. Bede is represented in this collection by his exultant Easter hymn, *Laetare caelum desuper* (hymn 65).[23] Alcuin of York (ca. 740–804) extended the Anglo-Saxon learned tradition, but the ten hymns edited by Dümmler[24] have an academic ring which detracts from their impact.

8

Alcuin's presence at the court of Aachen and subsequently at Tours helped to stimulate a renaissance in hymnology. Paul the Deacon has three hymns ascribed to him in *AH* 50, one of which, *Ut queant laxis resonare fibris*, a hymn in sapphics honoring John the Baptist, is regarded as one of the best of the Carolingian era, but the attribution is not wholly certain. Paulinus of Aquileia, a learned theologian whose compositions reflect deep meditation on the scriptures, is represented by nine hymns in *AH* 50. The famous *Ubi caritas et amor*, composed for Holy Thursday, has been ascribed to him,[25] but the attribution remains uncertain. Another outstanding hymnodist of the age is Theodulf of Orléans (ca. 750–821); of his four hymns in *AH* 50, the splendid *Gloria, laus, et honor*, traditionally the processional on Palm Sunday, has been included in this collection (hymn 74). It is clear from a reference in the hymn that it was composed after Theodulf was deposed from his see and was incarcerated in the monastery of Saint Aubin at Angers. A pervasive feature of Carolingian hymnody is the increasing deployment of classical meters and motifs, reflecting the increasing prominence of classical authors in the education of clerics.

9

The Carolingian revival of learning had a conspicuous effect on the German monasteries. Hrabanus Maurus, a pupil of Alcuin at Tours, and later abbot of Fulda and archbishop of Mainz, was a prolific versifier. Twenty-seven hymns are ascribed to him in *AH* 50, but scholars are skeptical about these attributions, especially for the hymn *Veni, creator Spiritus* (hymn 75 below).[26] This consecration hymn for bishops and monarchs became widely popular as the hymn sung at Vespers on Pentecost Sunday, and nowadays it is frequently heard at the conferment of the sacrament of Confirmation. Walahfrid Strabo of Reichenau, a pupil of Hrabanus Maurus at Fulda, had a deeper vein of talent, as shown in his eleven hymns in *AH* 50; they reflect a wide appreciation of earlier poetry, classical as well as Christian. Gottschalk of Fulda, the heterodox theologian, was, like his friend Walahfrid, impressively learned. Only six hymns are attributed to him in *AH* 50, but ten others are established as his; they are marked by a deep sense of remorse at human guilt, but this is combined with expression of hope in God's mercy.[27]

10

Meanwhile, at the Benedictine monastery of Saint Gall, the poetic form of the *tropus* and the Sequence were undergoing significant development. The *tropus* was initially a gloss on the Introit, Kyrie, Gradual, Offertory, or Communion of the Mass. Beginning as a prose piece, it gradually developed rhyme and assonance. The Sequence similarly arose from the Proper of the Mass; at the close of the Gradual, the prolonged final -*a* of the Alleluia began to be replaced by a prose meditation with a syllable for each note of the melisma, to aid in memorization of the music; the words of this became known as *prosa* or *sequentia*.[28] It was Notker Balbulus at Saint Gall who was responsible for the transformation into poetic form; whereas the earlier Sequences composed in France and Spain were unstructured and unlearned, the German compositions as shaped by Notker are more correct in their Latinity and more supple in their rhythm and rhyme.[29] The foundation was thus laid for the evolution of the genre, which attained an intermediate stage with Wipo and Hermannus Contractus (Hermann the Cripple). Wipo in the first half of the eleventh century composed the *Victimae paschali laudes* (hymn 76 in this collection), which became the Sequence for the Easter Sunday Mass; and to Hermann are assigned not only several Sequences, but more dubiously the celebrated Marian antiphon *Alma Redemptoris mater*.[30]

During the eleventh and twelfth centuries, the cathedral schools and monasteries of France were the source of a flood of fine hymns. At Chartres, Fulbert (970–1038) in promoting the new era of Christian humanism wrote hymns more literary than liturgical; of the twelve attributed to him in *AH* 50, only three are certainly his, though the rest are clearly products of his school.[31] Other important figures of this era who turned their talents to hymnody are Marbod of

Rennes, Baudri of Bourgueil, Guido of Bazoches, Peter the
Venerable, Bernard of Clairvaux (*Dulcis Iesu memoria* is not
his, though it has been attributed to him), and Aimar of Le
Puy, whose *Salve Regina* (hymn 77 in this collection) is regularly sung at Compline.[32]

The most original and powerful talent among the hymn
writers of the twelfth century is Peter Abelard (1079–1142).
At the request of Heloise and her community at the Oratory
of the Paraclete, Peter composed hymns for the whole cycle
of the year in his Paraclete hymnbook *(Hymnarius Paraclitensis).*[33] It falls into three parts: *Hymni nocturnales et diurni*
(twenty-nine hymns for the various hours of the daily Office), *Hymni festorum* (forty-seven hymns to celebrate major
feasts of the Church), and *Hymni sanctorum* (fifty-two hymns
for the feast days of saints). Though the compositions incorporate familiar motifs and techniques from the Old Testament, learned explanations of the senses of scripture, and
subtle evocations of earlier hymns that had become classics
in the genre, there are strikingly original features of content
and style, and they demand of the reader the most careful
attention and reflection. Peter's genius as hymnologist can
be classed with that of Ambrose, and for that reason thirteen of his hymns are included in this collection (hymns 78–
90). The first, *O quanta qualia,* is the most celebrated of
them; it appears among the "Day Hymns," to be sung at Vespers on the Sabbath, and its theme is the eternal Sabbath
that we are to enjoy in heaven. The other twelve comprise
three groups of four, each group celebrating a major feast
(Christmas, Epiphany, and Ascension). Peter also composed
a series of *planctus* (laments) on such Old Testament themes
as the murder of Jephtha's daughter.[34]

11

Another prominent hymn writer in Peter Abelard's day was Adam of Saint Victor (d. 1146), who is acknowledged as the master composer of the Sequence. Already by the end of the eleventh century, however, many Sequences had attained the technical perfection that we associate particularly with Adam: close correspondence of word accent with line stress, regular caesura, consistent double-syllabic rhyme, and couplets consisting of a combination of eight-syllable and seven-syllable lines. Thus the forty-five Sequences selected for their perfection of form from the earliest Victorine graduals, and assigned to Adam in *AH* 54, cannot all be attributed with certainty to Adam himself, though they will have originated in his abbey. *Salve, mater Salvatoris* (hymn 91 in this collection), the best-known of the Sequences attributed to him, illustrates the prominence of the Virgin Mary in these hymns and the fondness for elaborate symbolism that is a feature of Victorine Sequences. Another Augustinian, Alexander Neckham (1157–1217), and his contemporary Philip the Chancellor (d. 1236/7), composed Sequences on similar themes.[35]

Philip's *Pange, lingua, Magdalenae* (hymn 92 in this collection) is one of several hymns devoted to Mary Magdalene, whom he identified (perhaps wrongly) with the woman who washed and anointed Christ's feet. Perhaps the most celebrated of all these hymns is the so-called "Golden Sequence," *Veni, sancte Spiritus* (hymn 94 in this collection), which is sung at Pentecost. Although two possible authors of this hymn, Pope Innocent III and Stephen Langton, Archbishop of Canterbury (ca. 1150–1228),[36] are mentioned by contemporaries, the sequence is now regarded as anonymous.[37]

12

The grand climax of the medieval Latin hymn is reached in the thirteenth century with the advent of the new religious orders of friars. The Dominican Thomas Aquinas (1225–1274) composed the Office for the recently instituted feast of Corpus Christi at the request of Pope Urban IV. In the Sequence *Lauda, Sion, Salvatorem,* the hymn for Lauds *Verbum supernum prodiens,* and the hymn for Vespers *Pange, lingua* (96–98 in this collection), Thomas encapsulates in beautifully controlled rhyming verses the doctrine of the Real Presence in the Eucharist, which he later expounded at greater length in the *Summa theologiae* (3.75–77). There is also fair certainty that he composed the devotional hymn *Adoro devote.*[38] Aquinas's compositions inspired other Eucharistic hymns later in the century and in the next, including the anonymous *Ave, verum corpus,* which has become a perennial favorite in church liturgy because of the musical setting by Mozart.

In contrast to this controlled and philosophic hymnody of Saint Thomas, the contributions of the Franciscan hymnodists are more devotional and personal, being focused especially on the sufferings of Jesus and his mother. The most majestic of medieval Sequences, the *Dies irae* (hymn 95 in this collection), is usually credited to Thomas of Celano, disciple and biographer of Saint Francis; but his role may have been the more modest one of infusing an existing

Benedictine meditation with a more penitential flavor.[39] The hymn is a meditation on the Last Judgment, contrasting the awful justice of the Father in the Old Testament with the tender compassion of the Son in the New. The hymn owes much to the *responsorium* in the Mass for the Dead, *Libera me,* and to earlier poetic treatments from that of the Venerable Bede onward.[40]

Saint Bonaventure (1221–1274), better known as a scholastic theologian and philosopher in the Augustinian tradition, was another Franciscan who made a notable contribution to hymnody. Perhaps the best-known composition attributed to him is *Recordare sanctae crucis,* though like so many medieval hymns it is attributed to a variety of authors, including Bernard of Clairvaux, Alexander Neckham, and Jacopone da Todi.[41] Of the eight hymns which Bonaventure wrote for the Office of the Holy Cross, *In passione Domini* (93 in this collection) offers a characteristic example of authentically Franciscan subject and treatment. A similar judgment can be made of *Stabat mater* (100 in this collection), which is usually ascribed to Jacopone da Todi. The attribution is far from certain, but the hymn certainly breathes the spirituality of a Franciscan friar.[42]

13

With few exceptions these hymns have been incorporated into the Roman Breviary, but with some revision of the texts. Many hymns had of necessity to be abbreviated for liturgical use; in others a conventional doxology has been appended as the final stanza. In the seventeenth century a major revision was undertaken by Urban VIII (pope 1623–

1644), who enlisted the aid of four Jesuit scholars to meet humanist standards of metrics and Latinity.[43] Since then minor revisions have continued to be made, dictated by theological considerations on the one hand and by advances in the scholarship of hymnody on the other. The texts in this collection adhere to the original wordings, and accordingly differ in some instances from versions in the Breviary.

I would like to record my gratitude to the editorial committee of the Dumbarton Oaks project for their ready acceptance of my manuscript for publication and especially to the chief movers Professors Danuta Shanzer and Jan Ziolkowski. I also wish to thank Christopher Husch for his careful and perspicacious scrutiny of my typescript for publication. Thanks must also be extended to Professors Roger Wright, Danuta Shanzer, and Michael Winterbottom, who assisted with reviewing the manuscript at a crucial stage. The gracious assistance of members of my family was also most welcome in my hour of need.

P. G. Walsh

The translations given in the English do not reproduce the Latin rhyme-schemes, but imitate the Latin meters faithfully, with the following exceptions: the elegiac couplets of hymns 22 and 74 are rendered by iambic hexameters alternating with pentameters, and the iambic hexameter of hymn 78 by iambic pentameter. Hymn 53 is rendered in more loose iambic lines, rather than strict octosyllables. I have attempted to render the acrostic in hymn 64; Q was impossible, but it may amuse the reader to imagine the word *Who* which begins stanza 16 to be spelled in its archaic Scottish spelling *Quho*. In hymns 77 and 76 the translation loosely follows the rhythm of the original, in the interest of avoiding strained artificiality. The meter of the translation of 94 is two syllables shorter than the Latin, which allows for a leaner and more powerful rendering, and that of 95 catalectic, for convenience. Again for convenience, 99's trochaic trimeter catalectic is converted into iambs.

In the notes, translations from classical and patristic authors are taken from the Loeb editions where they exist and otherwise are Professor Walsh's or my own. Latin and English Bible quotations are taken from the DOML edition of the Vulgate and of the 1750/1752 Douay-Rheims translation.

Christopher Husch

The contents of this volume were prepared originally two decades ago but set aside. The general editor and especially the Medieval Latin editor, with considerable help from Roger Wright and Michael Winterbottom, have overseen its careful preparation for publication by Christopher Husch. Peter Walsh himself approved the manuscript after initial copyediting and made minor revisions, and many small changes and additions have been made for consistency and for updating. At the same time, no one involved in readying the book for print has believed that it would be necessary or desirable to tamper with the basic strength and character of Peter Walsh's voice and scholarship by revising extensively.

NOTES

1 So Mk 14:26, Mt 26:30.

2 Lk 1:46–55, 1:68–79; for the *Sanctus,* see hymn 15.3.1n. below.

3 *Ep.* 10.96.7, "Carmen Christo quasi deo dicere" (Singing a song to Christ as God). A. N. Sherwin-White's commentary on Pliny's letters (*The Letters of Pliny: A Historical and Social Commentary,* Oxford, 1966) has a full bibliography.

4 *Eccl. Hist.* 5.28.5–6

5 Tertullian, *Apol.* 39.18; Cyprian, *Ad Donat.* 16.

6 Ed. A. Feder, *CSEL* 65, 209–16; W. Bulst, *Hymni Latini Antiquissimi LXXV, Psalmi III* (Heidelberg, 1956), 31–35.

7 Ed. P. Lambot, *Revue Bénédictine* 47 (1935): 312–30.

8 So Augustine, *Conf.* 9.7.15.

9 Fontaine, *Hymnes.*

10 See N. B. McLynn, *Church and Court in a Christian Capital* (Berkeley, 1994).

11 Morin's ascription to Nicetas (see hymn 15n.) was supported by Burn, *Hymn Te Deum.* For a reassessment linking it with a Paschal Vigil, see E. Kahler, *Studien zum Te Deum und zur Geschichte des 24 Psalms in der alten Kirche* (Göttingen, 1958).

12 For the Mozarabic hymnary, see *AH,* vol. 27, and J. Szövérffy, *Iberian Hymnody* (Albany, 1971).

13 On Prudentius, see the edition of M. P. Cunningham, *CCL* 126 (1966). There are translations by H. J. Thomson in the Loeb series, by M. C. Eagan in the *Fathers of the Church* series, and by David R. Slavitt. On hymns 16 and 17 below there is an informative commentary by van Assendelft, *Sol ecce surgit igneus.*

14 The text of hymn 19 is presented with commentary by Walpole, *Early Latin Hymns,*151–58.

15 For Fortunatus and his background, see J. W. George, *Venantius Fortunatus, a Poet in Merovingian Gaul* (Oxford, 1992); on the hymns, J. Szövérffy, "Venantius Fortunatus and the Earliest Hymns to the Holy Cross," *Classical Folia* 20 (1966): 107–22.

16 I. B. Milfull, *The Hymns of the Anglo-Saxon Church,* 1–5.

17 See H. Gneuss, *Hymnar und Hymnen in englischen Mittelalter* (Göttingen, 1965), 443.

18 On the Durham Hymnary, see Milfull, *The Hymns of the Anglo-Saxon Church*. For the Canterbury Hymnal, see Wieland, *The Canterbury Hymnal*.

19 The Bangor Antiphonary is edited by P. S. Warren (London, 1893–1895), the *Liber Hymnorum* by J. H. Barnard and R. Atkinson (London, 1898).

20 Critical edition by C. Blume, *AH* 51, 275–83; annotation in Barnard–Atkinson, *Liber Hymnorum*, 2:142–69.

21 So Bede himself, *Eccl. Hist.* 5.24.

22 Bede was so proud of this hymn that he included it in his *Ecclesiastical History* (4.20).

23 Bede's hymns are assembled in *AH* 50 and in *CCL* 122; see also W. Bulst, *Zeitschrift für deutsches Altertum* 89 (1958–59): 83–91.

24 *MGH, Poetae Latini Aevi Carolini*, vol. 1; also in *AH* 50.

25 So D. L. Norberg, *La poésie latine rhythmique du Haut Moyen Âge* (Stockholm, 1954), 91–92.

26 For doubts, see Raby, *CLP* 183 with earlier scholars cited there. Some supporting evidence for Hrabanus Maurus's authorship appears in P. Godman, *Poetry of the Carolingian Renaissance* (London, 1985), 246–47.

27 On Walahfrid and Gottschalk, see Raby, *CLP* 183–89, 189–92. The additional hymns of Gottschalk are edited by Strecker–Schumann in *MGH, Poetae Latini*, vol. 6, pt. 1, 86–106.

28 On the origins of the Sequence, see W. von den Steinen, "Die Anfänge der Sequenzdichtung," *Zeitschrift für Schweizerische Kirchengeschichte* 40 (1946): 190–212; 41 (1947): 19–48, 122–162.

29 On Notker, see W. von den Steinen, *Notker der Dichter.*

30 On Wipo, see Raby, *CLP* 217–19; on Hermann and the authorship of *Alma Redemptoris mater,* Raby 226–27; M. Manitius, *Geschichte der lateinischen Literatur des Mittelalters* (Munich, 1923), 2:777.

31 On Fulbert's background, F. Behrends, ed., *The Letters and Poems of Fulbert of Chartres* (Oxford, 1976). On his hymns, Raby, *CLP* 258–64; J. Szövérffy, *Die Annalen der Lateinischen Hymnendichtung,* 1:353–57.

32 See Raby, *CLP* 227 (Aimar); 273–77 (Marbod); 277–85 (Baudri); 306–9 (Guido); 326–31 (Bernard). For the authorship of *Dulcis Iesu memoria,* see A. Wilmart, *Le "Jubilus" dit de Saint Bernard* (Rome, 1944).

33 Szövérffy, *Peter Abelard's Hymnarius Paraclitensis.* Also C. Waddell, ed., *Hymn Collections from the Paraclete,* 2 vols. (Gethsemani, 1987), which pays more attention to musical and liturgical aspects. For a judicious commen-

tary embracing the approaches of both these scholars, see the unpublished PhD thesis of Patricia H. Woods, *The Festival Hymns of Peter Abelard* (Glasgow, 1991).

34 See the editions of W. Meyer (Erlangen, 1890), and G. Vecchi (Modena, 1951).

35 Neckham's hymns are in *AH* 48, Philip the Chancellor's in *AH* 52.

36 See Raby, *CLP* 342–44.

37 See Petrus W. Tax, "Zur Verfasserschaft und Entstehungszeit der Pfingstsequenz 'Veni, sancte spiritus,'" *Zeitschrift für deutsches Altertum und deutsche Literatur* 135.1 (2006): 13–20.

38 For the ascription of *Adoro devote* (hymn 99 below) to Aquinas, see Raby, *Speculum* 20 (1945): 236–38.

39 See K. Vellekoop, *Dies Irae, Dies Illa: Studien zur Frühgeschichte einer Sequenz* (Bilthoven, 1978).

40 See the fine discussion in Raby, *CLP* 443–452.

41 Text in *AH* 50; see Raby, *CLP* 421–24.

42 Raby, *CLP* 437–43.

43 P. Battifol, *Histoire du Breviaire romain,* 2nd ed. (Paris, 1911; English translation 1912).

AMBROSE

I

Aeterne rerum conditor

1. Aeterne rerum conditor,
   noctem diemque qui regis,
   et temporum das tempora
   ut alleves fastidium,

2. Praeco diei iam sonat,
   noctis profundae pervigil,
   nocturna lux viantibus,
   a nocte noctem segregans.

3. Hoc excitatus lucifer
   solvit polum caligine,
   hoc omnis errorum chorus
   vias nocendi deserit.

4. Hoc nauta vires colligit,
   pontique mitescunt freta;
   hoc ipse petra ecclesiae
   canente culpam diluit.

5. Surgamus ergo strenue;
   gallus iacentes excitat
   et somnolentos increpat;
   gallus negantes arguit.

Hymn 1

Eternal founder of the world

1. Eternal founder of the world,
   who rule the night and day, and give
   the seasons their established times
   to lend relief to wearied lives:

2. The herald of the day sounds forth,
   unsleeping through the depths of night;
   a light to travelers in the dark,
   he splits the watches of the night.

3. His crowing stirs the light-bringer
   to liberate the sky from gloom;
   by him the vagrant demons' band
   does quit the paths where they deal harm.

4. By him the sailor stirs his strength,
   and the sea's rough waters calm themselves;
   by him the church's rock himself,
   hearing him crow, washed out his guilt.

5. So let us rise with forceful haste;
   the cock roots out the lie-abeds
   and castigates the sleepy-eyes;
   the cock rebukes those who deny.

6. Gallo canente spes redit,
   aegris salus refunditur,
   mucro latronis conditur,
   lapsis fides revertitur.

7. Iesu, labantes respice,
   et nos videndo corrige;
   si respicis, lapsus cadunt,
   fletuque culpa solvitur.

8. Tu lux refulge sensibus,
   mentisque somnum discute;
   te nostra vox primum sonet,
   et vota solvamus tibi.

II

Splendor paternae gloriae

1. Splendor paternae gloriae,
   de luce lucem proferens,
   lux lucis et fons luminis,
   dies dierum inluminans,

2. Verusque sol, inlabere,
   micans nitore perpeti,
   iubarque sancti Spiritus
   infunde nostris sensibus.

6.　　When the cock crows, hope is restored,
　　　well-being floods back on the sick,
　　　the highwayman's sword finds its sheath,
　　　the faith returns to who have slipped.

7.　　Jesus, observe the wavering,
　　　and by your glancing put us straight;
　　　when you look back, our failures fall,
　　　and guilt is washed away by tears.

8.　　Pour forth your light upon our hearts,
　　　and break the sleep that grips our minds.
　　　Your name let our voice first proclaim,
　　　and us our prayers to you discharge.

Hymn 2

O radiance of the Father's glory

1.　　O radiance of the Father's glory,
　　　from his light light engendering,
　　　the light of light and fount of light,
　　　the day that lend your light to days,

2.　　And the true sun, glide down on us,
　　　flashing with an enduring glow,
　　　and pour the Holy Spirit's bright rays
　　　deeply into our consciousness.

3. Votis vocemus et Patrem
—Patrem perennis gloriae,
Patrem potentis gloriae—
culpam releget lubricam,

4. Informet actus strenuos,
dentem retundat invidi,
casus secundet asperos,
donet gerendi gratiam,

5. Mentem gubernet et regat
casto fideli corpore;
fides calore ferveat,
fraudis venena nesciat.

6. Christusque nobis sit cibus,
potusque noster sit fides;
laeti bibamus sobriam
ebrietatem Spiritus.

7. Laetus dies hic transeat,
pudor sit ut diluculum,
fides sicut meridies,
crepusculum mens nesciat.

8. Aurora cursus provehit,
aurora totus prodeat,
in Patre totus Filius,
et totus in Verbo Pater.

3. The Father, too, let us implore
    —the Father of enduring fame,
    the Father of such potent glory—
    to banish our pernicious guilt,

4. To shape us to incisive action,
    to blunt the tooth of the envious one,
    to turn to good our harsh reverses,
    to grant us grace for what we do,

5. Our minds to rule and rightly steer,
    keeping our bodies faithful, pure;
    so let our faith with ardor glow,
    avoid the poisons of deceit.

6. Then let Christ be our sustenance,
    and let faith be the drink we seek;
    so may we joyfully imbibe
    the Spirit's sober drunkenness.

7. Joyfully may this day pass by,
    our purity be as the dawn,
    our faith as ardent as noonday,
    our minds not clouded when dusk falls.

8. The dawn advances forth its course,
    let our dawn in his wholeness come,
    the Son's whole essence in the Father,
    and the Father wholly in his Word.

III

Iam surgit hora tertia

1. Iam surgit hora tertia
   qua Christus ascendit crucem;
   nil insolens mens cogitet,
   intendat affectum precis.

2. Qui corde Christum suscipit
   innoxium sensum gerit,
   votisque praestat sedulis
   sanctum mereri Spiritum.

3. Haec hora quae finem dedit
   diri veterno criminis,
   mortisque regnum diruit,
   culpamque ab aevo sustulit.

4. Hinc iam beata tempora
   coepere Christi gratia;
   fidei replevit veritas
   totum per orbem ecclesias.

5. Celsus triumphi vertice
   matri loquebatur suae:
   "En, filius, mater, tuus";
   apostolo, "En mater tua,"

Hymn 3

Now dawns the third hour of the day

1. Now dawns the third hour of the day,
the hour when Christ mounted the cross;
let our minds harbor no proud thought,
but foster eagerness for prayer.

2. He who takes Christ into his heart
controls his thoughts all free of blame;
by constant prayers deserves to win
the Holy Spirit's presence there.

3. This is the hour that brought an end
to that long-standing grievous sin,
demolished then the realm of death,
and rid the world of ancient guilt.

4. From that time on our blessed days
began, through merit of Christ's grace;
through all the world the truth of faith
has filled the churches everywhere.

5. He on high from his triumph's peak
addressed his mother with these words:
"O mother, here behold your son";
to John: "Behold your mother here,"

6. Praetenta nuptae foedera
   alto docens mysterio,
   ne virginis partus sacer
   matris pudorem laederet.

7. Cui fidem caelestibus
   Iesus dedit miraculis,
   nec credidit plebs impia;
   qui credidit salvus erit.

8. Nos credimus natum Deum
   partumque virginis sacrae,
   peccata qui mundi tulit,
   ad dexteram sedens Patris.

IV

Deus, creator omnium

1. Deus, creator omnium
   polique rector, vestiens
   diem decoro lumine,
   noctem soporis gratia,

2. Artus solutos ut quies
   reddat laboris usui,
   mentesque fessas allevet,
   luctusque solvat anxios:

6.   Thus teaching that her bridal pact
    concealed this mystery profound:
    the virgin's sacred birth would not
    impair the mother's chastity.

7.   Jesus, by heavenly miracles,
    provided proof that this was so.
    The impious mob withheld belief;
    he who believed will sure be saved.

8.   We do believe the birth of God,
    sprung from the sacred virgin's womb;
    he bore the sins of all the world,
    and now sits at his Father's right.

Hymn 4

O God, creator of all things

1.   O God, creator of all things,
    the heavens' ruler, you who dress
    the day with its enhancing light,
    night with the welcome gift of sleep,

2.   That rest may let our limbs relax,
    restore them for the tasks of toil,
    and succor bring to wearied minds,
    relieve us from our harrowing griefs:

3. Grates peracto iam die,
    et noctis exortu preces
    voti reos ut adiuves,
    hymnum cantantes solvimus.

4. Te cordis ima concinant,
    te vox canora concrepet,
    te diligat castus amor,
    te mens adoret sobria,

5. Ut cum profunda clauserit
    diem caligo noctium,
    fides tenebras nesciat,
    et nox fide reluceat.

6. Dormire mentem ne sinas,
    dormire culpa noverit;
    castis fides refrigerans
    somni vaporem temperet.

7. Exuta sensu lubrico
    te cordis alta somnient,
    nec hostis invidi dolo
    pavor quietos suscitet.

8. Christum rogamus et Patrem,
    Christi Patrisque Spiritum,
    unum potens per omnia,
    fove precantes, Trinitas.

3. At this day's end we render thanks,
    singing this hymn to you; likewise
    now at the rising of the night
    we beg your aid to pay our vows.

4. May heartfelt feeling sing your name,
    may tuneful voices you proclaim,
    may our chaste love now cherish you,
    may sober minds now you adore,

5. That once the shadow of the night
    with its dark depths cuts short the day,
    our faith may know no shadowy gloom,
    and night may glitter with that faith.

6. Let not our minds succumb to sleep,
    but let our faults embrace that sleep;
    may faith refresh and cool chaste hearts
    and temper the hot fumes of sleep.

7. Dispelling every wicked thought,
    let our hearts' deepness dream of you,
    nor let the envious foe's deceit
    cause fear to stir us from our rest.

8. Christ and the Father we implore,
    the Spirit of Christ and the Father,
    one power that pervades all things,
    as we pray, aid us, Trinity.

V

Intende, qui regis Israel

1. Intende, qui regis Israel,
   super Cherubim qui sedes,
   appare Ephrem coram, excita
   potentiam tuam, et veni.

2. Veni, redemptor gentium;
   ostende partum virginis:
   miretur omne saeculum;
   talis decet partus Deo.

3. Non ex virili semine
   sed mystico spiramine
   Verbum Dei factum est caro,
   fructusque ventris floruit.

4. Alvus tumescit virginis,
   claustrum pudoris permanet;
   vexilla virtutum micant,
   versatur in templo Deus.

5. Procedat e thalamo suo,
   pudoris aula regia,
   geminae gigas substantiae
   alacris ut currat viam.

Hymn 5

Give ear, O king of Israel

1.   Give ear, O king of Israel,
     seated above the Cherubim,
     appear before Ephraim's face,
     stir up thy mightiness, and come.

2.   Redeemer of the Gentiles, come;
     show forth the birth from virgin's womb;
     let every age show wonderment;
     such birth is fitting for our God.

3.   Not issuing from husband's seed,
     but from the Spirit's mystic breath,
     God's Word was fashioned into flesh,
     and thrived as fruit of Mary's womb.

4.   The virgin's womb begins to swell;
     her maidenhead remains intact:
     the banners of her virtues gleam;
     God in his temple lives and stirs.

5.   From his chamber let him come forth,
     the royal court of chastity,
     as giant of his twin natures
     eager to hasten on his way.

6. Egressus eius a Patre,
    regressus eius ad Patrem;
    excursus usque ad inferos,
    recursus ad sedem Dei.

7. Aequalis aeterno Patri,
    carnis tropaeo accingere,
    infirma nostri corporis
    virtute firmans perpeti.

8. Praesepe iam fulget tuum,
    lumenque nox spirat novum,
    quod nulla nox interpolet,
    fideque iugi luceat.

VI

Amore Christi nobilis

1. Amore Christi nobilis,
    et filius tonitrui,
    arcana Ioannis Dei
    fatu revelavit sacro.

2. Captis solebat piscibus
    patris senectam pascere;
    turbante dum natat salo,
    immobilis fide stetit.

6. First from the Father he set forth,
   then to his Father he returns;
   he sallies to the realms below,
   then journeys back to God's abode.

7. You are the eternal Father's peer;
   gird on your trophy of the flesh,
   and strengthen with your constant power
   the frailties of our bodies' frame.

8. Your manger now is all aglow,
   the night breathes forth a light unknown;
   a light that never night may shroud,
   and that shall gleam with constant faith.

Hymn 6

John, celebrated by Christ's love

1. John, celebrated by Christ's love,
   and "son of thunder," did reveal
   in words of sacred utterance
   the hidden mysteries of God.

2. His custom was to harvest fish
   to feed his father in old age;
   while tossed upon the turbulent deep,
   he persevered, steadfast in faith.

3. Hamum profundo merserat,
    piscatus est verbum Dei,
    iactavit undis retia,
    vitam levavit omnium.

4. Piscis bonus pia est fides
    mundi supernatans salo,
    subnixa Christi pectore,
    sancto locuta Spiritu:

5. "In principio erat Verbum,
    et Verbum erat apud Deum,
    et Deus erat Verbum. Hoc erat
    in principio apud Deum.

6. Omnia per ipsum facta sunt."
    Sic laudet ipse, sic sonet,
    et laureatus Spiritu
    scriptis coronetur suis.

7. Commune multis passio,
    cruorque delictum lavans;
    hoc morte praestat martyrum
    quod fecit esse martyres.

8. Vinctus tamen ab impiis
    calente olivo dicitur
    tersisse mundi pulverem,
    stetisse victor aemuli.

3.   He plunged his hook into the deep,
the word of God was what he caught;
he cast his nets into the waves,
in them he raised true life for all.

4.   The good fish is devoted faith,
which swims upon the world's salt sea,
reclining on the breast of Christ,
and speaking with the Holy Spirit:

5.   "In the beginning was the Word,
and the Word was with God,
and the Word was God. The same
was in the beginning with God.

6.   All things were made by him." Just so
let him speak praise, just so sound forth;
for his writings let him be crowned
with laurel as the Spirit's gift.

7.   Many experience suffering,
and bloodshed that expunges sin;
but this transcends the martyrs' deaths,
this justifies their martyrdom.

8.   When cast in chains by wicked men,
with the hot oil, the story goes,
he cleansed the foul dust of this world,
stood victor over the envious one.

VII

Illuminans altissimus

1. Illuminans altissimus
   micantium astrorum globos,
   pax vita lumen veritas,
   Iesu, fave precantibus,

2. Seu mystico baptismate
   fluenta Iordanis retro
   conversa quondam tertio
   praesenti sacraris die;

3. Seu stella partum virginis
   caelo micans signaverit,
   et hoc adoratum die
   praesepe magos duxerit;

4. Vel hydriis plenis aquae
   vini saporem infuderis;
   hausit minister conscius
   quod ipse non impleverat,

5. Aquas colorari videns,
   inebriare flumina;
   mutata elementa stupent
   transire in usus alteros.

Hymn 7

O Christ most high, affording light

1. O Christ most high, affording light
    to the spheres of brightly gleaming stars,
    our peace and life and light and truth,
    Jesus, show favor when we pray,

2. Whether, by your mystic baptism,
    you consecrated on this day
    the waters of the Jordan, which
    three times of old turned back their course;

3. Or if the star flashing in heaven
    marked out the virgin's pangs of birth,
    and led the Magi on this day
    before the manger to adore;

4. Or if in vessels water-filled
    you introduced the taste of wine:
    the steward sampled it, and knew
    that this was not what he'd poured in,

5. Seeing the water change its hue,
    the poured-out stream cause drunkenness;
    the altered elements marvel
    that they pass to another use.

6. Sic quinque milibus virum
   dum quinque panes dividit,
   edentium sub dentibus
   in ore crescebat cibus,

7. Multiplicabatur magis
   dispendio panis suo.
   Quis haec videns mirabitur
   iugos meatus fontium?

8. Inter manus frangentium
   panis rigatur profluus;
   intacta quae non fregerant
   fragmenta subrepunt viris.

VIII

Agnes beatae virginis

1. Agnes beatae virginis
   natalis est, quo spiritum
   caelo refudit debitum
   pio sacrata sanguine.

2. Matura martyrio fuit,
   matura nondum nuptiis;
   nutabat in viris fides,
   cedebat et fessus senex.

6.   Thus, when unto five thousand men
      he portioned out five loaves of bread,
      the food grew greater in their mouths
      beneath their teeth that chewed on it;

7.   The bread increased in quantity
      the more it was itself used up.
      Who, noting this, will be surprised
      that springs issue perpetually?

8.   When broken by their clutching hands
      the bread pours forth abundantly;
      the fragments which they do not break
      creep whole into disciples' hands.

Hymn 8

It is the day of Agnes's birth

1.   It is the day of Agnes's birth,
      a virgin blessed; she on this day
      her life, to heaven owed, paid back,
      made holy with devoted blood.

2.   She was of age for martyrdom,
      but not yet old enough to wed;
      among men faith was wavering,
      and weary elders yielded too.

3. Metu parentes territi
    claustrum pudoris auxerant;
    solvit fores custodiae
    fides teneri nescia.

4. Prodire quis nuptum putet,
    sic laeta vultu ducitur,
    novas viro ferens opes,
    dotata censu sanguinis.

5. Aras nefandi numinis
    adolere taedis cogitur;
    respondet: "Haud tales faces
    sumpsere Christi virgines;

6. Hic ignis exstinguit fidem,
    haec flamma lumen eripit.
    Hic, hic ferite! Ut profluo
    cruore restinguam focos."

7. Percussa quam pompam tulit!
    Nam veste se totam tegens,
    curam pudoris praestitit
    ne quis retectam cerneret.

8. In morte vivebat pudor,
    vultumque texerat manu.
    Terram genu flexo petit,
    lapsu verecundo cadens.

3. Her parents, paralyzed by fear,
    reinforced her purity's defense.
    But faith, which recognized no bonds,
    unbarred the doors that guarded her.

4. You'd think she came forth to be wed,
    so glad she looked when led away,
    bearing fresh riches to her man;
    her dowry was the wealth of blood.

5. Compelled to kindle with the torch
    the altar of an impious god,
    she answered: "Torches such as these
    maidens of Christ have never borne;

6. This fire extinguishes true faith,
    this flame does tear away the light.
    Strike here, yes, here! So pouring forth
    my blood, I may put out the flames."

7. When struck, what majesty she showed!
    She draped her clothes all round herself,
    showing concern for modesty,
    that none might witness her unclothed.

8. In death her modesty still lived,
    and with her hand she veiled her face.
    She sank to earth on bended knee,
    her posture modest as she fell.

IX

Hic est dies verus Dei

1. Hic est dies verus Dei,
   sancto serenus lumine,
   quo diluit sanguis sacer
   probrosi mundi crimina,

2. Fidem refundens perditis
   caecosque visu inluminans.
   Quem non gravi solvit metu
   latronis absolutio?

3. Qui praemium mutans cruce
   Iesum brevi adquirit fide,
   iustosque praevio gradu
   praevenit in regno Dei.

4. Opus stupent et angeli
   poenam videntes corporis,
   Christoque adhaerentem reum
   vitam beatam carpere.

5. Mysterium mirabile!
   ut abluat mundi luem,
   peccata tollat omnium,
   carnis vitia mundans caro.

AMBROSE

Hymn 9

This is the true day of our God

1. This is the true day of our God;
   it is agleam with holy light,
   whereon his sacred blood expunged
   transgressions of an impious world,

2. Restoring faith unto the lost,
   enlightening the blind with sight.
   Who is there whom from heavy fear
   the thief's acquittal did not loose?

3. The cross he changed for a reward,
   gained Jesus by a moment's faith,
   and he came to God's kingdom first,
   given right of way before the just.

4. Even the angels gasped at this,
   seeing Christ's body marked with pain,
   yet close to Christ, the guilty thief
   enjoying now the blessed life.

5. A wondrous mystery indeed!
   That flesh should cleanse the world's foul sin,
   should take away the sins of all,
   cleansing them of the faults of flesh.

6. Quid hoc potest sublimius,
   ut culpa quaerat gratiam,
   metumque solvat caritas,
   reddatque mors vitam novam,

7. Hamum sibi mors devoret
   suisque se nodis liget,
   moriatur ut vita omnium
   resurgat ut vita omnium,

8. Cum mors per omnes transeat,
   omnes resurgant mortui,
   consumpta mors ictu suo
   perisse se solam gemat?

X

Victor Nabor Felix

1. Victor Nabor Felix, pii
   Mediolani martyres,
   solo hospites, Mauri genus,
   terrisque nostris advenae,

2. Torrens harena quos dedit,
   anhela solis aestibus,
   extrema terrae finium
   exsulque nostri nominis.

6.   What can be more sublime than this,
that fault itself should look for grace,
and love should put an end to fear,
and death should give back life anew,

7.   That death should swallow its own hook
and bind itself with its own bonds,
that all men's life should enter death
that all men's life may rise again,

8.   That when death all mankind pervades,
then all the dead should rise again,
that death destroyed by its own blow
should grieve that it alone has died?

Hymn 10

Victor, Nabor, Felix, all three

1.   Victor, Nabor, Felix, all three
devoted martyrs at Milan,
guests to our soil, Moorish by race,
and strangers to these realms of ours:

2.   The scorching desert brought them forth,
gasping beneath the sun's fierce heat,
remotest boundary of the earth
and exiled from the name we bear.

3. Suscepit hospites Padus
   mercede magna sanguinis;
   sancto replevit Spiritu
   almae fides ecclesiae,

4. Et se coronavit trium
   cruore sacro martyrum,
   castrisque raptos impiis
   Christo sacravit milites.

5. Profecit ad fidem labor,
   armisque docti bellicis
   pro rege vitam ponere,
   decere pro Christo pati,

6. Non tela quaerunt ferrea,
   non arma, Christi milites;
   munitus armis ambulat
   veram fidem qui possidet.

7. Scutum viro sua est fides,
   et mors triumphus, quem invidens
   nobis tyrannus ad oppidum
   Laudense misit martyres.

8. Sed reddiderunt hostias;
   rapti quadrigis corpora
   revecti in ora principum
   plaustri triumphalis modo.

3. The Po received them as its guests,
    but at the great price of their blood;
    the faith of our nourishing Church
    then filled them with the Holy Spirit.

4. She crowned herself with sacred blood
    that these three martyrs later shed;
    she snatched them from their godless camp
    and anointed them to fight for Christ.

5. Their training reinforced their faith,
    and, having learned in warlike arms
    to lay their lives down for their king,
    that suffering for Christ is meet,

6. They do not look for iron weapons,
    not arms, they soldiers of the Christ;
    he who possesses genuine faith
    has armor to protect his step.

7. A man's own faith is his true shield,
    and death his triumph; the tyrant then,
    grudging us it, sent them away
    to Lodi, to be martyrs there.

8. But yet the victims were restored;
    their bodies, drawn in chariots,
    were brought before our leaders' eyes
    as if in a triumphal car.

XI

Grates tibi, Iesu, novas

1. Grates tibi, Iesu, novas
   novi repertor muneris
   Protasio Gervasio
   martyribus inventis cano.

2. Piae latebant hostiae,
   sed non latebat fons sacer;
   latere sanguis non potest
   qui clamat ad Deum Patrem.

3. Caelo refulgens gratia
   artus revelavit sacros;
   nequimus esse martyres,
   sed repperimus martyres.

4. Hic quis requirat testium
   voces, ubi factum est fides?
   Sanatus impos mentium
   opus fatetur martyrum.

5. Caecus recepto lumine
   mortis sacrae meritum probat.
   Severus est nomen viro,
   usus minister publici.

Hymn 11

Jesus, to you new thanks I hymn

1. Jesus, to you new thanks I hymn
    for this new gift that I have found:
    Protasius and Gervasius,
    our martyrs both, have been unearthed.

2. These holy victims hid unseen,
    not hidden was their hallowed spring;
    that blood cannot remain unseen
    that unto God the Father cries.

3. The grace that cast its light from heaven
    revealed to us their sacred limbs;
    we cannot ourselves martyrs be,
    yet martyrs have we lighted on.

4. Who would demand for this the word
    of witnesses, when deeds give proof?
    One healed of his disordered mind
    attests the martyrs' power at work.

5. The blind man who regained his sight
    does prove the power of holy death.
    Severus is the name of him,
    official in the state's employ.

6.   Ut martyrum vestem attigit,
      et ora tersit nubila,
      lumen refulsit ilico
      fugitque pulsa caecitas.

7.   Soluta turba vinculis,
      spiris draconum libera,
      emissa totis urbibus
      domum redit cum gratia.

8.   Vetusta saecla vidimus:
      iactata semicinctia,
      tactuque et umbra corporum
      aegris salutem redditam.

XII

Apostolorum passio

1.   Apostolorum passio
      diem sacravit saeculi,
      Petri triumphum nobilem,
      Pauli coronam praeferens.

2.   Coniunxit aequales viros
      cruor triumphalis necis;
      Deum secutos praesulem
      Christi coronavit fides.

6.   When he had touched the martyrs' clothes,
and wiped his eyes, clouded by mist,
at once the light came flooding back
and blindness, banished, fled away.

7.   The crowd was loosened from its bonds,
freed from the evil serpents' coils;
having come forth from all the towns,
it journeyed home with thankfulness.

8.   We witnessed scenes from days of old:
men threw their garments on the bones,
and by the corpses' touch and shade
health was restored to the infirm.

Hymn 12

The suffering the apostles bore

1.   The suffering the apostles bore
has canonized this worldly day;
the glorious triumph Peter won
and crown of Paul are both displayed.

2.   These peers have been united by
the blood from their triumphal death;
they followed God to be their guide,
and faith in Christ has crowned them both.

3. Primus Petrus apostolus,
    nec Paulus impar gratia;
    electionis vas sacrae
    Petri adaequavit fidem.

4. Verso crucis vestigio
    Simon, honorem dans Deo,
    suspensus ascendit, dati
    non immemor oraculi.

5. Praecinctus, ut dictum est, senex
    et elevatus ab altero
    quo nollet ivit, sed volens
    mortem subegit asperam.

6. Hinc Roma celsum verticem
    devotionis extulit,
    fundata tali sanguine
    et vate tanto nobilis.

7. Tantae per urbis ambitum
    stipata tendunt agmina;
    trinis celebratur viis
    festum sacrorum martyrum.

8. Prodire quis mundum putet,
    concurrere plebem poli:
    electa, gentium caput,
    sedes magistri gentium.

3.   Peter is first among apostles,
     and Paul not unequal in grace;
     a vessel made by heaven's choice,
     he equaled Peter in his faith.

4.   Implanting upside down his cross,
     Simon, paying homage to his God,
     mounted on it and hung, mindful
     of the prophecy given to him.

5.   This old man, as was prophesied,
     girt up, raised by another's hand,
     went whither he was loath to go,
     but willingly subdued harsh death.

6.   From this foundation Rome has raised
     the head of its devotion high,
     established on such blood as this,
     ennobled by that mighty seer.

7.   Around the circuit of great Rome
     the serried columns make their way;
     on triple routes they celebrate
     the sacred martyrs' festive day.

8.   One could believe the world came forth,
     and heaven's citizens crowded there:
     O chosen city, Gentiles' head,
     seat of the Gentiles' preceptor.

XIII

Apostolorum supparem

1.   Apostolorum supparem
Laurentium archidiaconem
pari corona martyrum
Romana sacravit fides.

2.   Xystum sequens hic martyrem
responsa vatis rettulit:
"Maerere, fili, desine;
sequere me post triduum."

3.   Nec territus poenae metu,
heres futurus sanguinis
spectavit obtutu pio
quod ipse mox persolveret.

4.   Iam nunc in illo martyre
egit triumphum martyris,
successor aequus syngrapham
vocis tenens et sanguinis.

5.   Post triduum iussus tamen
census sacratos prodere;
spondet pie nec abnuit,
addens dolum victoriae.

Hymn 13

As one who runs the apostles close

1.   As one who runs the apostles close,
Lawrence, the deacons' president,
was hallowed by the faith at Rome,
with crown as martyr matching theirs.

2.   When Sixtus suffered martyrdom,
he followed, heard the prophet's words:
"Leave off, my son, from grieving so;
you'll follow me after three days."

3.   Unmoved by fear of punishment,
as future heir to bloodletting
he witnessed with devoted sight
the price that he was soon to pay.

4.   Already in Sixtus' martyrdom
a martyr's triumph he pursued;
a worthy successor, he owned
the bond of Sixtus's voice and blood.

5.   He was commanded, in three days
the sacred treasures to consign;
he piously pledged without demur,
harnessing guile to victory.

6.   Spectaculum pulcherrimum!
     egena cogit agmina,
     inopesque monstrans praedicat:
     "Hi sunt opes ecclesiae."

7.   Vere piorum perpetes
     inopes profecto sunt opes.
     Avarus inlusus dolet
     flammas et ultrices parat.

8.   Fugit perustus carnifex
     suisque cedit ignibus;
     "Versate me" martyr vocat,
     "Vorate, si coctum est" iubet.

6. O, what a noble sight was then!
He drew the impoverished up in lines,
showed forth the needy, and proclaimed:
"These are the riches of the Church."

7. The truly pious plainly count
the poor as their long-lasting wealth.
The greedy man, thus mocked, is pained,
and makes ready revengeful flames.

8. The executioner is scorched,
does flee and from his fires retreat.
The martyr calls out: "Turn me round,"
he orders: "Eat me, if I'm cooked!"

XIV

Aeterna Christi munera

1. Aeterna Christi munera
   et martyrum victorias
   laudes ferentes debitas
   laetis canamus mentibus.

2. Ecclesiarum principes,
   belli triumphales duces,
   caelestis aulae milites
   et vera mundi lumina,

3. Terrore victo saeculi
   poenisque spretis corporis,
   mortis sacrae compendio
   lucem beatam possident.

4. Traduntur igni martyres
   et bestiarum dentibus;
   armata saevit ungulis
   tortoris insani manus.

5. Nudata pendent viscera,
   sanguis sacratus funditur;
   sed permanent immobiles
   vitae perennis gratia.

Hymn 14

The eternal gifts that Christ bestowed

1. The eternal gifts that Christ bestowed
   and victories that martyrs won
   let us, according praises due,
   in song proclaim with joyful hearts.

2. As leaders of the churches all,
   triumphal generals in war,
   as soldiers of the court of heaven,
   and true lights of the universe,

3. They quashed their terror of the world
   and spurned the body's punishments;
   by the shortcut of holy death
   they now possess the blessed light.

4. These martyrs are consigned to flames
   and to the teeth of savage beasts;
   the maddened torturer, his hand
   armed with claws, vents his rage on them.

5. Their entrails, thus exposed, hang down,
   their consecrated blood is shed;
   but they abide unflinchingly,
   so as to gain eternal life.

6. Devota sanctorum fides,
   invicta spes credentium,
   perfecta Christi caritas
   mundi triumphat principem.

7. In his paterna gloria,
   in his voluntas Spiritus,
   exultat in his Filius;
   caelum repletur gaudio.

8. Te nunc, Redemptor, quaesumus
   ut martyrum consortio
   iungas precantes servulos
   in sempiterna saecula.

6. Devoted faith of saintly men,
    believers' hope invincible,
    the perfect love they show for Christ
    triumphs over the world's dark prince.

7. In them the Father's fame abides,
    in them resides the Spirit's will,
    in them the Son feels boundless joy;
    the heavens abound in happiness.

8. Now we, Redeemer, make this plea:
    join with the martyrs' company
    your own poor servants, now at prayer,
    for life abiding without end.

[NICETAS OF
REMESIANA]

XV

Te Deum laudamus

1. Te Deum laudamus,
   te Dominum confitemur,
   te aeternum Patrem
   omnis terra veneratur.

2. Tibi omnes angeli,
   tibi caeli et universae potestates,
   tibi cherubim et seraphim
   incessabili voce proclamant:

3. "Sanctus, sanctus, sanctus
   Dominus Deus Sabaoth.
   Pleni sunt caeli et terra
   maiestate gloriae tuae."

4. Te gloriosus apostolorum chorus,
   te prophetarum laudabilis numerus,
   te martyrum candidatus laudat exercitus,

5. Te per orbem terrarum
   sancta confitetur ecclesia,
   Patrem immensae maiestatis,

Hymn 15

We praise you as God

1. We praise you as God,
   we proclaim you as Lord,
   every land reveres you
   as its eternal Father.

2. All the angels,
   heaven and all the powers,
   the cherubim and seraphim,
   cry out in unceasing voice:

3. "Holy, holy, holy,
   Lord God of hosts.
   heaven and earth are filled
   with the majesty of your glory."

4. The exultant chorus of apostles,
   the praiseworthy band of prophets,
   the white-robed army of martyrs all praise you.

5. Throughout the world
   the holy Church praises you,
   the Father of boundless majesty,

venerandum tuum verum unigenitum filium,
sanctum quoque Paraclitum Spiritum.

6. Tu rex gloriae, Christe,
    tu Patris sempiternus es Filius,
    tu, devicto mortis aculeo,
    aperuisti credentibus regna caelorum.

7. Tu, ad dexteram Dei sedens
    in gloria Patris,
    iudex crederis esse venturus.

8. Te ergo quaesumus, tuis famulis subveni,
    quos pretioso sanguine redemisti;
    aeterna fac cum sanctis tuis
    in gloria numerari.

9. Salvum fac populum tuum, Domine,
    et benedic hereditati tuae,
    et rege eos, et extolle eos
    usque in aeternum.

10. Per singulos dies benedicimus te,
    et laudamus nomen tuum
    in saeculum et in saeculum saeculi.

11. Dignare, Domine, die isto
    sine peccato nos custodire.

12. Miserere nostri, Domine, miserere nostri,
    fiat misericordia tua, Domine, super nos,
    quemadmodum speravimus in te.

      your true, only-begotten Son worthy of
          adoration,
      and too the Holy Spirit, the Comforter.

6.   You, Christ, are the king of glory,
      you are the everlasting Son of the Father,
      you, having conquered the sting of death,
      opened the kingdom of heaven to believers.

7.   You, seated at God's right hand
      in the glory of the Father,
      will come, we believe, as judge.

8.   So we beg you, aid your servants,
      whom you redeemed with your precious blood;
      grant us to be numbered
      with your saints in eternal glory.

9.   Save your people, Lord,
      and bless your inheritance,
      and govern them, and raise them
      into eternal life.

10.   Every day we bless you,
      and praise your name
      forever and for ever and ever.

11.   Deign, Lord, on this day
      to keep us without sin.

12.   Have mercy on us, Lord, have mercy on us,
      may your mercy, Lord, be over us,
      as we have hoped in you.

PRUDENTIUS

XVI

Ales diei nuntius

1. Ales diei nuntius
    lucem propinquam praecinit;
    nos excitator mentium
    iam Christus ad vitam vocat.

2. "Auferte" clamat "lectulos
    aegros, soporos, desides,
    castique, recti, et sobrii,
    vigilate; iam sum proximus."

3. Post solis ortum fulgidi
    serum est cubile spernere,
    ni parte noctis addita
    tempus labori adieceris.

4. Vox ista, qua strepunt aves
    stantes sub ipso culmine
    paulo ante quam lux emicet,
    nostri figura est iudicis.

5. Tectos tenebris horridis
    stratisque opertos segnibus
    suadet quietem linquere,
    iam iamque venturo die,

Hymn 16

The winged herald of the day

1. The winged herald of the day
    foretells the near approach of light;
    now Christ, who wakes minds from the dead,
    bestirs us to embark on life.

2. "Carry away" he cries "these beds
    unwell, slumbrous, and sluggardly,
    while you, being pure, upright, and staid,
    be watchful; I am very near."

3. When once the gleaming sun has risen,
    it is too late to spurn your bed,
    unless some portion of the night
    you've added to the toil of day.

4. That cock crow, which the birds produce
    that perch themselves beneath our roof
    shortly before the gleam of day,
    is symbol of our judge's voice.

5. As we lie covered by grim night
    and buried in our idle beds,
    it urges us to abandon rest,
    for day will imminently break,

6. Ut cum coruscis flatibus
    aurora caelum sparserit,
    omnes labore exercitos
    confirmet ad spem luminis.

7. Hic somnus ad tempus datus
    est forma mortis perpetis;
    peccata, ceu nox horrida,
    cogunt iacere et stertere.

8. Sed vox ab alto culmine
    Christi docentis praemonet
    adesse iam lucem prope
    ne mens sopori serviat,

9. Ne somnus usque ad terminos
    vitae socordis opprimat
    pectus sepultum crimine
    et lucis oblitum suae.

10. Ferunt vagantes daemonas
    laetos tenebris noctium
    gallo canente exterritos
    sparsim timere et cedere.

11. Invisa nam vicinitas
    lucis salutis numinis
    rupto tenebrarum situ
    noctis fugat satellites.

12. Hoc esse signum praescii
    norunt repromissae spei,
    qua nos soporis liberi
    speramus adventum Dei.

6.   That he, when once the dawn has flecked
the heavens with its darting breaths,
may strengthen all oppressed by toil
to grasp the hope brought by the light.

7.   This sleep, bestowed for but a time,
prefigures an enduring death;
our sins, a sort of hideous night,
force us to lie down and to snore.

8.   But from the summit up on high
Christ's voice instructs and cautions us
that daylight is now close at hand,
lest our minds be enslaved to sleep,

9.   Lest slumber should oppress our hearts
even to the end of idle life,
as they lie buried deep in sin
and all unmindful of their light.

10.   Men say, as demons roam abroad,
rejoicing in the shades of night,
at cock crow they are terrified,
fearfully scatter and retire.

11.   For hateful to them is the approach
of light, salvation, godly power;
it cleaves the dark's unsightliness
and routs the henchmen of the night.

12.   From prior knowledge they well know
that this denotes our promised hope,
through which, delivered now from sleep,
we expect the arrival of our God.

13.   Quae vis sit huius alitis
      Salvator ostendit Petro,
      ter antequam gallus canat
      sese negandum praedicans.

14.   Fit namque peccatum prius
      quam praeco lucis proximae
      inlustret humanum genus
      finemque peccandi ferat.

15.   Flevit negator denique
      ex ore prolapsum nefas,
      cum mens maneret innocens
      animusque servaret fidem.

16.   Nec tale quidquam postea
      linguae locutus lubrico est,
      cantuque galli cognito
      peccare iustus destitit.

17.   Inde est quod omnes credimus
      illo quietis tempore
      quo gallus exultans canit
      Christum redisse ex inferis.

18.   Tunc mortis oppressus vigor,
      tunc lex subacta est Tartari,
      tunc vis diei fortior
      noctem coegit cedere.

19.   Iam iam quiescant improba,
      iam culpa furva obdormiat,
      iam noxa letalis suum
      perpessa somnum marceat.

13. The pregnant meaning of this bird
    the Savior once to Peter showed,
    when he proclaimed he'd be denied
    three times before the cock should crow.

14. For sinning has its place before
    the herald of the imminent light
    sheds brightness on the human race,
    and brings an end to wickedness.

15. The denier did bewail at last
    the blasphemy slipped from his mouth,
    although his mind stayed innocent
    and his heart likewise kept its faith.

16. Thereafter no such word he spoke
    through slippery utterance of the tongue,
    but, having recognized cock crow,
    the just man put away all sin.

17. This is wherefore we all believe
    that in that restful hour of night
    at which the cock in triumph sings
    Christ made his way back from the dead.

18. Then was the power of death brought low,
    then was the rule of hell suppressed,
    then did the mightier force of day
    compel the night to yield its place.

19. Now, now let wickedness die down,
    and gloomy sin now lie asleep;
    let deadly wrong now waste away,
    experiencing its own deep sleep.

20. Vigil vicissim spiritus
    quodcumque restat temporis
    dum meta noctis clauditur
    stans ac laborans excubet.

21. Iesum ciamus vocibus
    flentes precantes sobrii;
    intenta supplicatio
    dormire cor mundum vetat.

22. Sat, convolutis artibus,
    sensum profunda oblivio
    pressit gravavit obruit
    vanis vagantem somniis.

23. Sunt nempe falsa et frivola
    quae mundiali gloria
    ceu dormientes egimus;
    vigilemus: hic est Veritas.

24. Aurum voluptas gaudium
    opes honores prospera,
    quaecumque nos inflant mala:
    fit mane, nil sunt omnia.

25. Tu, Christe, somnum dissice;
    tu rumpe noctis vincula;
    tu solve peccatum vetus,
    novumque lumen ingere.

20. Our wakeful spirit in its turn
     must stand on guard in prayerful toil
     for the remaining hours of dark
     until night's boundary comes down.

21. Let us with voices Jesus call,
     weeping, beseeching, temperate;
     a concentrated plea for help
     lets not the pure heart lie asleep.

22. For, while our limbs lie intertwined,
     enough has deep forgetfulness
     oppressed, weighed down, and overwhelmed
     our minds, which roam in empty dreams.

23. Spurious indeed and trivial
     are those pursuits that we have sought
     in worldly fame, as though in sleep;
     let us be wakeful: Truth is here!

24. Gold and low pleasure and delight,
     wealth and distinctions and success,
     such evil things as puff us up:
     morning comes, they are all as naught.

25. Do you, O Christ, dispel our sleep,
     and break the shackles of the night;
     demolish our long-standing sin,
     bestow upon us your new light.

XVII

Nox et tenebrae et nubila

1. Nox et tenebrae et nubila,
    confusa mundi et turbida,
    lux intrat, albescit polus,
    Christus venit; discedite!

2. Caligo terrae scinditur
    percussa solis spiculo,
    rebusque iam color redit
    vultu nitentis sideris.

3. Sic nostra mox obscuritas,
    fraudisque pectus conscium
    ruptis retectum nubibus
    regnante pallescit Deo.

4. Tunc non licebit claudere
    quod quisque fuscum cogitat,
    sed mane clarescent novo
    secreta mentis prodita.

5. Fur ante lucem squalido
    impune peccat tempore,
    sed lux dolis contraria
    latere furtum non sinit.

6. Versuta fraus et callida
    amat tenebris obtegi,

Hymn 17

O night and darkness and dense clouds

1. O night and darkness and dense clouds,
    turmoil and maelstrom of the world,
    light enters in, the sky turns white,
    Christ is approaching; now depart!

2. The darkness on the earth is rent,
    pierced by the sharp dart of the sun,
    and color now returns to things
    beneath the gleaming daystar's face.

3. Just so our darkness is soon cleft,
    and our hearts, conscious of their guilt,
    exposed, their clouds of sin being rent,
    grow white beneath God's governance.

4. Then no one will be allowed
    his thoughts' dark workings to conceal;
    the secrets of our minds, betrayed,
    will with the new dawn be exposed.

5. In the foul time before the dawn
    the thief sins with impunity,
    but light which counteracts his wiles
    lets not his thieving lurk unseen.

6. Crafty and underhand deceit
    likes to be shrouded in the dark;

aptamque noctem turpibus
adulter occultus fovet.

7.   Sol ecce surgit igneus;
piget pudescit paenitet,
nec teste quisquam lumine
peccare constanter potest.

8.   Quis mane sumptis nequiter
non erubescit poculis,
cum fit libido temperans
castumque nugator sapit?

9.   Nunc, nunc severum vivitur,
nunc nemo temptat ludicrum;
inepta nunc omnes sua
vultu colorant serio.

10.   Haec hora cunctis utilis,
qua quisque quod studet gerat,
miles togatus navita
opifex arator institor.

11.   Illum forensis gloria,
hunc triste raptat classicum;
mercator hinc ac rusticus
avara suspirant lucra.

12.   At nos lucelli et faenoris
fandique prorsus nescii,
nec arte fortes bellica,
te, Christe, solum novimus.

the adulterer who works unseen
loves night, ideal for loathsome deeds.

7.   But see, the fiery sun comes up;
disgust, shame, and regret ensue;
before the witness of the light
none can persist in deeds of sin.

8.   Who does not blush when morning comes
at having drunk cups to excess?
For then the longing moderates,
and triflers taste sobriety.

9.   Now, now our life is serious,
now no one seeks frivolity;
now all men mask their foolishness,
wearing a sober countenance.

10.   This hour brings profit to us all,
when each performs his chosen work,
the soldier, lawyer, mariner,
the workman, plowman, peddler.

11.   Fame in the courts one man pursues,
another the harsh bugle call;
the merchant next and countryman
pant eager after greedy gain.

12.   But we, of gain and usury
and eloquence being ignorant,
nor being brave in arts of war,
have knowledge, Christ, of you alone.

13.   Te mente pura et simplici,
te voce, te cantu pio
rogare curvato genu
flendo et canendo discimus.

14.   His nos lucramur quaestibus,
hac arte tantum vivimus,
haec inchoamus munera
cum sol resurgens emicat.

15.   Intende nostris sensibus,
vitamque nostram despice:
sunt multa fucis inlita
quae luce purgentur tua.

16.   Durare nos tales iube
quales remotis sordibus
nitere pridem iusseras
Iordane tinctos flumine.

17.   Quodcumque nox mundi dehinc
infecit atris nubibus,
tu, rex Eoi sideris,
vultu sereno inlumina.

18.   Tu sancte, qui taetram picem
candore tingis lacteo
ebenoque crystallum facis,
delicta terge livida.

19.   Sub nocte Iacob caerula
luctator audax angeli,
eo usque dum lux surgeret,
sudavit impar proelium.

13. You, with a pure and single mind,
     you, with voice and devoted song,
     we learn to entreat on bended knee
     with tears that mingle with our song.

14. This is the gain that makes us rich,
     this skill alone supports our life,
     these are the tasks we undertake
     when the sun rising flashes forth.

15. Direct your gaze into our hearts,
     and cast your eyes on our whole lives:
     there is much that is smeared with grime,
     which by your light must be made clean.

16. Bid us continue as we were
     when, all our foulness once removed,
     you long ago bade us to shine
     when we were dipped in Jordan's stream.

17. Whatever gloomy stain since then
     world's night has brought with its black clouds,
     do you, king of the eastern star,
     illuminate with your bright face.

18. O holy one, you who transform
     foul pitch with brightness milky-white,
     and make crystal from ebony,
     so cleanse us of our murky sins.

19. When Jacob in the dark of night
     engaged the angel in bold fight,
     for long, until the light arose,
     he sweated in unequal strife.

20. Sed cum iubar claresceret,
    lapsante claudus poplite,
    femurque victus debile
    culpae vigorem perdidit.

21. Nutabat inguen saucium,
    quae corporis pars vilior
    longeque sub cordis loco
    diram fovet libidinem.

22. Hae nos docent imagines
    hominem tenebris obsitum,
    si forte non cedat Deo,
    vires rebelles perdere.

23. Erit tamen beatior
    intemperans membrum cui
    luctando claudum et tabidum
    dies oborta invenerit.

24. Tandem facessat caecitas,
    quae nosmet in praeceps diu
    lapsos sinistris gressibus
    errore traxit devio.

25. Haec lux serenum conferat
    purosque nos praestet sibi;
    nihil loquamur subdolum,
    volvamus obscurum nihil.

26. Sic tota decurrat dies,
    ne lingua mendax, ne manus
    oculive peccent lubrici,
    ne noxa corpus inquinet.

20. But when the orb's bright beam shone out,
his hams collapsing, feeble at once,
and overcome in crippled thigh,
he lost the crude force of his sin.

21. He grew weak in his wounded groin,
which, being the body's baser part
and lying far below the heart,
embraces lust unspeakable.

22. From such examples we are taught
that man, by darkness being beset,
should he refuse to yield to God,
forfeits his powers rebellious.

23. But he will be more blessed still
whose body, lacking modesty,
the dawning day will come upon
crippled and wasted in the fight.

24. At last may our blindness depart,
which dragged us headlong far too long,
as we slipped with misguided steps
along a wandering wayward path.

25. May this light bring bright clarity
and make us chaste before its face;
let us utter no guileful word,
revolve no dark thought in our minds.

26. So may the whole day run its course,
that neither lying tongue, nor hand,
nor wanton eyes indulge in sin,
that no guilt stain the body's frame.

27. Speculator adstat desuper,
    qui nos diebus omnibus
    actusque nostros prospicit
    a luce prima in vesperum.

28. Hic testis, hic est arbiter,
    hic intuetur quidquid est
    humana quod mens concipit;
    hunc nemo fallit iudicem.

XVIII

Deus, ignee fons animarum

1. Deus, ignee fons animarum,
   duo qui socians elementa,
   vivum simul ac moribundum,
   hominem, pater, effigiasti.

2. Tua sunt, tua, rector, utraque;
   tibi copula iungitur horum;
   tibi, dum vegetata cohaerent,
   et spiritus et caro servit.

3. Rescissa sed ista seorsum
   solvunt hominem perimuntque,
   humus excipit arida corpus,
   animae capit aura liquorem;

27. The watchman is at hand on high,
    who eyes us every single day
    and all our actions does descry
    from day's first dawn till eventide.

28. He is our witness, he our judge,
    he examines every single thing
    conceived of by the human mind;
    he is the judge no one deceives.

Hymn 18

O God, fiery source of all spirits

1. O God, fiery source of all spirits,
   you who, fusing our two forms of being,
   the living, and that doomed to perish,
   have, O Father, the human man fashioned.

2. O Ruler, both are your possession;
   by you they are merged and united;
   while they in rude health cleave together,
   both spirit and flesh are your servants.

3. But once they are torn from each other,
   they loose and destroy man's existence,
   dusty earth entertains the poor body,
   the air's breath bears the soul-fluid upward;

4. Quia cuncta creata necesse est
    labefacta senescere tandem,
    compactaque dissociari,
    et dissona texta retexi.

5. Hanc tu, Deus optime, mortem
    famulis abolere paratus,
    iter inviolabile monstras
    quo perdita membra resurgent;

6. Ut, dum generosa caducis
    ceu carcere clausa ligantur,
    pars illa potentior exstet,
    quae germen ab aethere traxit.

7. Si terrea forte voluntas
    luteum sapit et grave captat,
    animus quoque pondere victus
    sequitur sua membra deorsum.

8. At si generis memor ignis
    contagia pigra recusat,
    vehit hospita viscera secum
    pariterque reportat ad astra.

9. Nam quod requiescere corpus
    vacuum sine mente videmus,
    spatium breve restat, ut alti
    repetat conlegia sensus.

10. Venient cito saecula, cum iam
    socius calor ossa revisat,
    animataque sanguine vivo
    habitacula pristina gestet.

4.   For all things created are fated
     to become at last feeble and aged,
     and close-welded parts to be sundered,
     and discordant threads be unraveled.

5.   This death, noblest God, you did purpose
     should cease to exist for your servants,
     and you show us a path indestructible
     by which dead limbs gain resurrection;

6.   That, while what is noble is shackled
     to the fleeting, as though shut in prison,
     the more powerful part stands forth extant,
     which from heaven its seed has derived.

7.   If it hap that our will here on earth
     tastes of clay and embraces the leaden,
     the soul too, weighted down by the burden,
     does follow its limbs, heading downward.

8.   But the fiery spirit, if mindful
     of its birth it spurns sluggish contagion,
     playing host, it transports body with it,
     and conveys it alike to the heavens.

9.   For the body that we see reposing,
     lying empty with no mind within it,
     remains only briefly, and later
     reunites with the senses in heaven.

10.   The age will come soon, when directly
     allied heat will with bones reassemble,
     and, enlivened by blood which restores it,
     will don its original dwellings.

11.   Quae pigra cadavera pridem
      tumulis putrefacta iacebant,
      volucres rapientur in auras
      animas comitata priores.

12.   Hinc maxima cura sepulcris
      impenditur, hinc resolutos
      honor ultimus accipit artus,
      et funeris ambitus ornat.

13.   Candore nitentia claro
      praetendere lintea mos est,
      adspersaque myrrha Sabaeo
      corpus medicamine servat.

14.   Quidnam sibi saxa cavata,
      quid pulcra volunt monumenta,
      nisi quod res creditur illis
      non mortua, sed data somno?

15.   Hoc provida Christicolarum
      pietas studet, utpote credens
      fore protinus omnia viva
      quae nunc gelidus sopor urget.

16.   Qui iacta cadavera passim
      miserans tegit aggere terrae
      opus exhibet ille benignum
      Christo pius omnipotenti;

17.   Quia lex eadem monet omnes
      gemitum dare sorte sub una,
      cognataque funera nobis
      aliena in morte dolere.

11.   Corpses that for long have lain sluggish,
        having crumbled to dust in their barrows,
        will be swiftly rapt into the heavens,
        now joined to their previous spirits.

12.   This is why the most careful attention
        is bestowed on the tombs, why the last rites
        receive the limbs when they have gone slack,
        and the funeral's pomp bestows honor.

13.   'Tis the custom to cover the corpses
        with linen of dazzling whiteness,
        and the myrrh which is sprinkled upon them
        by its powers Sabaean embalms them.

14.   What point has a hollowed stone coffin,
        what point a sepulchre of beauty,
        except that to them is entrusted
        what is not dead, but ceded to slumber?

15.   The farseeing devotion of Christians
        does take zealous pains for such matters,
        believing that soon will be quickened
        all things that cold sleep now oppresses.

16.   He who pityingly raises an earth mound
        to cover men's corpses wide-scattered
        thereby demonstrates with compassion
        a kind deed unto Christ the Almighty;

17.   For the same law admonishes all men
        to bestow one's laments without bias,
        to feel grief for the death of one's kindred
        even in the death of a stranger.

18.   Sancti sator ille Tobiae,
   sacer ac venerabilis heros,
   dapibus iam rite paratis
   ius praetulit exsequiarum.

19.   Iam stantibus ille ministris
   cyathos et fercula liquit,
   studioque accinctus humandi
   fleto dedit ossa sepulchro.

20.   Veniunt mox praemia caelo
   pretiumque rependitur ingens,
   nam lumina nescia solis
   Deus inlita felle serenat.

21.   Iam tunc docuit pater orbis
   quam sit rationis egenis
   mordax et amara medela,
   cum lux animum nova vexat.

22.   Docuit quoque non prius ullum
   caelestia cernere regna,
   quam nocte et vulnere tristi
   toleraverit aspera mundi.

23.   Mors ipsa beatior inde est,
   quod per cruciamina leti
   via panditur ardua iustis
   et ad astra doloribus itur.

24.   Sic corpora mortificata
   redeunt melioribus annis
   nec post obitum recalescens
   compago fatiscere novit.

18.   The father of holy Tobias,
      that sacred and venerable hero,
      though a banquet was duly laid ready,
      put the duties of burial before it.

19.   As the servants already stood waiting,
      he abandoned the cups and the courses,
      then girt in his zeal for the burial,
      laid the bones in the tomb sore lamented.

20.   A reward soon descended from heaven,
      and there came an abundant repayment,
      for to eyes with no knowledge of sunlight
      God with smearing of gall did bring brightness.

21.   Even then the world's father had taught us
      how bitter and sharp is the healing
      for those who are wanting in reason,
      when the new light does dazzle their spirit.

22.   He taught too that no man is given
      prior sight of the kingdom of heaven,
      till enduring harsh wounding and darkness
      he has suffered such worldly affliction.

23.   Hence is death itself the more blessed,
      since by the torments of the deathbed
      the high path opens up for the righteous
      and the way to the stars is by suffering.

24.   Thus bodies enduring death's stresses
      return in an era more blessed,
      and our frame, after death new warmth gaining,
      is ignorant of all exhaustion.

25. Haec quae modo pallida tabo
color albidus inficit ora,
tunc flore venustior omni
sanguis cute tinget amoena.

26. Iam nulla deinde senectus
frontis decus invida carpet,
macies neque sicca lacertos
suco tenuabit adeso.

27. Morbus quoque pestifer, artus
qui nunc populatur anhelos,
sua tunc tormenta resudans
luet inter vincula mille.

28. Hunc eminus aere ab alto
victrix caro iamque perennis
cernet sine fine gementem
quos moverat ipse dolores.

29. Quid turba superstes inepta
clangens ululamina miscet?
Cur tam bene condita iura
luctu dolor arguit amens?

30. Iam maesta quiesce querella;
lacrimas suspendite, matres;
nullus sua pignora plangat;
mors haec reparatio vitae est.

31. Sic semina sicca virescunt
iam mortua iamque sepulta,
quae reddita caespite ab imo
veteres meditantur aristas.

25. These cheeks, to which, made pale with corruption,
   a ghastly white color adds tincture,
   blood will then lend a pleasing complexion,
   more beautiful than any blossom.

26. Hereafter no old age with envy
   will pluck from our visage its beauty,
   and no wasting process will shrivel
   our members by draining their juices.

27. And baneful Disease, which now plunders
   our bodies, and renders them breathless,
   will then, sweating under his tortures,
   suffer under a thousand strong shackles.

28. Then high above from the high heaven,
   victorious flesh, now immortal,
   will behold him without end lamenting
   the pains he himself had inflicted.

29. Why is it that throngs of survivors
   bawl out their loud howls in confusion?
   Why does senseless sorrow by grieving
   censure laws founded so rightly?

30. Fall silent, dejected complaining;
   hold back, O ye mothers, your tears;
   let no one lament for his loved ones;
   this death's nothing but life's renewal.

31. Dry seeds that are dead and lie buried
   thus do sprout and acquire fresh vigor,
   as from the earth's deep clods delivered
   they hearken to yesteryear's harvests.

32. Nunc suscipe, terra, fovendum
    gremioque hunc concipe molli;
    hominis tibi membra sequestro
    generosa et fragmina credo.

33. Animae fuit haec domus olim
    factoris ab ore creatae;
    fervens habitavit in istis
    sapientia principe Christo.

34. Tu depositum tege corpus;
    non immemor ille requiret
    sua munera fictor et auctor
    propriique aenigmata vultus.

35. Veniant modo tempora iusta
    cum spem Deus impleat omnem;
    reddas patefacta necesse est
    qualem tibi trado figuram.

36. Non, si cariosa vetustas
    dissolverit ossa favillis,
    fueritque cinisculus arens
    minimi mensura pugilli;

37. Nec, si vaga flamina et aurae,
    vacuum per inane volantes,
    tulerint cum pulvere nervos,
    hominem periisse licebit.

38. Sed dum resolubile corpus
    revocas, Deus, atque reformas,
    quanam regione iubebis
    animam requiescere puram?

32. Now, Earth, take this man to be cherished,
     and fold him in your gentle bosom;
     'tis a man's limbs I lodge in your keeping,
     august too the remains I entrust you.

33. Here a soul once established its dwelling,
     being formed from the breath of its Maker;
     in these lifeless remains there dwelt glowing
     wisdom, which in the Christ has its origin.

34. Do you keep secure this body laid here;
     not unmindful, its shaper and author
     sometime will reclaim what he gave you,
     his own countenance's mystic image.

35. May that proper time soon be upon us,
     when God shall fulfill all our longing;
     you must then open up and surrender
     this figure I attribute to you.

36. Even if the decay of long ages
     has dissolved these bones into ashes,
     and the dry residue of these ashes
     has measured the merest of handfuls;

37. Even if vagrant winds and the breezes,
     as they flit through the void of the heavens,
     shall have borne off his fibers and ashes,
     man shall not be permitted to perish.

38. But until you call back and refashion
     this body, O God, which unravels,
     in what region, pray, will you order
     that the unfettered soul should find respite?

39. Gremio senis addita sancti
    recubabit, ut est Eleazar,
    quem floribus undique saeptum
    dives procul adspicit ardens.

40. Sequimur tua dicta, redemptor,
    quibus atra morte triumphans
    tua per vestigia mandas
    socium crucis ire latronem.

41. Patet ecce fidelibus ampli
    via lucida iam Paradisi,
    licet et nemus illud adire,
    homini quod ademerat anguis.

42. Illic precor, optime ductor,
    famulam tibi praecipe mentem
    genitali in sede sacrari,
    quam liquerat exsul et errans.

43. Nos tecta fovebimus ossa
    violis et fronde frequenti,
    titulumque et frigida saxa
    liquido spargemus odore.

39.   It will rest in the aged saint's bosom
      where Lazarus now makes his lodging,
      at whom, girded on all sides with blossoms,
      the rich man, from afar, in flames, gazes.

40.   We attend on your words, O Redeemer,
      by which, over dark death prevailing,
      you did bid your crucified comrade,
      the thief, to walk in your footsteps.

41.   Behold: a bright path for the faithful
      lies open to Paradise spacious;
      that grove too is open for entry,
      from which man was debarred by the serpent.

42.   In that place I pray, noblest leader,
      command that the soul of your servant
      be enshrined in its native birthplace,
      which it quitted, a wandering exile.

43.   We shall keep these bones warm, being buried,
      with violets and layers of foliage,
      and these cold stones and the inscription
      we shall sprinkle with perfume libation.

SEDULIUS

XIX

A solis ortus cardine

1. A solis ortus cardine
   adusque terrae limitem
   Christum canamus principem
   natum Maria virgine.

2. Beatus auctor saeculi
   servile corpus induit,
   ut carne carnem liberans
   non perderet quod condidit.

3. Clausae puellae viscera
   caelestis intrat gratia;
   venter puellae baiulat
   secreta quae non noverat.

4. Domus pudici pectoris
   templum repente fit Dei;
   intacta nesciens virum
   verbo concepit filium.

5. Enixa est puerpera
   quem Gabriel praedixerat,
   quem matris alvo gestiens
   clausus Ioannes senserat.

Hymn 19

Away from the sunrise's hinge

1. Away from the sunrise's hinge
   unto the furthest zone of earth
   let us of Christ our leader sing,
   born of the virgin Mary's womb.

2. Blessed the maker of the world,
   who took the body of a slave,
   that he by flesh our flesh releasing
   might not destroy his creation.

3. Celestial grace does enter in
   the close-barred maiden's inner parts;
   the maiden's womb as burden bears
   such mysteries as she knew not.

4. Directly is the dwelling of
   her chaste bosom God's temple made;
   untouched and innocent of men,
   she by the word a son conceived.

5. Enduring childbirth, she brought forth
   the one whom Gabriel had foretold,
   whom John, closed in his mother's womb,
   leaping with joy did recognize.

6.   Faeno iacere pertulit,
   praesepe non abhorruit,
   parvoque lacte pastus est
   per quem nec ales esurit.

7.   Gaudet chorus caelestium
   et angeli canunt Deum,
   palamque fit pastoribus
   pastor, creator omnium.

8.   Hostis Herodes impie,
   Christum venire quid times?
   non eripit mortalia
   qui regna dat caelestia.

9.   Ibant magi qua venerant
   stellam sequentes praeviam;
   lumen requirunt lumine,
   Deum fatentes munere.

10.   Katerva matrum personat
    conlisa deflens pignora,
    quorum tyrannus milia
    Christo sacravit victimam.

11.   Lavacra puri gurgitis
    caelestis agnus attigit;
    peccata qui mundi tulit
    nos abluendo sustulit.

12.   Miraculis dedit fidem
    habere se Deum patrem,
    infirma sanans corpora
    et suscitans cadavera.

6. Fodder he suffered to lie in,
   the manger he did not disdain,
   and he who lets no bird go hungry
   with but a little milk was fed.

7. Gladdened is the heavenly chorus,
   and angels God in song proclaim,
   while there before the eyes of shepherds
   the shepherd lies, maker of all.

8. Herod, you irreligious foe,
   why fear that Christ is on his way?
   He does not wrest men's earthly realms,
   who heavenly kingdoms does bestow.

9. In that star's path that went before
   and led them, the Magi followed;
   by that light do they seek the Light,
   by gifts proclaiming him as God.

10. Keenly the crowd of mothers cries,
    weeping for children cruelly slain,
    thousands of whom the tyrant then
    devoted as victims to Christ.

11. Lamb of the heavens made his way
    unto the cleansed waters' streams;
    he who bore the whole world's sins
    washing us clean took them away.

12. Manifesting miracles,
    he proved his father to be God,
    by healing unwell bodies and
    by bringing corpses back to life.

13.   Novum genus potentiae!
        aquae rubescunt hydriae,
        vinumque iussa fundere
        mutavit unda originem.

14.   Orat salutem servulo
        nixus genu centurio;
        credentis ardor plurimus
        exstinxit ignes febrium.

15.   Petrus per undas ambulat
        Christi levatus dextera;
        natura quam negaverat
        fides paravit semitam.

16.   Quarta die iam fetidus
        vitam recepit Lazarus,
        mortisque liber vinculis
        factus superstes est sibi.

17.   Rivos cruoris torridi
        contacta vestis obruit;
        fletu rigante supplicis
        arent fluenta sanguinis.

18.   Solutus omni corpore
        iussus repente surgere,
        suis vicissim gressibus
        aeger vehebat lectulum.

19.   Tunc ille Iudas carnifex,
        ausus magistrum tradere,
        pacem ferebat osculo
        quam non habebat pectore.

13. Novel form of puissance!
    The water in the pot turns red,
    and, being bid to flow with wine,
    the stream transforms its very source.

14. On bent knees, the centurion
    begs that his servant be restored;
    his overwhelming zeal of faith
    put out the fever's burning fires.

15. Peter walks upright through the waves,
    supported by Christ's helping hand;
    the path that nature had denied
    faith then provided in its stead.

16. Quit of this life, already stinking,
    Lazarus gained life on the fourth day,
    and, from the chains of death released,
    he was his own survivor made.

17. Rivers of flowing blood are stemmed
    by the mere touch of his clothes;
    by the suppliant's moistening tears
    the running streams of blood run dry.

18. Still from weakness in his limbs,
    the sick man, bidden suddenly
    to rise, transformed, on his own feet
    unaided bears away his bed.

19. Then Judas, executioner,
    presumed his master to betray;
    a kiss he gave as sign of peace
    that in his heart he did not feel.

20. Verax datur fallacibus,
    pium flagellat impius,
    crucique fixus innocens
    coniunctus est latronibus.

21. Xeromyrram post sabbatum
    quaedam ferebant compares,
    quas adlocutus angelus
    vivum sepulcro non tegi.

22. Ymnis venite dulcibus;
    omnes canamus subditum
    Christi triumpho Tartarum,
    qui nos redemit venditus.

23. Zelum draconis invidi
    et os leonis pessimi
    calcavit unicus Dei
    seseque caelis reddidit.

20. Upright men are betrayed to liars,
the impious scourges the pious,
and on a cross the innocent
is fixed, his lot with robbers joined.

21. Xeromyrrh after the Sabbath day
his woman comrades brought to him,
to whom an angel then declared:
alive, he lay not in the tomb.

22. Ye all, come near with dulcet hymns;
let us all sing that Tartarus
has by Christ's triumph been subdued,
who redeemed us, though he was sold.

23. Zealous envy of the serpent
and heinous lion's savage maw
under his heel God's sole son crushed
and up to heaven betook himself.

VENANTIUS
FORTUNATUS

XX

Pange, lingua

1. Pange, lingua, gloriosi
   proelium certaminis,
   et super crucis tropaeo
   dic triumphum nobilem,
   qualiter redemptor orbis
   immolatus vicerit.

2. De parentis protoplasti
   fraude factor condolens,
   quando pomi noxialis
   morte morsu conruit,
   ipse lignum tunc notavit,
   damna ligni ut solveret.

3. Hoc opus nostrae salutis
   ordo depoposcerat,
   multiformis perditoris
   arte ut artem falleret,
   et medelam ferret inde
   hostis unde laeserat.

4. Quando ergo venit sacri
   plenitudo temporis,

Hymn 20

Sing, my tongue, of that engagement

1.   Sing, my tongue, of that engagement
     of the struggle glorious;
  tell too of that famous triumph
     on the trophy of the cross:
  how the world's redeemer was,
     sacrificed, victorious.

2.   Owing to our first-formed parent's
     injury, the maker grieved;
  when he bit the baleful apple
     and thereby collapsed in death,
  he himself the wood then marked out
     that wood's damage to repair.

3.   The due course of our salvation
     had demanded such a deed,
  that he frustrate by guile the guile
     of the assassin many-shaped,
  and bring healing from that quarter
     whence the foe inflicted harm.

4.   Therefore when at last the fullness
     of the sacred age emerged,

missus est ab arce patris
    natus, orbis conditor,
atque ventre virginali
    carne factus prodiit.

5.   Vagit infans inter arta
        conditus praesepia,
    membra pannis involuta
        virgo mater adligat,
    et pedes manusque, crura
        stricta pingit fascia.

6.   Lustra sex qui iam peracta
        tempus implens corporis,
    se volente, natus ad hoc,
        passioni deditus,
    agnus in crucis levatus
        immolandus stipite.

7.   Hic acetum, fel, harundo,
        sputa, clavi, lancea;
    mite corpus perforatur;
        sanguis, unda profluit.
    Terra, pontus, astra, mundus
        quo lavantur flumine.

8.   Crux fidelis, inter omnes
        arbor una nobilis;
    nulla talem silva profert
        flore, fronde, germine;
    dulce lignum dulce clavo
        dulce pondus sustinens.

from the Father's stronghold was his
    son sent, founder of the world,
and from virgin's womb, a creature
    made of flesh, he issued forth.

5.   Set within the narrow manger,
    lacking speech, the infant wails;
virgin mother binds his body
    all wrapped up in tattered rags,
both the feet and hands, while tightly
    swaddling bands adorn his legs.

6.   Thirty years he had completed,
    thus fulfilling days on earth;
of his own will, born for this end,
    to his passion given o'er,
as Lamb he was on the crosstree
    hoisted to be sacrificed.

7.   Here see vinegar, bitter gall,
    the reed, the spit, the nails, the lance;
pierced through is his gentle body;
    blood, water are oozing forth.
By this stream the earth, the ocean,
    stars and universe are cleansed.

8.   Cross so faithful, tree of all trees
    glorious, having no peer;
such a tree no forest brought forth
    with such blossom, leaf, and bud;
sweet the wood, which with sweet nails
    its sweet burden undergoes.

9.   Flecte ramos, arbor alta,
        tensa laxa viscera,
    et rigor lentescat ille
        quem dedit nativitas,
    ut superni membra regis
        mite tendas stipite.

10.   Sola digna tu fuisti
        ferre pretium saeculi,
    atque portum praeparare
        nauta mundo naufrago,
    quem sacer cruor perunxit
        fusus agni corpore.

XXI

Vexilla regis prodeunt

1.   Vexilla regis prodeunt,
    fulget crucis mysterium,
    quo carne carnis conditor
    suspensus est patibulo.

2.   Confixa clavis viscera,
    tendens manus, vestigia,
    redemptionis gratia
    hic immolata est hostia.

VENANTIUS FORTUNATUS

9.   Bend your branches, tree so lofty,
           loose your tight-knit inner core;
      let that stiffness grow more supple
           which your native birth imposed,
      that you may stretch forth the limbs
           of heaven's king from gentle trunk.

10.   You alone were then found worthy
           all the world's ransom to bear,
      yachtsman to prepare the harbor
           for our shipwrecked universe,
      you whom sacred blood anointed,
           pouring from the Lamb's spent frame.

Hymn 21

The standards of the king advance

1.   The standards of the king advance,
      the mystery of the cross shines forth,
      whereby the founder of our flesh
      in flesh upon a gibbet hung.

2.   Here, his body pierced by nails,
      and stretching forth his hands, his feet,
      for the redemption of the world
      as victim was he sacrificed.

3. Quo vulneratus insuper
   mucrone diro lanceae,
   ut nos lavaret crimine
   manavit unda et sanguine.

4. Impleta sunt quae concinit
   David fideli carmine,
   dicendo nationibus,
   "Regnavit a ligno Deus."

5. Arbor decora et fulgida,
   ornata regis purpura,
   electa digno stipite
   tam sancta membra tangere!

6. Beata, cuius bracchiis
   pretium pependit saeculi!
   Statera facta est corporis,
   praedam tulitque Tartari.

7. Fundis aroma cortice;
   vincis sapore nectare;
   iucunda fructu fertili
   plaudis triumpho nobili.

8. Salve ara, salve victima,
   de passionis gloria,
   qua vita mortem pertulit,
   et morte vitam reddidit.

3.   Upon this gibbet, wounded sore,
     pierced by the grim point of the lance,
     that he might cleanse us of our sins
     he dripped with water and with blood.

4.   Thus were the prophecies fulfilled
     that David sang in truthful strain,
     proclaiming to the world at large
     that God did reign from on the tree.

5.   O beautiful and shining tree,
     adorned with purple of the king,
     selected, as its trunk deserved,
     to touch so close such sacred limbs!

6.   O blessed tree, upon whose arms
     there hung the ransom of the world!
     It weighed his body in its scales,
     and bore away the prey of hell.

7.   From your bark fragrance you diffuse;
     sweeter than nectar is your taste;
     rejoicing in your fecund fruit,
     that splendid triumph you applaud.

8.   All hail, O altar; victim, hail,
     for sake of his passion's great fame,
     by which our Life endured his death,
     and by his death restored our life.

XXII

Crux benedicta nitet

Crux benedicta nitet, Dominus qua carne pependit
    atque cruore suo vulnera nostra lavit;
mitis amore pio pro nobis victima factus
    traxit ab ore lupi qua sacer agnus oves;
5   transfixis palmis ubi mundum a clade redemit
    atque suo clausit funere mortis iter.
Hic manus illa fuit clavis confixa cruentis,
    quae eripuit Paulum crimine, morte Petrum.
Fertilitate potens, O dulce et nobile lignum,
10   quando tuis ramis tam nova poma geris!
Cuius odore novo defuncta cadavera surgunt,
    et redeunt vitae qui caruere diem.
Nullum uret aestus sub frondibus arboris huius,
    luna nec in nocte sol neque meridie.

Hymn 22

The blessed cross gleams forth

The blessed cross gleams forth, where hung the Lord
   in flesh,
    and with his blood washed clean our gaping wounds;
where, made a meek victim for us, with pious love
    the sacred lamb his sheep from wolf jaws saved,
where, palms transfixed, from ruin he redeemed the   5
   world,
    and through his dying closed the road to death.
Hereon was impaled with bloody nails that hand
    that rescued Paul from sin, Peter from death.
How powerful your fruitfulness, sweet, noble wood,
    since on your branches such new fruits you bear!   10
By whose fresh fragrance bodies cold in death now
   rise,
    and those bereft of day return to life.
'Neath this tree's leaves the swelling heat will no man
   burn,
    nor moon at night nor sun at middle day.

15   Tu plantata micas, secus est ubi cursus aquarum,
        spargis et ornatas flore recente comas.
      Appensa est vitis inter tua bracchia, de qua
        dulcia sanguineo vina rubore fluunt.

You shine forth, rooted by the waters' running streams.　　15
　　And dapple your decked foliage with fresh blooms.
Between your outstretched arms there hangs the vine,
　　　from which
　　sweet wines pour forth with redness of his blood.

THE OLD HYMNAL

XXIII

Te lucis ante terminum

1. Te lucis ante terminum,
    rerum creator, poscimus
    ut pro tua clementia
    sis praesul ad custodiam.

2. Procul recedant somnia
    et noctium phantasmata,
    hostemque nostrum comprime
    ne polluantur corpora.

3. Praesta, Pater omnipotens,
    per Iesum Christum Dominum,
    qui tecum in perpetuum
    regnat cum sancto Spiritu.

Hymn 23

Before the closing of the light

1. Before the closing of the light,
   creator of the world, we pray
   that with your wonted clemency
   as leader you may guard our souls.

2. May dreams be banished far away,
   and apparitions of the night,
   and do you check our enemy,
   corrupted lest our bodies be.

3. Almighty Father, grant this prayer
   through Jesus Christ, who is our Lord,
   who reigns with you for evermore,
   together with the Holy Ghost.

XXIV

Iam lucis orto sidere

1. Iam lucis orto sidere
Deum precemur supplices
ut in diurnis actibus
nos servet a nocentibus.

2. Linguam refrenans temperet
ne litis horror insonet;
visum fovendo contegat
ne vanitates hauriat.

3. Sint pura cordis intima,
absistat et vecordia;
carnis terat superbiam
potus cibique parcitas,

4. Ut cum dies abscesserit
noctemque sors reduxerit,
mundi per abstinentiam
ipsi canamus gloriam.

Hymn 24

Now that the star of light has risen

1.   Now that the star of light has risen,
let us as suppliants pray to God
that he in all our deeds this day
may save us from the things that harm.

2.   May he restrain and check our tongue,
that awful strife may not resound;
may his warm presence shield our eyes
from entertaining vanities.

3.   Deep in our hearts may we be pure,
and folly have no part in us;
may sparing use of food and drink
wear down the arrogance of our flesh,

4.   So that, when daylight will depart,
and night return, as is its wont,
as we abstain from worldly things,
his glory we may hymn to him.

XXV

Aeterne lucis conditor

1. Aeterne lucis conditor,
   lux ipse totus et dies,
   noctem nec ullam sentiens
   natura lucis perpeti,

2. Iam cedit pallens proximo
   diei nox adventui,
   obtendens lumen siderum
   adest et clarus lucifer.

3. Iam stratis laeti surgimus,
   grates canentes et tuas,
   quod caecam noctem vicerit
   revectans rursus sol diem.

4. Te nunc, ne carnis gaudia
   blandis subrepant aestibus,
   dolis ne cedat saeculi
   mens nostra, sancte, quaesumus;

5. Ira ne rixam provocet,
   gula ne ventrem incitet,
   opum pervertat ne famis,
   turpis ne luxus occupet,

Hymn 25

Eternal founder of the light

1. Eternal founder of the light,
    yourself wholly both light and day,
    with no experience of night,
    your nature ever one of light,

2. The ghostly night is in retreat
    before the imminence of day;
    the shining light-bringer too is here,
    shrouding the light of other stars.

3. We rise in gladness from our beds,
    and sing our gratitude to you,
    because the sun has beaten back
    blind night, reushering the day.

4. We now entreat you, lest the joys
    of flesh by luring heat creep in,
    lest our minds to the world's traps
    succumb, O holy one, we pray;

5. That anger may not foster brawls,
    nor gluttony rouse our appetite,
    nor greed for wealth pervert our hearts,
    nor grisly luxury take hold;

6.   Sed firma mente sobrii
casto manentes corpore,
totum fideli spiritu
Christo ducamus hunc diem.

XXVI

Fulgentis auctor aetheris

1.   Fulgentis auctor aetheris,
qui lunam lumen noctibus,
sólem dierum cursibus
certo fundasti tramite,

2.   Nox atra iam depellitur,
mundi nitor renascitur,
novusque iam mentis vigor
dulces in actus erigit.

3.   Laudes sonare iam tuas
dies relatus admonet,
vultusque caeli blandior
nostra serenat pectora.

4.   Vitemus omne lubricum,
declinet prava spiritus,
vitam facta non inquinent,
linguam culpa non implicet.

6. Instead, with sober, steadfast minds
  let us remain of body chaste,
  and live out with the faithful spirit
  the whole length of this day for Christ.

Hymn 26

Creator of the gleaming heavens

1. Creator of the gleaming heavens,
  who set the moon to light the nights,
  who launched the sun on its fixed path
  to illuminate the course of days,

2. The soot-black night is banished now,
  the world's bright luster is reborn,
  and newfound liveliness of mind
  rouses us unto pleasant tasks.

3. Praises of you now to sound out
  returning day advises us,
  and heaven's face now kindlier
  induces brightness in our hearts.

4. Let us avoid all slippery ways;
  perverseness let our spirits shun;
  let not our deeds debase our lives;
  let guilt not intertwine our tongues.

5. Sed sol diem dum conficit,
    fides profunda ferveat,
    spes ad promissa provocet,
    Christo coniungat caritas.

XXVII

Deus, qui caeli lumen es

1. Deus, qui caeli lumen es
    satorque lucis, qui polum
    paterno fultum bracchio
    praeclara pandis dextera:

2. Aurora stellas iam tegit
    rubrum sustollens gurgitem,
    umectis namque flatibus
    terram baptizans roribus.

3. Currum iam poscit Phosphorus
    radiis rotisque flammeis,
    quod caeli scandens verticem
    profectus moram nesciens.

4. Iam noctis umbra linquitur,
    polum caligo deserit;
    typusque Christi lucifer
    diem sopitum suscitans.

5. But when the sun shuts down the day,
    let our faith ferment deep within,
    hope spur us to our promises,
    and love unite us close to Christ.

Hymn 27

O God, who are the light of heaven

1. O God, who are the light of heaven
    and father of the light, the sky,
    which rests on your paternal arm,
    you open with your famed right hand:

2. The dawn does now enshroud the stars,
    raising aloft her crimson flood,
    for she baptizes all the earth
    with dew borne on the moistening winds.

3. Now Phosphorus demands his car,
    its spokes and wheels a rosy red,
    for as he mounts to heaven's peak
    his setting-out knows no delay.

4. The shades of night are left behind,
    the murk vanishes from the sky;
    the light-bearer, symbol of Christ,
    awakens now the slumbrous day.

5. Dies dierum hagius es,
    lucisque lumen ipse es,
    unum potens per omnia,
    potens in unum Trinitas.

6. Te nunc, Salvator, quaesumus
    tibique genu flectimus;
    Patrem cum sancto Spiritu
    totis rogamus viribus.

XXVIII

Mediae noctis tempus est

1. Mediae noctis tempus est;
    prophetica vox admonet
    dicamus laudes ut Deo,
    Patri semper ac Filio,

2. Sancto quoque Spiritui;
    perfecta enim Trinitas
    uniusque substantiae
    laudanda semper nobis est.

3. Terrorem tempus hoc habet,
    quo, cum vastator angelus
    Aegypto mortes intulit,
    delevit primogenita.

5.   You are the holy day of days,
      you are yourself the light of light;
      one power, which pervades all things,
      you wield yourself the Triune power.

6.   O Savior, we beseech you now
      and unto you we bend the knee;
      the Father with the Holy Ghost
      with all our strength we supplicate.

Hymn 28

Now that the midnight hour is here

1.   Now that the midnight hour is here
      the prophet's words their warning give
      that we must utter praise to God,
      to the Father always and the Son,

2.   And to the Holy Spirit too;
      for to the Trinity perfect
      and in one substance consisting
      must we forever utter praise.

3.   This moment inculcates much fear,
      for the destroying angel then,
      inflicting deaths on Egypt's land,
      did slaughter all of its firstborn.

4. Haec hora iustis salus est,
    quos ibidem tunc angelus
    ausus punire non erat,
    signum formidans sanguinis.

5. Aegyptus flebat fortiter
    tantorum dira funera;
    solus gaudebat Israhel
    agni protectus sanguine.

6. Nos verus Israhel sumus;
    laetamur in te, Domine,
    hostem spernentes et malum
    Christi defensi sanguine.

7. Ipsum profecto tempus est
    quo voce evangelica
    venturus sponsus creditur,
    regni caelestis conditor.

8. Occurrunt sanctae virgines
    obviam tunc adventui,
    gestantes claras lampadas,
    magno laetantes gaudio.

9. At stultae vero remanent,
    quia stinctas habent lampadas,
    frustra pulsantes ianuam:
    clausa iam regni regia.

10. Quare vigilemus sobrie,
    gestantes mentes splendidas,
    advenienti ut Iesu
    digni curramus obviam.

4. This hour is safety to the just,
    whom in that place the angel then
    did not presume to punish, since
    he did respect the mark of blood.

5. The Egyptians then wept bitter tears
    over so many gruesome deaths;
    but Israel alone rejoiced,
    protected by the lamb's own blood.

6. We are true Israel indeed;
    we take our joy in you, O Lord,
    and guarded by the blood of Christ,
    we view with scorn the evil foe.

7. This is indeed the very time
    at which, as gospel words proclaim,
    the bridegroom, we believe, will come,
    creator of the heavenly realm.

8. The holy virgins issue forth
    to meet his coming at that hour,
    bearing in hand their shining lamps,
    rejoicing with unbounded joy.

9. The foolish ones remain behind,
    since they hold lamps no longer lit;
    in vain they hammer at the door:
    the kingdom's palace now is barred.

10. So let us keep watch soberly,
    maintaining brightly lit our minds,
    so we, when Jesus will arrive,
    may run to meet him worthily.

11.   Noctisque mediae tempore
           Paulus quoque et Sileas
           Christum, vincti in carcere,
           conlaudantes soluti sunt.

12.   Nobis hic mundus carcer est;
           te laudamus, Christe Deus;
           solve vincla peccatorum
           in te sancte credentium.

13.   Dignos nos fac, rex hagie,
           venturi regni gloria,
           aeternis ut mereamur
           te laudibus concinere.

14.   Gloria Patri ingenito,
           gloria unigenito,
           simul cum sancto Spiritu
           in sempiterna saecula.

XXIX

Aurora lucis rutilat

1.   Aurora lucis rutilat,
           caelum laudibus intonat,
           mundus exultans iubilat,
           gemens infernus ululat,

11. So also at the midnight hour
     did Paul and Silas, lying bound
     in prison, utter praise of Christ,
     and there and then gained their release.

12. For us a prison is this world;
     we give you praise, O Christ our God;
     release us from our bonds of sin,
     who put our sacred trust in you.

13. And make us worthy, holy king,
     of glory in the realm to come,
     that we together may deserve
     to hymn you with eternal praise.

14. Glory to Father unconceived,
     and to his sole-begotten son,
     and to the Holy Spirit too,
     for ages that will never end.

Hymn 29

The dawn of day now crimson glows

1. The dawn of day now crimson glows,
    the sky with praises does resound,
    the universe exults with joy,
    the nether world laments and groans,

2. Cum rex ille fortissimus,
   mortis confractis viribus,
   pede conculcans Tartara,
   solvit catena miseros.

3. Ille, qui clausus lapide
   custoditur sub milite,
   triumphans pompa nobili
   victor surgit de funere.

4. Solutis iam gemitibus
   et inferni doloribus,
   "quia surrexit Dominus,"
   resplendens clamat angelus.

5. Tristes erant apostoli
   de nece sui Domini,
   quem poena mortis crudeli
   servi damnarunt impii.

6. Sermone blando angelus
   praedixit mulieribus:
   "In Galilaea Dominus
   videndus est quantocius."

7. Illae dum pergunt concite
   apostolis hoc dicere,
   videntes eum vivere
   osculant pedes Domini.

8. Quo agnito discipuli
   in Galilaeam propere
   pergunt videre faciem
   desideratam Domini.

2. Because that King, most brave of all,
   having destroyed the power of death,
   treading Tartarus underfoot,
   has freed the wretched from their chains.

3. He, who was closed up by a stone
   with soldiers mounting guard outside,
   exultant, with a proud display,
   rises victorious over death.

4. When once the groans and grievous pains
   of hell below have been dispelled,
   "The Lord has risen" cries aloud
   an angel, gleaming splendidly.

5. The apostles meanwhile were downcast,
   mourning the murder of their Lord,
   whom wicked servants had condemned
   to cruel punishment of death.

6. The angel then with soothing words
   unto the women told this news:
   "Upon this hour in Galilee
   the Lord is to be seen by men."

7. As they with all speed made their way
   this to the apostles to report,
   they beheld him now alive,
   and to the Lord's feet kisses laid.

8. Then his disciples, hearing this,
   with all haste into Galilee
   direct their course, to see the face,
   so sorely yearned for, of the Lord.

9. Claro paschali gaudio
    sol mundo nitet radio,
    cum Christum iam apostoli
    visu cernunt corporeo.

10. Ostensa sibi vulnera
    in Christi carne fulgida;
    resurrexisse Dominum
    voce fatentur publica.

11. Rex Christe clementissime,
    tu corda nostra posside,
    ut tibi laudes debitas
    reddamus omni tempore.

XXX

Diei luce reddita

1. Diei luce reddita,
    primis post somnum vocibus
    Dei canamus gloriam,
    Christi fatentes gratiam,

2. Per quem creator omnium
    diem noctemque condidit,
    aeterna lege sanciens
    ut semper succedant sibi.

9. The sun, with Easter's glowing joy,
   shines on the world with spotless ray,
   when now the apostles gaze on Christ
   with vision of him in the flesh.

10. His glowing wounds were shown to them,
    marks in the Christ's flesh visible;
    "The Lord has risen," they proclaim
    with voices loud, for all to hear.

11. O Christ, our King most merciful,
    take now possession of our hearts,
    that praises that are owed to you
    we may at all times offer up.

Hymn 30

Now that the daylight is restored

1. Now that the daylight is restored,
   with our first words which follow sleep
   let us sing out the glory of God,
   confessing too the grace of Christ,

2. Through whom the creator of all things
   established both the day and night,
   and by eternal law prescribed
   each ever to succeed the other.

3. Tu, vera lux fidelium,
  quem lex veterna non tenet,
  noctis nec ortus succedens,
  aeterno fulgens lumine,

4. Christe, precamur, adnue
  orantibus servis tuis,
  iniquitas haec saeculi
  ne nostram captivet fidem.

5. Non cogitemus impie,
  invideamus nemini,
  laesi non reddamus vicem,
  vincamus in bono malum.

6. Absit nostris a cordibus
  ira, dolus, superbia;
  absistat avaritia,
  malorum radix omnium.

7. Vinum mentem non occupet
  ebrietate perdita,
  sed nostro sensui competens
  tuum bibamus poculum.

8. Conservet pacis foedera
  non simulata caritas;
  sit illibata castitas
  credulitate perpeti.

9. Addendis non sit praediis
  malesuada semper famis;
  si adfluant divitiae,
  prophetae nos psalmus regat.

3. You, the true light of faithful souls,
    untrammeled by that law of old,
    or by the night's successive rise,
    gleaming with everlasting light,

4. Dear Christ, we beg you, bend an ear
    to these your servants' fervent prayers;
    let not the iniquity of this world
    imprison our faith in its bonds.

5. Let us no impious thought pursue,
    nor envy any living soul,
    no injury reciprocate,
    but conquer evil by the good.

6. Let anger, guile, and arrogance
    not find a lodging in our hearts;
    nor let greed have a place in us,
    the root of every evil thing.

7. Let wine not dominate our minds
    with drunkenness beyond control;
    let us drink rather of your cup
    as is appropriate to our minds.

8. Let charity that is unfeigned
    maintain alliances of peace;
    let chastity remain intact
    and faith abide enduringly.

9. Let not greed, ever prompting ill,
    lead us to add to our estates;
    if riches should unto us flow,
    the prophet's psalm must govern us.

10. Praesta, pater ingenite,
totum ducamus iugiter
Christo placentes hunc diem,
sancto repleti Spiritu.

XXXI

Certum tenentes ordinem

1. Certum tenentes ordinem,
pio poscamus pectore
hora diei tertia
trinae virtutis gloriam,

2. Ut simus habitaculum
illi sancto Spiritui,
qui quondam in apostolis
hac hora distributus est.

3. Hoc gradientes ordine
ornavit cuncta splendide
regni caelestis conditor
aeternae vitae praemiis.

10.   Grant, Father who were never born,
      that through the course of this whole day
      we may conduct it, pleasing Christ,
      and with the Holy Spirit filled.

Hymn 31

Keeping the fixed order of the hours

1.   Keeping the fixed order of the hours,
     let our devoted hearts invoke
     at this, the third hour of the day,
     the glory of the triune power,

2.   That we may be the dwelling place
     for the Holy Spirit of Pentecost,
     who unto the apostles once
     was at this very hour bestowed.

3.   Those who in this fixed order walk
     he who created heaven's realm
     has splendidly in all ways adorned
     with blessings of eternal life.

XXXII

Dei fide, qua vivimus

1. Dei fide, qua vivimus,
   spe perenni, qua credimus,
   per caritatis gratiam,
   Christo canamus gloriam.

2. Qui ductus hora tertia
   ad passionis hostiam,
   crucis ferens suspendia,
   ovem reduxit perditam.

3. Precemur ergo subditi
   redemptione liberi,
   ut eruat a saeculo
   quos solvit a chirographo.

XXXIII

Dicamus laudes Domino

1. Dicamus laudes Domino
   fervente prompto spiritu;

Hymn 32

By faith in God, by which we live

1. By faith in God, by which we live,
   by lasting hope, source of belief,
   through grace bestowed by charity,
   let us proclaim to Christ his fame.

2. When he was led at that third hour
   to sacrificial suffering,
   enduring hanging on the cross,
   he regained the sheep which had been lost.

3. So let us pray on bended knee,
   since by redemption we are freed,
   that he may save us from the world,
   as he has loosed us from our bond.

Hymn 33

Let us sound praises to the Lord

1. Let us sound praises to the Lord
   with ready and devoted heart;

hora voluta sexies
nos ad orandum provocat,

2. Quia in hac fidelibus
verae salutis gratia
beati Agni hostia
crucis virtute redditur,

3. Cuius luce clarissima
tenebricat meridies;
sumamus toto pectore
tanti splendoris gratiam.

XXXIV

Deus, qui claro lumine

1. Deus, qui claro lumine
diem fecisti, Domine,
tuam rogamus gloriam
dum pronus volvitur dies.

2. Iam sol urgente Vespero
occasum suum graditur,
mundum concludens tenebris,
suum observans ordinem.

the hour has six times circled round,
and summons us to make our prayers,

2.   For at this hour for faithful souls
the grace of true salvation was
by sacrifice of the blessed Lamb
by power of the cross restored,

3.   By whose exceeding brilliant light
the brightness of midday goes dark;
let us embrace with our whole heart
the grace that such bright radiance brings.

Hymn 34

O Lord our God, who did create

1.   O Lord our God, who did create
the day with brilliance of light,
you in your glory we invoke
as day rolls on its downward course.

2.   The sun, hard-pressed by Hesperus,
embarks on his downward descent,
the world in darkness folding up
as he maintains his ordered course.

3.   Sed tu, excelse Domine,
precantes tuos famulos
labore fessos diei
quietos nox suscipiat,

4.   Ut non fuscatis mentibus
dies abscedat saeculi,
sed tua tecti gratia
cernamus lucem prosperam.

XXXV

Sator princepsque temporum

1.   Sator princepsque temporum,
clarum diem laboribus
noctemque qui soporibus
fixo distinguis ordine,

2.   Mentem tu castam dirige
obscura ne silentia
ad dira cordis vulnera
telis patescant invidi.

3.   Somno non cedat spiritus
vigilque custos corporis
metus inanes arceat,
fallax depellat gaudium.

3. But you, O Lord, who dwell on high,
   your servants here, making their prayers,
   exhausted by their day's hard work,
   let night take up in tranquil rest,

4. So that, our minds of darkness free,
   this worldly day may disappear;
   but we, protected by your grace,
   may look upon a happy dawn.

Hymn 35

Creator and the prince of days

1. Creator and the prince of days,
   with fixed arrangement you divide
   the bright day for our heavy toils
   from night allotted to our sleep;

2. Direct our mind in chastity,
   lest in the shadowed silence, we,
   by darts of the envious one, should be
   exposed to grave wounds of the heart.

3. Let not our spirit yield to sleep,
   but as the body's watchful guard
   let it ward off all empty fears
   and put to flight deceiving joy.

4. Vacent ardore pectora
    faces nec ullas sentiant,
    adfixae ne praecordiis
    mentis vigorem saucient.

5. Sed cum defessa corpora
    somni tenebunt gratiam,
    caro quietis sit memor,
    fides soporem nesciat.

4. May hearts be wholly free of heat
    and feel no flames of lustful thoughts,
    lest if they fasten on our hearts
    they impair the vigor of our minds.

5. But when our bodies wearily
    embrace the welcome charm of sleep,
    may our flesh recollect its rest,
    but faith no slumber entertain.

THE NEW HYMNAL

XXXVI

Rector potens, verax Deus

1. Rector potens, verax Deus
   qui temperas rerum vices,
   splendore mane instruis
   et ignibus meridiem,

2. Exstingue flammas litium,
   aufer calorem noxium,
   confer salutem corporum,
   veramque pacem cordium.

XXXVII

Rerum Deus tenax vigor

1. Rerum Deus tenax vigor,
   immotus in te permanens,
   lucis diurnae tempora
   successibus determinans,

Hymn 36

Ruler of power, God of truth

1. Ruler of power, God of truth,
    who control changes in the world,
    you dress the dawn with its bright gleam,
    and noonday with its blazing fires;

2. Put out the flames of our disputes,
    temper the heat which brings us harm,
    grant unto us our bodies' health,
    and on our hearts confer true peace.

Hymn 37

O God, the strength that binds all things

1. O God, the strength that binds all things,
    remaining unchanged in yourself,
    the periods of each day's light
    you limit by due sequences;

2. Largire clarum vespere,
   quo vita nusquam decidat,
   sed praemium mortis sacrae
   perennis instet gloria.

XXXVIII

Primo dierum omnium

1. Primo dierum omnium
   quo mundus exstat conditus,
   vel quo resurgens conditor
   nos morte victa liberat,

2. Pulsis procul torporibus
   surgamus omnes ocius,
   et nocte quaeramus pium,
   sicut prophetam novimus,

3. Nostras preces ut audiat
   suamque dextram porrigat,
   et hic piatos sordibus
   reddat polorum sedibus;

4. Ut quique sacratissimo
   huius diei tempore
   horis quietis psallimus,
   donis beatis muneret.

2.   Grant us clear skies at eventide,
so life at no point slips away,
but as reward for holy death
let lasting glory follow close.

Hymn 38

On this, the first day of all days

1.   On this, the first day of all days
on which the world, being made, emerged,
on which the maker rose again
and freed us, having conquered death,

2.   Let us, sloth driven far away,
rise all together urgently,
in darkness beg the holy one,
as we know that the prophet did,

3.   That he might hearken to our prayers
and offer unto us his hand,
and render us, here cleansed of filth,
unto the heavenly demesnes;

4.   And that whoever on this day,
which is the holiest of all,
do hymn him in these hours of rest
be endowed by him with blessed gifts.

XXXIX

Summae Deus clementiae

1. Summae Deus clementiae
mundique factor machinae,
unus potentialiter,
trinusque personaliter,

2. Nostros pius cum canticis
fletus benigne suscipe,
quo corda pura sordibus
te perfruamur largius;

3. Lumbos iecurque morbidum
adure igne congruo,
accincti ut sint perpetim
luxu remoto pessimo,

4. Ut quique horas noctium
nunc concinendo rumpimus,
donis beatae patriae
ditemur omnes adfatim.

Hymn 39

O God of greatest clemency

1. O God of greatest clemency,
   who made the fabric of the world,
   in exercise of power one,
   incorporate as persons three,

2. Devotedly, with kindly heart,
   receive our tears mingled with songs,
   so that we, hearts of foulness pure,
   may find in you more generous joy;

3. Our loins and liver, sore diseased,
   treat with appropriate cautery,
   that with their evil lust excised
   they may be girt continually.

4. So we who break the hours of night
   united in harmonious song
   may all be copiously enriched
   with gifts of our blessed fatherland.

XL

Consors paterni luminis

1. Consors paterni luminis,
   lux ipse lucis et dies,
   noctem canendo rumpimus;
   adsiste postulantibus.

2. Aufer tenebras mentium,
   fuga catervas daemonum;
   expelle somnolentiam,
   ne pigritantes obruat.

3. Sic, Christe, nobis omnibus
   indulgeas credentibus
   ut prosit exorantibus
   quod praecinentes psallimus.

4. Praesta, Pater piissime,
   Patrique compar unice,
   cum Spiritu Paraclito
   regnans per omne saeculum.

Hymn 40

O sharer in the Father's light

1. O sharer in the Father's light,
   yourself the light of light and day,
   singing we break the hours of night;
   be with us as we make our prayers.

2. Remove the shadows of our minds,
   and put to flight the demon hordes;
   dismiss from us our drowsiness,
   lest it submerge our sluggish minds.

3. O Christ, since all have faith in you,
   show kindness to us, one and all,
   that as we make our prayers to you
   the hymns we sing may benefit us.

4. O Father of devoted love,
   and you, the Father's only peer,
   who with the Spirit, Comforter,
   for ever rule, grant this our prayer.

XLI

Somno refectis artubus

1. Somno refectis artubus,
   spreto cubili surgimus;
   nobis, Pater, canentibus
   adesse te deposcimus.

2. Te lingua primum concinat,
   te mentis ardor ambiat,
   ut actuum sequentium
   tu, sancte, sis exordium.

3. Cedant tenebrae lumini
   et nox diurno sideri,
   ut culpa quam nox intulit
   lucis labascat munere.

4. Precamur idem supplices
   noxas ut omnes amputes,
   et ore te canentium
   lauderis in perpetuum.

Hymn 41

Our limbs being now refreshed from sleep

1.   Our limbs being now refreshed from sleep,
spurning our beds we gladly rise;
and, Father, in our hymn to you
we beg your presence close to us.

2.   Our tongues must hymn you first in praise,
our eager hearts solicit you,
holy one, that you be the start
of all our actions following.

3.   The darkness must give place to light,
and night before the star of day,
so that the sin that night brought in
may vanish with the gift of light.

4.   We pray too on our bended knees
that you may excise all our sins,
and by the tongues that sing your praise
may you be hymned for evermore.

XLII

Aeterna caeli gloria

1. Aeterna caeli gloria,
   beata spes mortalium,
   celsitonantis unice,
   castaeque proles virginis,

2. Da dexteram surgentibus,
   exsurgat et mens sobria,
   flagransque in laudem Dei
   grates rependat debitas.

3. Hortus refulget lucifer
   ipsamque lucem nuntiat:
   kadit caligo noctium;
   lux sancta nos illuminet,

4. Manensque nostris sensibus
   noctem repellat saeculi,
   omnique fine diei
   purgata servet pectora.

5. Quaesita iam primum fides
   radicet altis sensibus;
   secunda spes congaudeat,
   tunc maior exstet caritas.

Hymn 42

Eternal glory of the heavens

1.   Eternal glory of the heavens,
     O blessed hope of mortal men,
     sole son of the high thunderer,
     offspring of virgin's chastity,

2.   Lend us your hand as we arise,
     let our minds also sober rise,
     and as they burn in praise of God
     render the thanks that are his due.

3.   Rising, the morning star shines bright,
     reports the coming of the light:
     the darkness of the night falls back;
     may sacred light shine bright on us,

4.   And as it in our minds abides
     let it repel the world's dark night,
     and at the every end of day
     preserve our hearts once they are cleansed.

5.   Let faith, which is to be first sought,
     take root, lodged deep within our hearts;
     let hope as second share its joy,
     let love, the greatest, then stand out.

XLIII

Lucis creator optime

1. Lucis creator optime,
    lucem dierum proferens,
    primordiis lucis novae
    mundi parans originem,

2. Qui mane iunctum vesperi
    diem vocari praecipis:
    taetrum chaos inlabitur;
    audi preces cum fletibus.

3. Ne mens gravata crimine
    vitae sit exsul munere,
    dum nil perenne cogitat
    seseque culpis inligat.

4. Caelorum pulset intimum,
    vitale tollat praemium;
    vitemus omne noxium,
    purgemus omne pessimum.

Hymn 43

Noblest creator of the light

1. Noblest creator of the light,
    who activate the light of days,
    and with beginnings of new light
    furnish the origin of the world,

2. Who, joining morning to the eve,
    do bid that it be called the day:
    foul chaos now comes stealing in;
    so hearken to our tearful prayers.

3. Let not our mind, burdened with sin,
    be exiled from the gift of life,
    nor be involved in sinful acts
    with no thought of eternity.

4. May it at inmost heaven knock,
    let it there gain the prize of life;
    let us avoid all that will harm,
    of every worst sin cleanse ourselves.

XLIV

Immense caeli conditor

1.   Immense caeli conditor,
qui, mixta ne confunderent,
aquae fluenta dividens
caelum dedisti limitem,

2.   Firmans locum caelestibus
simulque terrae rivulis,
ut unda flammas temperet,
terrae solum ne dissipet,

3.   Infunde nunc, piissime,
donum perennis gratiae,
fraudis novae ne casibus
nos error adterat vetus.

4.   Lucem fides inveniat,
sic luminis iubar ferat:
haec vana cuncta terreat;
hanc falsa nulla comprimant.

Hymn 44

Boundless creator of the heavens

1.   Boundless creator of the heavens,
who, bisecting the water-floods,
set up the sky as boundary,
lest mingling they should swamp the world,

2.   And fortified the beds for streams
in heaven and on the earth below,
so water could restrain the flames
and not destroy the face of earth,

3.   Pour down now, most devoted one,
your gift of never-failing grace,
lest by hazards of fresh deceit
the ancient sin may wear us down.

4.   May faith gain knowledge of the light,
the beam of brightness thus obtain:
so let that light all vain things deter;
let no falsehoods suppress that faith.

XLV

Telluris ingens conditor

1. Telluris ingens conditor,
   mundi solum qui eruens,
   pulsis aquae molestiis
   terram dedisti immobilem,

2. Ut germen aptum proferens,
   fulvis decora floribus,
   fecunda fructu sisteret
   pastumque gratum redderet,

3. Mentis perustae vulnera
   munda viroris gratia,
   ut facta fletu diluat
   motusque pravos adterat.

4. Iussis tuis obtemperet,
   nullis malis approximet,
   bonis repleri gaudeat,
   et mortis actum nesciat.

Hymn 45

O mighty founder of the earth

1. O mighty founder of the earth,
   by rescuing the world's firm ground,
   driving the irksome waters back,
   you made the land immovable,

2. That it, bearing appropriate seeds,
   and beauteous with golden flowers,
   might be fertile with yield of fruit,
   and offer welcome sustenance.

3. Now cleanse the wounds of our parched minds,
   restoring them with verdant grace,
   that it may purge our deeds with tears,
   and evil inclinations quell.

4. So may our minds heed your commands,
   draw never near to evil things,
   rejoice in blessings' goodly store,
   know nothing of the works of death.

XLVI

Caeli Deus sanctissime

1. Caeli Deus sanctissime,
   qui lucidum centrum poli
   candore pingis igneo
   augens decoro lumine,

2. Quarto die qui flammeam
   solis rotam constituens,
   lunae ministrans ordini
   vagos recursus siderum,

3. Ut noctibus vel lumini
   diremptionis terminum,
   primordiis et mensium
   signum dares notissimum:

4. Illumina cor hominum,
   absterge sordes mentium,
   resolve culpae vinculum,
   everte moles criminum.

Hymn 46

Most holy God of heaven above

1. Most holy God of heaven above,
    who with your fiery brightness paint
    the shining center of the sky,
    enhancing it with beauteous light,

2. Who on that fourth day did create
    the fiery circle of the sun,
    supplying to the moon's fixed route
    the wandering courses of the stars;

3. You thus imposed on night and day
    the limits of their separate reigns,
    and to the beginnings of the months
    the clearest indication gave.

4. Pour light into the hearts of men,
    wipe clean the foulness in our minds;
    release us from the chains of guilt,
    dislodge the heavy weight of sins.

XLVII

Magnae Deus potentiae

1. Magnae Deus potentiae,
   qui ex aquis ortum genus
   partim remittis gurgiti,
   partim levas in aera,

2. Demersa lymphis imprimens,
   subvecta caelis inrogans,
   ut stirpe una prodita
   diversa rapiant loca,

3. Largire cunctis servulis,
   quos mundat unda sanguinis,
   nescire lapsus criminum
   nec ferre mortis taedium,

4. Ut culpa nullum deprimat,
   nullum levet iactantia,
   elisa mens ne concidat,
   elata mens ne corruat.

Hymn 47

O God, whose power is so great

1. O God, whose power is so great,
   who of the race sprung from the deep
   remit some to the ocean swell
   but others raise into the air,

2. Confining those plunged in the deep,
   assigning those raised to the sky,
   that each sprung from that single stock
   may occupy diverse abodes,

3. Pour grace on all poor servants here,
   cleansed by the issue of your blood,
   to know no lapses into sins
   nor bear the weariness of death,

4. That guilt may nobody oppress,
   no one may boastfulness inflate,
   nobody's mind be crushed and fall,
   nor be puffed up and tumble down.

XLVIII

Conditor alme siderum

1. Conditor alme siderum,
   aeterna lux credentium,
   Christe, redemptor omnium,
   exaudi preces supplicum,

2. Qui condolens interitu
   mortis perire saeculum,
   salvasti mundum languidum,
   donans reis remedium,

3. Vergente mundi vespere,
   uti sponsus de thalamo,
   egressus honestissima
   virginis matris clausula:

4. Cuius forti potentiae
   genu curvantur omnia,
   caelestia terrestria
   nutu fatentur subdita,

5. Occasum sol custodiens,
   luna pallorem retinens,
   candor in astris relucens
   certos observans limites.

6. Te deprecamur, hagie,
   venture iudex saeculi,

Hymn 48

O kindly founder of the stars

1. O kindly founder of the stars,
    believers' everlasting light,
    O Christ, redeemer of all men,
    hear now the prayers your suppliants make,

2. You who, grieving as our world perished,
    lying prostrate in the grip of death,
    did save the sick and weary world,
    giving a cure to guilty men;

3. You, as the world's evening drew nigh,
    just as a bridegroom from his room,
    came out your virgin mother's womb,
    greatly honored receptacle:

4. To your indomitable power
    all things created bend the knee,
    the things of heaven, the things of earth
    confess subjection to your sway,

5. The sun maintaining its descent,
    the moon retaining its pale light,
    the brightness shining in the stars
    observing their fixed journeying.

6. We here beseech you, holy one,
    you who will come to judge the world,

conserva nos in tempore
hostis a telo perfidi.

7. Laus honor virtus gloria
Deo Patri cum Filio,
sancto simul Paraclito
in sempiterna saecula.

XLIX

O lux beata Trinitas

1. O lux beata Trinitas
et principalis unitas,
iam sol recedit igneus;
infunde lumen cordibus.

2. Te mane laudum carmine,
te deprecamur vespere,
te nostra supplex gloria
per cuncta laudet saecula.

preserve us at this present time
from weapons of the faithless foe.

7. Praise, honor, strength, and glory too
to God the Father with the Son,
and to the holy Comforter,
while endless ages run their course.

Hymn 49

O Trinity, our blessed light

1. O Trinity, our blessed light
and primal sovereign unity,
the fiery sun by now departs;
pour light instead into our hearts.

2. You in the morn with song of praise,
you in the evening we beseech;
so may our suppliant words in praise
hymn you through all ages to come.

L

Christe, redemptor omnium

1. Christe, redemptor omnium,
    ex Patre, Patris unice,
    solus ante principium
    natus ineffabiliter,

2. Tu lumen, tu splendor Patris,
    tu spes perennis omnium;
    intende quas fundunt preces
    tui per orbem famuli.

3. Memento, salutis auctor,
    quod nostri quondam corporis
    ex illibata virgine
    nascendo formam sumpseris.

4. Hic praesens testatur dies
    currens per anni circulum
    quod solus a sede Patris
    mundi salus adveneris.

5. Hunc caelum, terra, hunc mare,
    hunc omne quod in eis est,
    auctoris adventu sui
    laudat, exultans cantico.

Hymn 50

O Christ, redeemer of all men

1. O Christ, redeemer of all men,
   the Father's sole-begotten son,
   who alone before the world began
   were born (mystery ineffable!),

2. You are the Father's light so bright,
   the hope enduring of us all;
   hear now the prayers poured out to you
   by your servants throughout the world.

3. Remember, our salvation's author,
   that long ago you took the form
   of our own body, and were born
   out of a virgin without stain.

4. This present day to us attests
   throughout the cycle of the year
   that you did quit your Father's seat,
   and came alone to save the world.

5. Sky and earth praise him, him the sea,
   him all things that abide in these,
   now that their Maker has drawn near,
   as they all in their song rejoice.

6.   Nos quoque, qui sancto tuo
redempti sanguine sumus,
ob diem natalis tui
hymnum novum concinimus.

LI

Ex more docti mystico

1.   Ex more docti mystico
servemus, en, ieiunium,
denum dierum circulo
ducto quater notissimo.

2.   Lex et prophetae primitus
hoc praetulerunt, postmodum
Christus sacravit, omnium
rex atque factor temporum.

3.   Utamur ergo parcius
verbis, cibis, et potibus,
somno, iocis, et artius
perstemus in custodia.

4.   Vitemus autem pessima
quae subruunt mentes vagas,
nullumque demus callido
hosti locum tyrannidis.

6.   We also, who have been redeemed
      by power of your holy blood,
      on the occasion of your birth
      a new hymn sing in unison.

Hymn 51

Instructed by the mystic norm

1.   Instructed by the mystic norm
      let us our fasting now maintain;
      the familiar cycle has now begun,
      extending for four times ten days.

2.   The law and prophets anciently
      proclaimed this, and then after them
      Christ sanctified it, he who is
      the king and maker of all times.

3.   So let us use more sparingly
      exchange of words and food and drink,
      and sleep and joking; let us stay
      more stringently upon our guard.

4.   Let us avoid those wicked things
      that undermine our wandering minds,
      nor grant to our foul-scheming foe
      a vantage point of tyranny.

5. Dicamus omnes cernui,
    clamemus atque singuli;
    ploremus ante iudicem,
    flectamus iram vindicem.

6. Nostris malis offendimus
    tuam, Deus, clementiam;
    effunde nobis desuper
    remissor indulgentiam.

7. Memento quod sumus tui,
    licet caduci plasmatis;
    ne des honorem nominis
    tui, precamur, alteri.

8. Laxa malum quod fecimus,
    auge bonum quod poscimus,
    placere quo tandem tibi
    possimus hic et perpetim.

LII

Audi, benigne conditor

1. Audi, benigne conditor,
    nostras preces cum fletibus,
    in hoc sacro ieiunio
    fusas quadragenario.

5.   Let us all speak on bended knee,
and each and all cry out aloud;
let us lament before the judge,
let us divert his vengeful wrath.

6.   By our so wicked deeds, O God,
your kindly mercy we offend;
forbearing be, and from on high
pour on us mercy for our sins.

7.   Remember we belong to you,
though members of the fallen flesh;
do not, we pray, to others give
the signal glory of your name.

8.   Dissolve the evil we have done,
increase the blessings that we seek,
so that both now and ever more
we may at last your favor win.

Hymn 52

O kind creator, bend your ear

1.   O kind creator, bend your ear
and hearken to our tearful prayers
poured out during this holy fast
lasting the course of forty days.

2. Scrutator alme cordium,
    infirma tu scis virium;
    ad te reversis exhibe
    remissionis gratiam.

3. Multum quidem peccavimus,
    sed parce confitentibus;
    ad laudem tui nominis
    confer medelam languidis.

4. Sic corpus extra conteri
    dona per abstinentiam
    ieiunet ut mens sobria
    a labe prorsus criminum.

5. Praesta, beata Trinitas,
    concede, simplex unitas,
    ut fructuosa sint tuis
    ieiuniorum munera.

LIII

Iesu, nostra redemptio

1. Iesu, nostra redemptio,
    amor et desiderium,
    Deus, creator omnium,
    homo in fine temporum,

2.   O kindly searcher of men's hearts,
     you know the weakness of our powers;
     now that we turn back unto you,
     grant us to have forgiveness' grace.

3.   We have indeed sinned direly,
     but spare us, for we do confess;
     to glorify your name, bestow
     a remedy, for we are sick.

4.   Grant that our flesh by abstinence
     may be so chastened outwardly
     that sober hearts within may fast
     entirely from all stain of sins.

5.   Ensure, O blessed Trinity,
     grant, you who are one unity,
     that fruitful may be the rewards
     your servants reap by fasting thus.

Hymn 53

O Jesus, our redemption

1.   O Jesus, our redemption,
     our love and our desire,
     God, who all things created,
     man, at the close of times,

2. Quae te vicit clementia
    ut ferres nostra crimina,
    crudelem mortem patiens
    ut nos a morte tolleres,

3. Inferni claustra penetrans
    tuos captivos redimens,
    victor triumpho nobili
    ad dextram Patris residens?

4. Ipsa te cogat pietas
    ut mala nostra superes
    parcendo, et voti compotes
    nos tuo vultu saties.

5. Tu esto nostrum gaudium
    qui es futurum praemium,
    sit nostra in te gloria
    per cuncta semper saecula.

LIV

Aeterne rex altissime

1. Aeterne rex altissime
    redemptor et fidelium,
    quo mors soluta deperit,
    datur triumphus gratiae,

2. What kindness overcame you,
   that you should bear our sins,
   a cruel death enduring
   to rescue us from death?

3. Hell's gate you penetrated,
   your captives you redeemed,
   victor in noble triumph
   on the Father's right you sit.

4. Let that devotion press you
   to overcome our sins
   by pardon; our wish granted,
   give full sight of your face.

5. Now be our present joy,
   and next our future prize,
   may our glory stay in you
   through every age to come.

Hymn 54

Eternal king set high above

1. Eternal king set high above,
   and redeemer of faithful souls,
   by whom death is loosed and destroyed,
   and the triumph of grace is given,

2. Scandens tribunal dexterae
    Patris, potestas omnium
    conlata est, Iesu, caelitus,
    quae non erat humanitus,

3. Ut trina rerum machina,
    caelestium, terrestrium,
    et infernorum condita
    flectat genu iam subdita.

4. Tremunt videntes angeli
    versam vicem mortalium;
    culpat caro, purgat caro,
    regnat Deus Dei caro.

5. Tu, Christe, nostrum gaudium,
    manens Olympo praeditum,
    mundi regis qui fabricam
    mundana vincens gaudia.

6. Hinc te precantes quaesumus,
    ignosce culpis omnibus,
    et corda sursum subleva
    ad te superna gratia.

7. Et cum repente coeperis
    clarere nube iudicis,
    poenas repellas debitas,
    reddas coronas perditas.

2. As you climb to the judgment seat,
   positioned at the Father's right,
   that power in heaven was granted you
   that you did not possess as man:

3. The threefold fabric of the world,
   created things in heaven and earth
   and those which lie below the earth,
   now subjected, must bend the knee.

4. The angels tremble to behold
   the lot of mortal men transformed;
   the flesh sins, the flesh purifies,
   the flesh of God now reigns as God.

5. You, Christ, are source of our delight,
   who are possessed of heaven for ever,
   who rule the fabric of the world,
   surpassing every earthly joy.

6. So now we beg you in our prayers
   to pardon us for all our sins,
   and raise our hearts aloft to you
   by means of grace bestowed from heaven.

7. So when suddenly you begin
   to gleam bright on the judgment-cloud,
   remit the punishments we owe,
   restore the crowns we forfeited.

LV

Optatus votis omnium

1. Optatus votis omnium
   sacratus inluxit dies,
   quo Christus, mundi spes, Deus
   conscendit caelos arduos.

2. Ascendens in altum Dominus,
   propriam ad sedem remeans,
   gavisa sunt caeli regna
   reditu unigeniti.

3. Magno triumpho proelii,
   mundi perempto principe,
   Patris praesentans vultibus
   victricis carnis gloriam,

4. Est elevatus in nubibus,
   et spem fecit credentibus,
   aperiens Paradisum,
   quem protoplasti clauserant.

5. O grande cunctis gaudium,
   quo partus nostrae virginis
   post sputa, flagra, post crucem
   paternae sedi iungitur!

Hymn 55

That day for which all longed in prayer

1. That day for which all longed in prayer,
   that sacred day, at last has dawned,
   on which Christ, world's hope, as God
   did rise up to the lofty skies.

2. So when the Lord mounted on high,
   returning to his native seat,
   heaven's kingdom was suffused with joy
   at the return of the sole-born.

3. In glorious triumph from the fight,
   having slain the prince who ruled the world,
   showing unto his Father's face
   the glory of victorious flesh,

4. He was raised up among the clouds,
   and to believers he brought hope,
   as he laid open Paradise,
   which our first parents had foreclosed.

5. O boundless joy to everyone,
   that our virgin's offspring, who
   endured the spits, the whips, the cross,
   does now attain his Father's seat!

6. Agamus ergo gratias
    nostrae salutis vindici,
    nostrum quod corpus vexerit
    sublimem ad caeli regiam.

7. Sit nobis cum caelestibus
    commune manens gaudium,
    illis quod se praesentavit,
    nobis quod se non abstulit.

8. Nunc provocatis actibus
    Christum exspectare nos decet
    vitaque tali vivere
    quae possit caelum scandere.

LVI

Iam Christus astra ascenderat

1. Iam Christus astra ascenderat,
    regressus unde venerat,
    promisso Patris munere
    sanctum daturus Spiritum.

2. Sollemnis surgebat dies
    quo mystico septemplici
    orbis volutus septies
    signat beata tempora.

6.   So let us now express our thanks
      to our salvation's rescuer,
      for he has borne our bodily form
      to heaven's palace up on high.

7.   May we with denizens of heaven
      abiding joy in common share,
      since he joined those who dwell above,
      yet did not separate from us.

8.   Now, as we rouse our energies,
      our duty is to wait on Christ,
      and here to live the kind of life
      that may on high to heaven climb.

Hymn 56

Now Christ had mounted to the stars

1.   Now Christ had mounted to the stars,
      returning to his former home,
      the Holy Spirit to bestow
      as promised by the Father's gift.

2.   That solemn day was dawning now
      to which the globe had circled round
      seven times its mystic number seven,
      denoting now the blessed time.

3. Cum hora cunctis tertia
repente mundus intonat,
apostolis orantibus
Deum venisse nuntians.

4. De Patris ergo lumine
decorus ignis almus est,
qui fida Christi pectora
calore verbi compleat.

5. Impleta gaudent viscera
adflata sancto lumine;
voces diversae consonant,
fantur Dei magnalia.

6. Ex omni gente cogitur
Graecus Latinus barbarus,
cunctisque admirantibus
linguis loquuntur omnium.

7. Iudaea tunc incredula
vesano turba spiritu
ructare musti crapulam
alumnos Christi concrepat.

8. Sed signis et virtutibus
occurrit et docet Petrus
falsa profari perfidos
Iohele teste comprobans.

3.   On all, when that third hour had come,
     the world in sudden thunder broke,
     according to the apostles' prayers
     announcing God's arrival here.

4.   So downward from the Father's light
     the beauteous, fostering fire descends,
     to fill the hearts that trust in Christ
     with the burning impact of the word.

5.   Men's hearts are full, and feel the joy
     as holy light is breathed on them;
     their diverse voices harmonize
     and tell of God's glorious deeds.

6.   From every race is gathered there
     the Greek, Latin, barbarian,
     and to the astonishment of all
     they speak in universal tongues.

7.   The unbelieving crowd of Jews
     being then possessed by lunacy
     together shout: "Christ's fosterlings
     are belching, reeling with new wine!"

8.   But Peter, wielding signs and powers,
     confronts them, teaching them the truth,
     that they are faithless, telling lies,
     with Joel his witness giving proof.

LVII

Beata nobis gaudia

1. Beata nobis gaudia
   anni reduxit orbita,
   cum Spiritus Paraclitus
   effulsit in discipulos.

2. Ignis vibrante lumine
   linguae figuram detulit,
   verbis ut essent proflui
   et caritate fervidi.

3. Linguis loquuntur omnium;
   turbae pavent gentilium;
   musto madere deputant
   quos Spiritus repleverat.

4. Patrata sunt haec mystice
   Paschae peracto tempore,
   sacro dierum numero
   quo lege fit remissio.

5. Te nunc, Deus piissime,
   vultu precamur cernuo,
   illapsa nobis caelitus
   largire dona Spiritus.

Hymn 57

These joys so blessed unto us

1. These joys so blessed unto us
   the year's orbit has rendered back,
   when the Spirit the Comforter
   on Christ's disciples shone his rays.

2. He chose the appearance of a tongue
   endowed with quivering light of fire,
   so they might speak with fluency
   and burn within with Christian love.

3. They spoke in universal tongues;
   the crowds of Gentiles showed their fear;
   those whom the Spirit had possessed
   they thought were tipsy with new wine.

4. These deeds were done in mystery
   once Eastertide had run its course,
   at that sacred number of days
   when by the law release is given.

5. We now, O most devoted God,
   beseech you with our faces bowed,
   to grant the Spirit's gifts to us
   that glide down from the heaven above.

6.   Dudum sacrata pectora
tua replesti gratia;
dimitte nunc peccamina
et da quieta tempora.

LVIII

Rex gloriose martyrum

1.   Rex gloriose martyrum,
corona confitentium,
qui respuentes terrea
perducis ad caelestia,

2.   Aurem benignam protinus
adpone nostris vocibus:
tropaea sacra pangimus;
ignosce quod deliquimus.

3.   Tu vincis in martyribus;
parcendo confitentibus
tu vince nostra crimina,
donando indulgentiam.

6.　You filled those consecrated hearts
　　of old with your abundant grace;
　　now grant us pardon from our sins,
　　and grant to us untroubled times.

Hymn 58

O king of martyrs, glorious

1.　O king of martyrs, glorious,
　　the crown of those who praise your name,
　　you who lead them that do despise
　　earthly affairs to things of heaven,

2.　Your kindly ear without delay
　　to our entreating voices bend:
　　of sacred trophies we do sing;
　　grant pardon wherein we do sin.

3.　In martyrs lies your victory;
　　by sparing those proclaiming you
　　gain victory over our sins,
　　bestowing pardon on our faults.

LIX

Deus, tuorum militum

1. Deus, tuorum militum
   sors et corona, praemium,
   laudes cantantes martyris
   absolve nexu criminis.

2. Hic nempe mundi gaudia
   et blandimenta noxia
   caduca rite deputans
   pervenit ad caelestia.

3. Poenas cucurrit fortiter
   et sustulit viriliter;
   pro te effundens sanguinem
   aeterna dona possidet.

4. Ob hoc precatu supplici
   te poscimus, piissime:
   in hoc triumpho martyris
   dimitte noxam servulis.

Hymn 59

O God, the portion, crown, and prize

1.   O God, the portion, crown, and prize
   of us your soldiers here on earth,
   as we proclaim your martyr's praise
   deliver us from bonds of sin.

2.   For, surveying this world's delights
   and mischievous alluring charms,
   he rightly judged them perishable,
   and so attained to heavenly joys.

3.   Unflinching, he passed through his pains
   and suffered them in manly wise;
   by pouring out his blood for you
   he now has gained eternal gifts.

4.   This prompts us now with suppliant prayer
   to beg you, most devoted one:
   forgive your lowly servants' guilt
   on this, your martyr's triumph day.

LX

Iesu, corona virginum

1. Iesu, corona virginum,
   quem mater illa concipit,
   quae sola virgo parturit,
   haec vota clemens accipe,

2. Qui pascis inter lilia
   saeptus choreis virginum,
   sponsus decorus gloria,
   sponsisque reddens praemia;

3. Quocumque pergis, virgines
   sequuntur, atque laudibus
   post te canentes cursitant
   hymnosque dulces personant.

4. Te deprecamur, largius
   nostris adauge mentibus
   nescire prorsus omnia
   corruptionis vulnera.

Hymn 60

Jesus, you are the virgins' crown

1. Jesus, you are the virgins' crown,
   whom that famed mother did conceive,
   sole virgin to have borne a child;
   these prayers indulgently receive,

2. You who among the lilies feast,
   enclosed by bands of virgins there,
   a bridegroom handsome in your fame,
   and rendering prizes to your brides;

3. Whithersoever you advance
   the virgins follow you, and race,
   singing your praises, in your wake,
   and make their sweet hymns to resound.

4. We pray you now, more generously
   give added vision to our minds,
   to have no truck with any wounds
   inflicted by corruption's dart.

LXI

Iesu, redemptor omnium

1. Iesu, redemptor omnium,
   perpes corona praesulum,
   in hac die clementius
   nostris faveto vocibus,

2. Tui sacri qua nominis
   confessor almus claruit,
   cuius celebrat annua
   devota plebs sollemnia.

3. Qui rite mundi gaudia
   huius caduca respuens
   cum angelis caelestibus
   laetus potitur praemiis.

4. Huius benigne adnue
   nobis sequi vestigia;
   huius precatu servulis
   dimitte noxam criminis.

Hymn 61

Jesus, redeemer of all men

1. Jesus, redeemer of all men,
   of leaders the enduring crown,
   upon this day lend kindly ear
   more leniently to these our prayers,

2. On which day your most holy name's
   kindly confessor won great fame,
   in whose honor this annual feast
   the people with devotion keep.

3. Since he so rightly did reject
   this world's perishable delights,
   he now obtains rewards in heaven,
   rejoicing with the angels there.

4. Now in your kindness grant that we
   may in his traces plant our feet,
   and through his prayers pardon the guilt
   of your poor servants' sinning ways.

LXII

Quem terra pontus aethera

1. Quem terra pontus aethera
   colunt adorant praedicant,
   trinam regentem machinam,
   claustrum Mariae baiulat.

2. Cui luna, sol, et omnia
   deserviunt per tempora
   perfusa caeli gratia
   gestant puellae viscera.

3. Mirentur ergo saecula
   quod angelus fert semina,
   quod aure virgo concipit
   et corde credens parturit.

4. Beata mater munere,
   cuius supernus artifex
   mundum pugillo continens
   ventris sub arca clausus est.

5. Benedicta caeli nuntio,
   fecunda sancto Spiritu
   desideratus gentibus
   cuius per alvum fusus est.

Hymn 62

He whom the earth and sea and sky

1. He whom the earth and sea and sky
   worship, adore, and loud proclaim
   (for he the triple fabric guides)
   is in the womb of Mary borne.

2. He whom the moon, the sun, and all
   through their appointed seasons serve
   is in the maiden's womb enclosed,
   a womb imbued with heavenly grace.

3. So let the ages wonder that
   the angel bore with him the seed,
   the virgin through her ear conceived
   and bore the child with inner faith.

4. Blessed the mother with that gift;
   her heavenly maker from on high,
   who held the world within his fist,
   was closed within her belly's ark.

5. She was by heaven's herald praised,
   and fertile by the Holy Ghost,
   that maiden from out of whose womb
   burst he whom nations longed to see.

6. O gloriosa femina,
   excelsa super sidera!
   Qui te creavit provide
   lactas sacrato ubere.

7. Quod Eva tristis abluit
   tu reddis almo germine;
   intrent ut astra flebiles,
   caeli fenestra facta es.

8. Tu regis alti ianua
   et porta lucis fulgida;
   vitam datam per virginem
   gentes redemptae plaudite.

LXIII

Ave, maris stella

1. Ave, maris stella,
   Dei mater alma,
   atque semper virgo,
   felix caeli porta.

2. Sumens illud *Ave*
   Gabrielis ore,
   funda nos in pace
   mutans nomen Evae.

6.   O woman of such splendid fame,
      exalted high above the stars!
      Him who with forethought gave you life
      you suckle at your holy breast.

7.   What Eve so sadly washed away
      you with your fostering seed restored;
      that woeful men might mount the stars,
      the heavens' window you became.

8.   You are the door to the high king,
      and gleaming portal to the light;
      that life through the virgin bestowed
      applaud ye, nations now redeemed.

Hymn 63

Hail, star of the ocean

1.   Hail, star of the ocean,
      God's own gracious mother,
      and a virgin always,
      blessed gate to heaven.

2.   You, who took that *Ave*
      from the lips of Gabriel,
      in peace us establish,
      Eva's name transforming.

3. Solve vincla reis,
   profer lumen caecis;
   mala nostra pelle,
   bona cuncta posce.

4. Monstra te esse matrem;
   sumat per te precem
   qui pro nobis natus
   tulit esse tuus.

5. Virgo singularis,
   inter omnes mitis,
   nos culpis solutos
   mites fac et castos.

6. Vitam praesta puram,
   iter para tutum,
   ut videntes Iesum
   semper collaetemur.

7. Sit laus Deo Patri,
   summum Christo decus,
   Spiritui sancto
   honor, tribus unus.

3. From our guilt unloose us,
    give sight to our blindness;
    drive out all our evils,
    draw out all our virtues.

4. Show your role maternal;
    let him hear prayers through you,
    he who born for our sakes
    deigned to be your offspring.

5. Virgin like no other,
    gentler than all maidens,
    from guilty deeds free us;
    make us pure and gentle.

6. Make our lives unspotted,
    grant us a safe journey,
    that, beholding Jesus,
    we may share joy ever.

7. Praise be to the Father,
    to Christ greatest glory,
    to the Holy Spirit
    honor, all three sharing.

COLUMBA OF IONA

LXIV

Altus Prosator

1. Altus Prosator, vetustus
    dierum et ingenitus,
    erat absque origine
    primordii et crepidine.
    Est et erit in saecula
    saeculorum infinita.
    Cui est unigenitus
    Christus et sanctus Spiritus
    coaeternus in gloria
    deitatis perpetua.
    Non tres deos depromimus,
    sed unum Deum dicimus,
    salva fide in personis
    tribus gloriosissimis.

2. Bonos creavit angelos
    ordines et archangelos
    principatuum ac sedium,
    potestatum, virtutium,
    uti non esset bonitas
    otiosa ac maiestas

Hymn 64

Ancient in days, the high Creator

1. Ancient in days, the high Creator,
    unbegotten, lacked a source
    of origin or foundation.
    He is and shall be without end
    through boundless ages yet to be.
    With him the sole-begotten Christ
    and Holy Spirit eternal stand,
    in godhead's glory perpetual.
    It is not three gods we proclaim,
    but one God only we affirm,
    by faith's integrity, in three
    persons exceeding glorious.

2. Brought he the good angels to be,
    and archangels, and further ranks
    of principalities and thrones
    and powers and virtues, to ensure
    that the Trinity's goodness and
    high dignity would not be slow

Trinitatis in omnibus
largitatis muneribus,
sed haberet caelestia
in quibus privilegia
ostenderet magnifice
possibili fatimine.

3. Caeli de regni apice,
stationis angelicae
claritate, prae fulgoris
venustate speciminis
superbiendo, ruerat
Lucifer, quem formaverat,
apostataeque angeli
eodem lapsu lugubri
auctoris cenodoxiae
pervicacis invidiae,
ceteris remanentibus
in suis principatibus.

4. Draco magnus, taeterrimus,
terribilis et antiquus,
qui fuit serpens lubricus,
sapientior omnibus
bestiis et animantibus
terrae ferocioribus,
tertiam partem siderum
traxit secum in barathrum
locorum infernalium
diversorumque carcerum,
refugas veri luminis
parasito praecipites.

in granting all the gifts of its
generosity, but would have
agents through which it might dispense
with splendor heavenly privileges
through utterance replete with power.

3. Cast down from heaven's kingdom's peak,
    which is the angels' bright abode,
    at his refulgent, beauteous form
    in arrogance exulting there,
    bright Lucifer, whom God had made,
    went hurtling down to hell below,
    and the apostate angels too
    in the same melancholy fall
    of that author of empty pomp
    whose envy unremitting raged;
    meanwhile the other angels stayed
    on their princely abodes above.

4. Dreadful and massive, the dragon
    fearsome of form and ancient,
    who was the serpent slippery,
    wiser than wild beasts, and wiser
    than fiercer creatures of the earth,
    dragged down a third part of the stars
    with him down into the abyss
    of the infernal realms of hell
    and of the diverse prisons there,
    as fugitives from the true light
    by the deceiver thrown headlong.

5. Excelsus mundi machinam
praevidens et harmoniam,
caelum et terram fecerat,
mare, aquas condiderat.
Herbarum quoque germina,
virgultorum arbuscula,
solem, lunam, ac sidera,
ignem ac necessaria,
aves, pisces, et pecora,
bestias, animalia,
hominem demum regere
protoplastum praesagmine.

6. Factis simul sideribus,
aetheris luminaribus,
collaudaverunt angeli
factura pro mirabili
immensae molis Dominum
opificem caelestium
praeconio laudabili
debito et immobili,
concentuque egregio
grates egerunt Domino
amore et arbitrio
non naturae donario.

7. Grassatis primis duobus
seductisque parentibus,
secundo ruit zabulus
cum suis satellitibus,
quorum horrore vultuum
sonoque volitantium

5.   Exalted, foreseeing the frame
and harmony of the world, he made
the heavens and the earth, the sea
and waters did he put in place.
The seeds of plants he also made,
the slender growth of thickets too,
the sun, the moon, and too the stars,
and fire and all things that men use,
the birds, the fish, the cattle too,
wild animals, all living things,
and lastly man, destined to rule
first-formed with power of prophecy.

6.   Formed he the stars, put in their place
as lamps to light the firmament;
the angels joined in eulogy,
for his wondrous creation of
that boundless mass, praising the Lord,
the craftsman of the heavens above,
in proclamation that wins praise,
with utterance meet that knows no change,
and sang in noble harmony,
discharging thanks unto the Lord,
doing this out of love and will,
not from the gift that nature prompts.

7.   Guiling and seducing then
our firstborn parents, both of them,
the devil fell a second time,
together with his satellites,
at the terror of whose aspect
and sound produced by flitting wings,

consternarentur homines
metu territi fragiles,
non valentes carnalibus
haec intueri visibus,
qui nunc ligantur fascibus
ergastulorum nexibus.

8. Hic sublatus e medio
deiectus est a Domino;
cuius aeris spatium
constipatur satellitum
globo invisibilium
turbido perduellium,
ne malis exemplaribus
imbuti ac sceleribus,
nullis umquam tegentibus
saeptis ac parietibus,
fornicarentur homines
palam omnium oculis.

9. Invehunt nubes pontias
ex fontibus brumalias,
tribus profundioribus
oceani dodrantibus,
maris caeli climatibus
caeruleis turbinibus,
profuturas segetibus,
vineis, et germinibus,
agitatae flaminibus
thesauris emergentibus,
quique paludes marinas
evacuant reciprocas.

frail men would be quite paralyzed,
and be by terror horrified,
unable with their body's eyes
to gaze upon such ghastly sights;
but now they are confined in bonds
by chains of their harsh prison cells.

8.   Here removed from earthly place,
Satan was cast down by the Lord;
the expanse of air is thronged throughout
with his disordered whirling mob
of warring satellites, unseen
lest men, infected by their crimes
and evil precedents they set,
should play the wanton, not concealed
by walls and barriers, open to
the searching eyes of everyone.

9.   Inward the clouds bear wintry floods
that stem from waters of the sea,
from out the ocean's deeper floods,
comprising three fourths of the expanse,
up to the regions of the sky
in whirlwinds of deep azure hue,
where they will nourishment supply
unto the corn and vines and buds,
these clouds being driven by the winds
emerging from their treasure stores;
they drain the shallows of the coasts,
which ebb and flow continuously.

10. Kaduca ac tyrannica
    mundique momentanea
    regum praesentis gloria
    nutu Dei deposita;
    ecce gigantes gemere
    sub aquis magno ulcere
    comprobantur, incendio
    aduri ac supplicio
    Cocytique Charybdibus
    strangulati turgentibus,
    Scyllis obtecti fluctibus
    eliduntur et scrupibus.

11. Ligatas aquas nubibus
    frequenter crebrat Dominus,
    ut ne erumpant protinus
    simul ruptis obicibus,
    quarum uberioribus
    venis velut uberibus
    pedetemptim natantibus
    telli per tractus istius
    gelidis ac ferventibus
    diversis in temporibus
    usquam influunt flumina
    nunquam deficientia.

12. Magni Dei virtutibus
    appenditur dialibus
    globus terrae et circulus
    abysso magnae inditus
    suffultu Dei, iduma
    omnipotentis valida,

10.   Keeling and tyrannical fame
of monarchs of this present world
is short-lived, ended by God's will;
see how the giants, as all know,
submerged by waters, utter groans,
suffering great torments, scorched by fire
and punishment, and strangled by
Cocytus's Charybdean whirls,
engulfed by Scyllan snarling cliffs,
are buffeted by waves and rocks.

11.   Locked up in the clouds, the waters
the Lord filters in frequent showers,
lest they should burst forth suddenly
and break their barriers all at once,
from whose more fertilizing streams,
as from a woman's fecund breasts,
as they pursue their gradual course
throughout the regions of the earth,
being hot or cold at diverse times,
the never-failing rivers run.

12.   Mighty powers of our great God
make the earth's globe suspended stand,
its circle poised in the abyss
by God's support beneath, and by
the almighty one's strong right hand,

columnis velut vectibus
eundem sustentantibus,
promontoriis et rupibus
solidis fundaminibus
velut quibusdam basibus
firmatus immobilibus.

13. Nulli videtur dubium
in imis esse infernum,
ubi habentur tenebrae,
vermes et dirae bestiae,
ubi ignis sulphureus
ardens flammis edacibus,
ubi rugitus hominum,
fletus et stridor dentium,
ubi Gehennae gemitus
terribilis et antiquus,
ubi ardor flammaticus,
sitis famisque horridus.

14. Orbem infra, ut legimus,
incolas esse novimus,
quorum genu precario
frequenter flectit Domino,
quibusque impossibile
librum scriptum revolvere
obsignatum signaculis
septem de Christi monitis,
quem ideo resignaverat
postquam victor exstiterat,
explens sua praesagmina
adventus prophetalia.

with columns like crowbars underneath
bearing it up, with promontories
and rocks as solid fundaments,
firmly established as though on
bases immovable as supports.

13. No one, it seems, is left in doubt
that hell exists in realms below,
in that abode where darkness dwells
with worms and terrifying beasts,
where that sulfurous fire rages
ablaze with fierce devouring flames,
where too are men's bellowing cries,
their wailing moans and gnashing teeth,
where Gehenna's groan resounds,
fearsome of form and ancient,
where too the burning heat of flames
and thirst and hunger, dreadful pains.

14. On the earth's nether side, we read,
people dwell there, as we know,
whose knees are often bent in prayer
in homage to the Lord above,
and quite beyond whose power it lies
to unroll and read the written book,
sealed as it is with seven seals
in keeping with Christ's warning words,
which book he had himself unsealed
when he emerged victorious,
fulfilling his prophetic words
in which his coming was foretold.

15. Plantatum a prooemio
     paradisum a Domino
     legimus in primordio
     Genesis nobilissimo,
     cuius ex fonte flumina
     quattuor sunt manantia,
     cuius etiam florido
     lignum vitae in medio,
     cuius non cadunt folia
     gentibus salutifera,
     cuius inenarrabiles
     deliciae ac fertiles.

16. Quis ad condictum Domini
     montem ascendit Sinai?
     Quis audivit tonitrua
     ultra modum sonantia,
     quis clangorem perstrepere
     enormitatis bucinae?
     Quis quoque vidit fulgura
     in gyro coruscantia,
     quis lampades et iacula
     saxaque collidentia,
     praeter Israhelitici
     Moysem iudicem populi?

17. Regis regum rectissimi
     prope dies est Domini,
     dies irae et vindictae,
     tenebrarum et nebulae,
     diesque mirabilium
     tonitruorum fortium,

15. Planted the Lord in the beginning
    his paradise, a garden fair:
    thus do we read in Genesis'
    exordium of greatest fame,
    from which rich source four rivers flow,
    and at whose flowering center stands
    the tree of life, whose foliage,
    which bears salvation to mankind,
    does never fall or fade, whose fruits
    untellable and fecund are.

16. Who up the Lord's appointed mount
    of Sinai did make his climb?
    Who has heard the thunder-roll
    resound far louder than its wont,
    who has heard noise out the raucous din
    of the trumpet massively huge?
    And who has witnessed lightning-flames,
    flashing, exploding all around,
    who fires and darts, and clashing rocks,
    save Moses, Israel's people's judge?

17. Righteous ruler of rulers, the Lord,
    his appointed day is near,
    that day of anger and revenge,
    of darkness and oppressive cloud,
    the day when savage thunderclaps
    of power wonderful resound,

dies quoque angustiae,
maeroris et tristitiae,
in quo cessabit mulierum
amor ac desiderium,
hominumque contentio
mundi huius et cupido.

18.   Stantes erimus pavidi
ante tribunal Domini,
reddemusque de omnibus
rationem affectibus,
videntes quoque posita
ante obtutus crimina,
librosque conscientiae
patefactos in facie,
in fletus amarissimos
ac singultus erumpemus,
subtracta necessaria
operandi materia.

19.   Tuba primi archangeli
strepente admirabili,
erumpent munitissima
claustra ac polyandria
mundi praesentis frigora
hominum liquescentia,
undique conglobantibus
ad compagines ossibus,
animabus aethralibus
eisdem obviantibus
rursumque redeuntibus
debitis mansionibus.

the day too when oppression comes,
a day of sadness and of grief,
on which day will cease utterly
love and desire for womankind,
and so too all striving of men
and lusting for this present world.

18.   So trembling shall we shall take our stand
before the dais of the Lord,
and we shall render an account
of all desires that we held dear;
our sins too there we shall behold
plainly set out before our gaze,
and books that document our guilt
will be exposed before our face.
Most bitter then will be the tears
and sobs that burst forth from our lips,
since any opportunity
for saving action will be lost.

19.   The horn of the first archangel
will blast forth with a wondrous sound,
then vaults and sepulchres secure
will burst apart and open wide,
unfreezing all the glacial cold
of human bodies in this world,
their bones from every quarter then
welding together at their joints,
their souls now poised in heaven above,
coming to meet them, and again
returning to their meet abodes.

20. Vagatur ex climactere
    Orion caeli cardine,
    derelicto Vergilio,
    astrorum splendidissimo;
    per metas Thetis ignoti
    orientalis circuli
    girans certis ambagibus
    redit priscis reditibus,
    oriens post biennium
    Vesperugo in vesperum;
    sumpta in problematibus
    tropicis intellectibus.

21. Xristo de caelis Domino
    descendente celsissimo,
    praefulgebit clarissimum
    signum crucis et vexillum,
    tectisque luminaribus
    duobus principalibus,
    cadent in terram sidera
    ut fructus de ficulnea,
    eritque mundi spatium
    ut fornacis incendium;
    tunc in montium specubus
    abscondent se exercitus.

22. Ymnorum cantionibus
    sedulo tinnientibus,
    tripudiis sanctis milibus
    angelorum vernantibus,
    quattuorque plenissimis
    animalibus oculis,

20.   Voyaging from his high point,
the pivot of the heavens, Orion
leaves behind the Pleiades,
most bright of constellations;
beyond the limits of the ring
of eastern Thetis' unknown tracts
the evening star on its fixed course
gyrates, by former paths returns,
rising after two years' delay
as evening star at eventide;
these constellations, seen as types,
have figurative significance.

21.   Christ, the loftiest of lords,
from heaven making his descent,
the sign and standard of the cross
will gleam before him, shining bright,
and when the two chief orbs of light
are shrouded and hidden from view,
the stars shall tumble to the earth
as fruit that from a fig tree falls,
and then the world's circumference
will like a fiery furnace blaze;
then will the hosts conceal themselves
within the caverns in the hills.

22.   Hymns are chanted, with their sound
continually ringing out,
as angels in their thousands there
express their joy with holy dance,
and the four beasts all full of eyes,

cum viginti felicibus
quattuor senioribus
coronas admittentibus
Agni Dei sub pedibus,
laudatur tribus vicibus
Trinitas aeternalibus.

23. Zelus ignis furibundus
consumet adversarios
nolentes Christum credere
Deo a Patre venisse.
Nos vero evolabimus
obviam ei protinus,
et sic cum ipso erimus
in diversis ordinibus
dignitatum pro meritis
praemiorum perpetuis,
permansuri in gloria
e saeculis in saecula.

with the four-and-twenty elders blessed,
as they lay down their gleaming crowns
beneath the feet of the Lamb of God;
the Trinity is praised by all
in threefold chorus without end.

23. Zealous fury of the fire
will then consume those enemies,
who are reluctant to believe
that Christ from God the Father came.
But we shall fly up to the heavens
so as to meet him there and then,
and we shall be his comrades there,
drawn up in all our diverse ranks
of dignities, according to
enduring merits of rewards,
and shall abide in glory there
eternally, for ever and ever.

THE VENERABLE BEDE

LXV

Laetare, caelum, desuper

1. Laetare, caelum, desuper,
   applaude, tellus ac mare:
   Christus resurgens post crucem
   vitam dedit mortalibus.

2. Iam tempus acceptum redit,
   dies salutis cernitur,
   quo mundus agni sanguine
   refulsit a nigredine.

3. Crux namque sacratissima
   ligni prioris vulnera
   in patre nostri seminis
   sanavit, hostem saucians.

4. Mors illa, mortis passio,
   est criminis remissio;
   illaesa virtus permanet,
   victus dedit victoriam.

5. Miretur omne saeculum
   crucis triumphum mysticae;
   haec signa congruentia
   velut tropaeum praesto sunt.

Hymn 65

Rejoice, you heavens, from above

1. Rejoice, you heavens, from above,
    now give ye praise, O earth and sea:
    Christ, risen again after the cross,
    new life has given unto men.

2. The acceptable time returns,
    salvation's day we now behold,
    on which the world by the Lamb's blood
    shone brightly, from darkness transformed.

3. For that most hallowed cross of Christ
    has healed the wounds from that first tree
    that the father of our seed sustained,
    dealing our foe a serious hurt.

4. That death, the suffering of death,
    is the remittance of our sins;
    his power continues unimpaired,
    defeated he gained victory.

5. Let every age show wonder at
    the triumph of the mystic cross;
    these signs, befitting the event,
    furnish a trophy of a kind.

6. Sol namque, magnum luminar,
    horas dierum permanens,
    viso novo mysterio
    decepit orbem territus.

7. Velans caput caligine
    exstinxit omnem lampadem,
    errare noctem passus est
    meridiano tempore.

8. Finduntur et fortes petrae,
    hiantur saxa plurima,
    defuncta surgunt corpora,
    vitae redduntur mortui.

9. Immitis ille Tartarus
    ad se trahentis omnia
    praesentiam non sustinens
    animas sanctas reddidit.

10. Nostrae fuit gustus spei
    hic, ut fideles crederent
    se posse post resurgere,
    vitam beatam sumere.

11. Nunc ergo Pascha candidum
    causa bonorum talium
    colamus omnes strenue,
    tantis renatis fratribus.

6.   For then the sun, which casts great light,
     abiding through the daylight hours,
     on sighting this new mystery
     being terrified, puzzled the world.

7.   Enveloping its head in mist
     it quenched the entire light of day,
     permitted night to roam abroad,
     though in the middle of the day.

8.   Then rocks were split, however hard,
     innumerable tombs gaped wide,
     lifeless cadavers rose again,
     dead men were to their life restored.

9.   Then Tartarus, so merciless,
     could not endure his presence there
     who all things to himself did draw,
     but yielded up its holy souls.

10.   He was the flavor of our hope,
     that faithful souls might then believe
     that they could later rise again,
     could enter upon blessed life.

11.   Now therefore this radiant Pasch,
     of our so great blessings the cause,
     let us all earnest celebrate,
     for all our brothers now reborn.

ANONYMOUS

LXVI

Agnoscat omne saeculum

1. Agnoscat omne saeculum
   venisse vitae praemium;
   post hostis asperi iugum
   apparuit redemptio.

2. Esaias quae praecinit
   completa sunt in virgine;
   annuntiavit angelus,
   sanctus replevit Spiritus.

3. Maria ventre concepit
   verbi fidelis semine;
   quem totus orbs non baiulat
   portant puellae viscera.

4. Radix iam Iesse floruit,
   et virga fructum edidit;
   fecunda partum protulit
   et virgo mater permanet.

5. Praesepe poni pertulit
   qui lucis auctor exstitit;
   cum Patre caelos condidit,
   sub matre pannos induit.

Hymn 66

Let every age now recognize

1. Let every age now recognize
   the advent of the prize of life;
   though we beneath the cruel foe's yoke
   did lie, redemption has appeared.

2. What Isaiah had prophesied
   is in a virgin now fulfilled;
   an angel was the messenger,
   the Holy Spirit filled her up.

3. So Mary in her womb conceived
   by seed bestowed by faithful word;
   him whom a world does not sustain
   a maiden's belly now contains.

4. The root of Jesse now has bloomed,
   and that branch has produced a fruit;
   the fertile maid did bear the child,
   and though mother, virgin remained.

5. A manger's confines he endured
   who author was of light itself;
   he with the Father formed the sky,
   his mother's swaddling he put on.

6. Legem dedit qui saeculo,
   cuius decem praecepta sunt,
   dignando factus est homo
   sub legis esse vinculo.

7. Adam vetus quod polluit
   Adam novus hoc abluit;
   tumens quod ille deiecit,
   humillimus hic erigit.

8. Iam nata lux est et salus,
   fugata nox et victa mors;
   venite, gentes, credite:
   Deum Maria protulit.

LXVII

Lucis largitor splendide

1. Lucis largitor splendide,
   cuius sereno lumine
   post lapsa noctis tempora
   dies refusus panditur,

2. Tu verus mundi lucifer,
   non is qui parvi sideris
   venturae lucis nuntius
   angusto fulget lumine,

6. He who gave law unto the world
   (the ten commandments he enjoined)
   became a human being, and
   deigned to be bound by that same law.

7. What that old Adam had defaced
   the new Adam again wiped clean;
   what Adam in his pride threw down,
   Christ's deep humility restored.

8. Light and salvation now are born,
   night put to flight, death overcome;
   you nations, come, and credence lend:
   Mary has given birth to God.

Hymn 67

O you bright giver of the light

1. O you bright giver of the light,
   by whose unclouded brilliance,
   once night's dark hours have slipped away,
   the day floods back and is revealed,

2. You true light-bringer of the world,
   not he who, with his tiny star's
   restricted gleam, as herald shines
   to announce the coming of the light,

3. Sed toto sole clarior
    lux ipse totus et dies,
    interna nostri pectoris
    illuminans praecordia,

4. Adesto, rerum conditor,
    paternae lucis gloria,
    cuius amota gratia
    nostra patescunt corpora,

5. Tuo quae plena Spiritu
    secum Deum gestantia
    nil rapientis perfidi
    diris pateant fraudibus,

6. Ut inter actus saeculi,
    vitae quos usus exigit,
    omni carentes crimine
    tuis vivamus legibus.

7. Probrosas mentis castitas
    carnis vincat libidines,
    sanctumque puri corporis
    delubrum servet Spiritus.

8. Haec spes precantis animae,
    haec sunt votiva munera,
    ut matutina nobis sit
    lux in noctis custodiam.

3. But brighter than the sun's full orb
   yourself wholly the light and day,
   shedding light on the vital parts
   that lie within our outer breasts,

4. Be with us, founder of the world,
   the glory of the Father's light,
   for if your grace is once removed
   our bodies lie exposed to ill;

5. May they be with your Spirit filled,
   bearing God in their company,
   nor to the dread wiles be exposed
   of that perfidious ravisher,

6. That, as we ply our worldly tasks,
   demanded by the needs of life,
   forgoing every sin, we may
   live life according to your laws.

7. So may our chastity of mind
   subdue the shameful lusts of flesh,
   and in our bodies free from sin
   preserve the Spirit's holy shrine.

8. This is the hope of our souls' prayer,
   these are our prayers in duty bound,
   that for us may the morning light
   remain until the watch of night.

LXVIII

Rerum Deus fons omnium

1. Rerum Deus fons omnium,
   qui rebus actis omnibus
   totius orbis ambitum
   censu replesti munerum,

2. Non actibus fessus manens,
   laboribus non saucius,
   cunctis quietem das, aegris
   curis ruant ne morbidi.

3. Concede nunc temporibus
   uti malorum consciis,
   instare iam virtutibus,
   et munerari prosperis,

4. Terroris ut cum iudicis
   horror supremus ceperit,
   laetemur omnes in vicem
   pacis repleti munere.

Hymn 68

O God, the source of all that is

1.   O God, the source of all that is,
who, having created everything,
the whole wide world's circumference
with riches of your gifts did fill,

2.   Your deeds leave you unwearied still,
your toils have not disabled you,
and you grant rest to all, lest they
be stricken with enfeebling cares.

3.   Grant now that, conscious of our ills,
we may exploit the present time,
strive to pursue the virtues close,
and be rewarded with success,

4.   That when that final, awful fear
before the Judge shall seize us all,
each may have joy as recompense,
all filled up with the gift of peace.

LXIX

Nunc, sancte nobis Spiritus

1. Nunc, sancte nobis Spiritus,
unum Patri cum Filio,
dignare promptus ingeri
nostro refusus pectori.

2. Os lingua mens sensus vigor
confessionem personent;
flammescat igne caritas,
accendat ardor proximos.

LXX

Qua Christus hora sitiit

1. Qua Christus hora sitiit
crucem vel in qua subiit,
quos praestat in hac psallere
ditet siti iustitiae.

Hymn 69

Deign, Holy Spirit, at this hour

1.   Deign, Holy Spirit, at this hour,
   one with the Father and the Son,
   your ready presence to bestow;
   instill your breath into our hearts.

2.   Let mouth, tongue, mind, thought, strength
   declare
   a proud confession of their faith;
   let charity blaze forth with fire,
   our neighbors let its heat ignite.

Hymn 70

The hour on which Christ thirsted

1.   The hour on which Christ thirsted, or
   endured the torment of the cross:
   let him a thirst for justice grant
   to us, prompted that hour to sing.

2. Quibus sit et esuries
de se quam ipse satiet,
crimen sit ut fastidium
virtusque desiderium.

3. Charisma sancti Spiritus
sic influat psallentibus
ut carnis aestus frigeat
et mentis algor ferveat.

LXXI

Iam, Christe, sol iustitiae

1. Iam, Christe, sol iustitiae,
mentis dehiscant tenebrae
virtutum ut lux redeat
terris diem cum reparas.

2. Das tempus acceptabile;
et paenitens cor tribue,
convertat ut benignitas
quos longa suffert pietas.

3. Quiddamque paenitentiae
da ferre, quamvis grandium
maiore tui munere
quo demptio sit criminum.

2. May we a hunger also feel
   for him that he can satisfy,
   that sin may be a loathsome thing,
   and virtue be our heartfelt need.

3. And may the Holy Spirit's gift
   so pour into us as we sing
   that flesh's burning heat may cool,
   and our minds' coldness ardent burn.

Hymn 71

Now Christ, O sun of justice

1. Now Christ, O sun of justice, let
   the darkness of our minds be cleft,
   that light of virtues may return
   as you bring daylight back to earth.

2. You grant a time acceptable:
   bestow even a contrite heart,
   that your kindness may us transform,
   whom your long-suffering love has borne.

3. Some penitential hardship too
   grant us to bear, so that our sins,
   however great, by your greater gift
   may be removed from guilty hearts.

4. Dies venit, dies tua,
   per quam reflorent omnia;
   laetemur in hac, ut tuae
   per hanc reducti gratiae.

5. Te rerum universitas,
   clemens, adoret, Trinitas,
   et nos novi per veniam
   novum canamus canticum.

LXXII

Tu, Trinitatis unitas

1. Tu, Trinitatis unitas,
   orbem potenter qui regis,
   attende laudum cantica
   quae excubantes psallimus.

2. Nam lectulis consurgimus
   noctis quieto tempore,
   ut flagitemus vulnerum
   a te medelam omnium,

3. Quo fraude quidquid daemonum
   in noctibus deliquimus,
   abstergat illud caelitus
   tuae potestas gloriae,

4.   The day approaches, your own day,
by which all things blossom afresh;
let us rejoice in it, for we
through it are brought back to your grace.

5.   The whole vast content of the world
must worship you, kind Trinity,
and we, renewed through pardoning,
will have to sing another song.

Hymn 72

You, oneness of the Trinity

1.   You, oneness of the Trinity,
who rule the universe with power,
pay heed now to these hymns of praise,
which keeping vigil we declaim.

2.   For from our narrow beds we rise
during the silent hours of night,
intending to demand of you
a remedy for all our wounds,

3.   That such sins we commit at night,
deceived by evil spirits' guile,
the power of your heavenly fame
may them in turn obliterate,

4. Ne corpus adsit sordidum,
   nec torpor instet cordium,
   et criminis contagio
   tepescat ardor spiritus.

5. Ob hoc, Redemptor, quaesumus,
   reple tuo nos lumine,
   per quod dierum circulis
   nullis ruamus actibus.

LXXIII

A Patre unigenitus

1. A Patre unigenitus
   ad nos venit per virginem,
   baptisma cruce consecrans,
   cunctos fideles generans.

2. De caelo celsus prodiit,
   excepit formam hominis,
   facturam morte redimens,
   gaudia vitae largiens.

3. Hoc te, Redemptor, quaesumus,
   inlabere propitius,
   klarumque nostris sensibus
   lumen praebe fidelibus.

4. That our bodies may not be stained,
   nor lethargy of hearts afflict,
   nor by the contagion of our guilt
   the warmth of spirit lose its heat.

5. So this, Redeemer, is our prayer:
   do you fill us up with your light,
   through whose power in the round of days
   no deeds of ours will make us fall.

Hymn 73

The Father's sole-begotten Son

1. The Father's sole-begotten Son
   did through a virgin come to us,
   hallowing our baptism by the cross,
   begetting all his faithful souls.

2. He left his lofty seat in heaven,
   he took on him a human form,
   creation by death redeeming,
   granting to us the joys of life.

3. Redeemer, this we beg of you,
   show kindness and steal into us,
   direct the brightness of your light
   into our minds, and give them faith.

4. Mane nobiscum, Domine,
    noctem obscuram remove;
    omne delictum ablue,
    piam medelam tribue.

5. Quem iam venisse novimus
    redire item credimus;
    sceptrum tuum inclitum
    tuo defende clipeo.

6. Vita, salus, et veritas,
    Xriste, rogantes adiuva;
    ymnum sonantes iubilo,
    zelum vincamus lubricum.

4. O Lord, abide with us, we pray,
   dispel the darkness of our night;
   wash clean away our every sin,
   bestow devoted remedy.

5. We know that earlier you came,
   and we believe you will return;
   defend your scepter of fair fame
   behind the buttress of your shield.

6. O life, salvation, and the truth,
   Christ, lend us aid, as this we beg:
   may we who sing this hymn with joy
   defeat the envious Satan's guile.

THEODULF OF
ORLÉANS

LXXIV

Gloria, laus, et honor

Gloria, laus, et honor tibi sit, rex Christe redemptor,
    cui puerile decus prompsit hosanna pium.
Israel es tu rex, Davidis et inclita proles,
    nomine qui in Domini, rex benedicte, venis.
5 Coetus in excelsis te laudat caelicus omnis,
    et mortalis homo et cuncta creata simul.
Plebs Hebraea tibi cum palmis obvia venit;
    cum prece voto hymnis adsumus ecce tibi.
Hi tibi passuro solvebant munia laudis;
10   nos tibi regnanti pangimus ecce melos.
Hi placuere tibi; placeat devotio nostra,
    rex pie, rex clemens, cui bona cuncta placent.
Fecerat Hebraeos hos gloria sanguinis alti;
    nos facit Hebraeos transitus ecce pius.
15 Inclita terrenis transitur ad aethera victis;
    virtus a vitiis nos capit alma tetris.

Hymn 74

Fame, honor, praise

Fame, honor, praise be yours, O Christ redeemer-king,
    to whom our graceful youth hosannas sang.
You are the king of Israel, David's famed son,
    who in the Lord's name, O blest king, did come.
All heaven's assembly sounds your praises up on high,   5
    and mortal man and all creation too.
The Hebrew people came to meet you with their
      palms;
    see how we attend you with prayers, vows, hymns.
They paid their dues of praise when you were soon to
      suffer;
    but we now hymn you, seated on your throne.   10
You found them pleasing; let too our devotion please,
    kind king, devoted king; all good things please you.
What formed the Hebrews was their famed ancestral
      blood;
    see how our holy passage Hebrews of us makes.
By conquering earthly things we pass to fame in   15
      heaven;
    kind virtue rescues us from grisly faults.

Nequitia simus pueri, virtute vieti;
  quod tenuere patres, da ut teneamus iter,
degeneresque patrum ne simus ab arte piorum;
20 nos tua post illos gratia sancta trahat.
Sis pius ascensor, tuus et nos simus asellus;
  tecum nos capiat urbs veneranda Dei.

Be we as babes in wickedness, in virtue old;
    grant us to tread the path the ancestors trod,
nor let us lapse from our devoted fathers' ways;
    may your blest grace draw us to follow them.   20
Be our devoted rider, and be we your donkey;
    and let God's august city welcome us.

LXXV

Veni, creator Spiritus

1.   Veni, creator Spiritus,
mentes tuorum visita;
imple superna gratia
quae tu creasti pectora,

2.   Qui Paraclitus diceris,
donum Dei altissimi,
fons vivus, ignis, caritas,
et spiritalis unctio.

3.   Tu septiformis munere,
dextrae Dei tu digitus,
tu rite promisso Patris
sermone ditans guttura.

4.   Accende lumen sensibus,
infunde amorem cordibus,
infirma nostri corporis
virtute firmans perpeti.

5.   Hostem repellas longius,
pacemque dones protinus;
ductore sic te praevio
vitemus omne noxium.

Hymn 75

Creator Spirit, come

1. Creator Spirit, come, and in
   the minds of your servants descend;
   fill up with grace from heaven on high
   those hearts that you yourself have made,

2. You who are called the Comforter,
   the gift of God who dwells on high,
   the living spring, and fire, and love,
   anointing of the spirit too.

3. You are sevenfold in your gift,
   you are God's right hand's finger, you
   are he who by the Father's pledge
   enriches throats with power of speech.

4. Ignite our thoughts with blazing light,
   and inject love into our hearts,
   our bodies' weakness strengthening
   with virtue's long-enduring power.

5. Drive back our foe remote from us,
   and grant us peace continually;
   if we have you to lead the way,
   we can avoid all harmful things.

6. Per te sciamus da Patrem,
    noscamus atque Filium,
    te utriusque Spiritum
    credamus omni tempore.

6. Through you grant us that we may know
    the Father, and may know the Son,
    that in you, Spirit of them both,
    we may at all times have belief.

WIPO

LXXVI

Victimae paschali laudes

1. Victimae paschali laudes
   immolent Christiani.

2. Agnus redemit oves.
   Christus innocens Patri
   reconciliavit
   peccatores.

3. Mors et vita duello
   conflixere mirando.
   dux vitae mortuus
   regnat vivus.

4. "Dic nobis, Maria,
   quid vidisti in via?"
   "Sepulchrum Christi viventis,
   et gloriam vidi resurgentis,

5. "Angelicos testes,
   sudarium et vestes.
   Surrexit Christus spes mea;
   praecedet suos in Galilaea."

Hymn 76

To the paschal victim, praises

1. To the paschal victim, praises
   let the Christians sacrifice.

2. The Lamb has redeemed the sheep.
   The sinless Christ
   has reconciled sinners
   to the Father.

3. Death and life have grappled
   in a wondrous duel.
   The leader of life, dead,
   does reign, alive.

4. "Tell us, Mary,
   what did you see on the way?"
   "I saw the tomb of Christ who lives,
   and his glory as he rose again,

5. "His witnesses angelic,
   the shroud cloth and the garments.
   Christ my hope has risen,
   will precede his followers in Galilee."

6. Credendum est magis soli
   Mariae veraci
   quam Iudaeorum turbae fallaci.

7. Scimus Christum surrexisse
   a mortuis vere;
   tu nobis, victor rex, miserere!

6. We must believe
    the truthful Mary and no other,
    rather than the deceiving crowd of Jews.

7. We know that Christ has risen up
    from the dead, verily;
    have mercy on us, victorious king!

.

AIMAR OF LE PUY

LXXVII

Salve, regina misericordiae

1. Salve, regina misericordiae,
    vita, dulcedo, et spes nostra, salve!

2. Ad te clamamus, exsules filii Evae,
    ad te suspiramus, gementes et flentes,
    in hac lacrimarum valle.

3. Eia ergo, advocata nostra,
    illos tuos misericordes oculos
    ad nos converte.

4. Et Iesum benedictum
    fructum ventris tui
    nobis post hoc exsilium ostende.

5. O clemens, O pia,
    O dulcis Maria.

Hymn 77

Greetings, queen of mercy

1. Greetings, queen of mercy,
   our life, sweetness, and hope, greetings!

2. To you we cry, we exiled children of Eve,
   to you we sigh, mourning and weeping,
   in this vale of tears.

3. Come then, our advocate,
   those pitying eyes of yours,
   turn them toward us.

4. And Jesus, the blessed
   fruit of your womb,
   show him to us after this our exile.

5. O clement, O loving,
   O sweet Mary.

PETER ABELARD

LXXVIII

O quanta qualia sunt
illa sabbata

1. O quanta qualia sunt illa sabbata,
   quae semper celebrat superna curia,
   quae fessis requies, quae merces fortibus
   cum erit omnia Deus in omnibus!

2. Vere Ierusalem est illa civitas,
   cuius pax iugis est, summa iucunditas,
   ubi non praevenit rem desiderium,
   nec desiderio minus est praemium.

3. Quis rex, quae curia, quale palatium,
   quae pax, quae requies, quod illud gaudium,
   huius participes exponant gloriae,
   si quantum sentiunt possint exprimere.

4. Nostrum est interim mentem erigere
   et totis patriam votis appetere,
   et ad Ierusalem ab Babylonia
   post longa regredi tandem exsilia.

Hymn 78

How great, how splendid will that Sabbath be

1. How great, how splendid will that Sabbath be,
   which heaven's court observes eternally,
   what rest for weary souls, and what reward
   the brave will win, when God is all in all!

2. That city truly is Jerusalem,
   whose peace unending is, joy unconfined,
   where longing does not its object precede,
   nor less than longing is the prize obtained.

3. The nature of the king, the palace, the court,
   the peace, the rest, the joy that there obtains,
   the souls who share this glory would explain,
   if feelings into words they could translate.

4. Meantime our task is to apply our minds,
   to seek that native land in all our prayers,
   and to Jerusalem from Babylon
   after long exile to return at last.

5.   Illic molestiis finitis omnibus
securi cantica Sion cantabimus,
et iuges gratias de donis gratiae
beata referet plebs tibi, Domine.

6.   Illic ex sabbato succedet sabbatum,
perpes laetitia sabbatizantium,
nec ineffabiles cessabunt iubili
quos decantabimus et nos et angeli.

7.   Perenni Domino perpes sit gloria,
ex quo sunt, per quem sunt, in quo sunt omnia;
ex quo sunt, Pater est; per quem sunt, Filius;
in quo sunt, Patris et Filii Spiritus.

LXXIX

Verbo Verbum

1.   Verbo Verbum
virgo concipiens,
ex se verus
ortus est Oriens,
a quo vera
diffusa claritas

5.   In heaven when all our griefs are at an end,
untroubled, we shall render Zion's songs,
and to you, Lord, the people who are blessed
will give eternal thanks for gifts of grace.

6.   There Sabbath after Sabbath will succeed,
unending joy for those observing them;
never the hymns of joy ineffable
shall cease, which we with angels will declaim.

7.   Unending praise be to the undying Lord,
from whom, through whom, in whom all things
       exist;
the Father is from whom, the Son through
       whom,
in whom, the Spirit of both Father and Son.

Hymn 79

When the virgin conceived by word the Word

1.   When the virgin
       conceived by word the Word,
from her arose
       the true dawn from the east,
from whom the true
       brightness of day diffused,

    circumductas
       abduxit tenebras.

2.   Felix dies,
       dierum gloria,
    huius ortus
       quae vidit gaudia.
    Felix mater
       quae Deum genuit,
    felix stella
       quae solem peperit.

3.   Quam beata
       pauper puerpera,
    cuius partus
       ditavit omnia.
    Pauper, inquam,
       sed celsa genere
    pontificum
       et regum sanguine.

4.   Vitae viam
       in via peperit;
    hospitium,
       non domum, habuit.
    Regum proles
       et caeli domina
    pro cameris
       intravit stabula.

and did dispel
    the darkness gathered round.

2.   How blessed is
    this day, glory of days,
which did behold
    the joys of this rising.
Blessed the mother
    who brought forth our God,
blessed the star
    that begot the true sun.

3.   How blessed though poor
    the mother in travail,
for by her labor
    all things she enriched.
Poor indeed, I declare,
    but noble in her birth
from stock of priests
    and from the blood of kings.

4.   The way to life
    she brought forth on the way;
she rested in
    an inn and not a house.
Offspring of kings,
    and mistress of the heavens,
instead of rooms
    she quartered in a stable.

5. Obstetrices
  in partu deerant,
sed angeli
  pro eis aderant.
Quorum statim
  chorus non modica
huius ortus
  edixit gaudia.

6. Defuerunt
  fortassis balnea,
sed quam lavent
  non erat macula.
Non est dolor
  quam illa relevent,
nec scissura
  quam illa reparent.

7. In excelsis
  sit Deo gloria,
pacis nobis
  in terra foedera.
Quam super his
  voces angelicae
decantasse
  noscuntur hodie.

5.   There were no midwives
          present at the birth,
     but angels were there
          to lend help instead.
     Large choirs among them
          then burst into song,
     and did proclaim
          the joys of this rising.

6.   Perhaps there was
          no water to be found,
     but no stain was there
          for water to cleanse.
     There was no pain
          that water might relieve,
     no tearing of the flesh
          it might repair.

7.   In the highest
          to God let glory be,
     a covenant
          of peace to us on earth.
     Which to us men
          upon this blessed day
     angelic voices,
          as we know, have sung.

LXXX

Dei patris

1. Dei patris
    et matris unicus,
   in praesepi
    pro cunis positus
   angustias
    praesepis sustinet,
   quem ambitus
    caeli non continet.

2. Excipitur
    vili tugurio
   qui praesidet
    caeli palatio.
   Quis super hoc,
    quis non obstupeat?
   Cuius mentem
    hoc non commoveat?

3. Pauper Deus,
    immo pauperrimus,
   sic factus est
    pro nobis omnibus.
   Quae sunt grates,
    quae retributio,
   super istis
    a nobis Domino?

Hymn 80

His father God

1. His father God
   and mother's sole-born son,
   laid in a manger
   instead of a cradle,
   the confines of
   the manger he endures,
   whom the expanse
   of heaven does not contain.

2. He is given
   this lowly hut's lodging,
   though he sits in command
   of heaven's palace.
   Who, seeing this,
   would not be astonished?
   What person's mind
   would not wonder at this?

3. God became poor,
   not just poor, but the poorest;
   he thus became
   for every one of us.
   What thanks, or what
   return can we supply
   to the Lord our God
   for a gesture like this?

4. In praesepi
   vagit ut parvulus,
  qui concutit
   caelum tonitribus.
  Stratum habet
   faeni reliquias
  qui regibus
   largitur purpuras.

5. Bestiarum
   infertur pabulo
  angelorum
   ipsa refectio.
  Instat inde
   grex animalium,
  hinc angeli
   praebent obsequium.

6. In excelsis
   sit Deo gloria,
  pacis nobis
   in terra foedera.
  Quam super his
   voces angelicae
  decantasse
   noscuntur hodie.

4.   In the manger
      he whimpers as a child,
  though he shatters
      the heavens above with thunder.
  Leavings of hay
      he lies on for his bed,
  though he on kings
      purple garments bestows.

5.   On beasts' fodder
      he is laid down within,
  though he is the refreshment
      of the angels.
  The herd of beasts
      on one side presses close,
  on the other
      the angels offer homage.

6.   In the highest
      to God let glory be,
  a covenant
      of peace to us on earth.
  Which to us men
      upon this blessed day
  angelic voices,
      as 'tis known, have sung.

LXXXI

Quam beatum stratum

1. Quam beatum
      stratum hoc straminis,
   tantae latus
      quod pressit virginis,
   quo parvulus
      nascens excipitur
   cuius palmo
      caelum concluditur.

2. In sericis
      reginae ceterae
   summo solent
      dolore parere;
   vilis strati
      beatus lectulus
   omnis fuit
      doloris nescius.

3. Regum satis
      in alimonia
   sunt subacta
      nutricum ubera.
   Educatur
      lacte virgineo,
   virgo clauso
      quem fudit utero.

Hymn 81

How blessed was that bed of straw

1. How blessed was
        that bed of straw, on which
    rested the flank
        of that virgin so great,
    on which was laid
        that baby at his birth,
    in whose small palm
        the heavens are enclosed.

2. In silken cloths
        all other queens are wont
    with utmost pain
        to give birth to their child;
    this blessed couch
        made out of worthless straw
    had no knowledge
        of any pain at all.

3. For the nurture
        of them begot of kings
    the breasts of wet nurses
        are commandeered;
    this child was reared
        upon a virgin's milk;
    the virgin bore him
        with hymen intact.

4. Nulli regum
        inter tot epulas,
    inter tantas
        et tot delicias,
    concessum est
        ut lacte virginis
    quis de suis
        alatur parvulis.

5. Virgo pauper
        fortassis esurit,
    quae parvulum
        hoc lacte reficit.
    Stupent caeli,
        mirantur angeli,
    obsequio
        lactantis seduli.

6. In excelsis
        sit Deo gloria,
    pacis nobis
        in terra foedera.
    Quam super his
        voces angelicae
    decantasse
        noscuntur hodie.

4.   To not one king
         amidst so many feasts,
     amidst so many
         and great luxuries,
     was it granted
         that any of their infants
     should be nourished
         upon a virgin's milk.

5.   The virgin poor
         strong hunger felt perhaps,
     as she refreshed
         her infant with this milk.
     The heavens gaped,
         the angels were amazed,
     ready to obey her
         as she gave him suck.

6.   In the highest
         to God let glory be,
     a covenant
         of peace to us on earth.
     Which to us men
         upon this blessed day
     angelic voices,
         as we know, have sung.

LXXXII

Gaude, virgo

1. Gaude, virgo,
       virginum gloria,
    matrum decus
       et mater, iubila,
    quae commune
       sanctorum omnium
    meruisti
       conferre gaudium.

2. Patriarchis
       sanctis ac regibus
    te filiam
       promisit Dominus.
    Te figurant
       legis aenigmata;
    prophetarum
       canunt oracula.

3. Te requirunt
       vota fidelium,
    ad te corda
       suspirant omnium.
    Tu spes nostra
       post Deum unica
    advocata
       nobis es posita.

PETER ABELARD

Hymn 82

Rejoice, virgin

1. Rejoice, virgin,
      who are glory of virgins;
    adornment of mothers
      and mother yourself, be glad:
    you were found worthy
      to bestow the joy
    that all the saints
      in common do possess.

2. To holy patriarchs,
      to kings as well,
    the Lord did promise you
      as their daughter.
    The mysteries of the law
      prefigured you,
    and oracles
      of prophets sang of you.

3. The prayers of the faithful
      aspire to you;
    the hearts of all
      breathe out their sighs to you.
    You and none else
      after God are our hope;
    you were appointed
      advocate for us.

4. Ad iudicis
       matrem confugiunt,
    qui iudicis
       iram effugiunt.
    Supplicare
       pro eis cogitur,
    quae pro reis
       mater efficitur.

5. Pia mater,
       pietas filius;
    ad hoc gignit,
       ad hoc est genitus,
    ut salventur
       servi per gratiam
    quam exhibet
       haec dies maximam.

6. In excelsis
       sit Deo gloria,
    pacis nobis
       in terris foedera.
    Quam super his
       voces angelicae
    decantasse
       noscuntur hodie.

4. Those who take refuge
        from the Judge's wrath
    flee for safe keeping
        to the Judge's mother.
    She is constrained
        to plead their case for them,
    who has become
        the mother for us sinners.

5. The mother is loving,
        and the Son is love;
    for this she gave birth,
        for this he was born,
    that slaves be set free
        by means of that grace
    that in its fullness
        this day brings to view.

6. In the highest
        to God let glory be,
    a covenant
        of peace to us on earth.
    Which to us men
        upon this blessed day
    angelic voices,
        as we know, have sung.

LXXXIII

Christiani, plaudite

1. Christiani, plaudite,
    resurrexit Dominus,
   victo mortis principe
    Christus imperat.
   Victori occurrite,
    qui nos liberat.

2. Superato zabulo,
    resurrexit Dominus,
   spoliato barathro
    suos eruit.
   Stipatus angelico
    coetu rediit.

3. Fraus in hamo fallitur,
    resurrexit Dominus,
   quae dum carne vescitur
    circumposita,
   virtute transfigitur
    carni insita.

4. Captivatis inferis,
    resurrexit Dominus,
   ditatisque superis
    caelum iubilat.
   Hymnis, psalmis, canticis
    terra resonat.

Hymn 83

O you Christians, clap your hands

1.   O you Christians, clap your hands,
  for the Lord has risen;
  conquered is the prince of death,
    and Christ now commands.
  Run to meet the victorious one,
    who has set us free.

2.   Vanquished is the devil now,
  for the Lord has risen,
  plundered are the depths of hell,
    Christ rescued his own.
  Circled by the angelic throng,
    he has now returned.

3.   By the hook is Fraud deceived,
  for the Lord has risen;
  as she fed upon the flesh
    that lay all around,
  she was pierced through by the power
    implanted in that flesh.

4.   He imprisoned those below,
  for the Lord has risen;
  those above are now enriched:
    heaven sings for joy.
  With their hymns, psalms, canticles
    the earth below resounds.

5. Deo Patri gloria,
      resurrexit Dominus,
    salus et victoria
      Christo Domini;
    par honor per saecula
      sit Spiritui.

LXXXIV

Da Mariae tympanum

1. Da Mariae tympanum
      resurrexit Dominus,
    Hebraeas ad canticum
      cantans provocet,
    Holocausta carminum
      Iacob immolet.

2. Subvertens Aegyptios,
      resurrexit Dominus,
    Rubri Maris alveos
      replens hostibus,
    quos involvit obrutos
      undis pelagus.

3. Dicat tympanistria,
      Resurrexit Dominus,

5. Glory be to God the Father,
     for the Lord has risen,
   health restored and victory
        to the Lord's anointed;
   equal honor through the years
        to the Holy Spirit.

Hymn 84

Give Mary a tambourine

1. Give Mary a tambourine,
     for the Lord has risen;
   as she sings, let her incite
        Hebrew women to song;
   let too Jacob sacrifice
        holocausts of songs.

2. Egyptians he did overwhelm,
     for the Lord has risen,
   filled the Red Sea's submerged caves
        with his enemies,
   whom the sea caught and buried
        in the waves below.

3. Let the timbrel player sing,
     For the Lord has risen,

illa quidem altera
 re, non nomine,
resurgentem merita
 prima cernere.

4. Cantet carmen dulcius,
 resurrexit Dominus,
reliquis fidelibus
 mixta feminis,
cum ipsa narrantibus
 hoc discipulis.

5. Deo patri gloria,
 resurrexit Dominus,
salus et victoria
 Christo Domini;
par honor per saecula
 sit Spiritui.

LXXXV

Golias prostratus est

1. Golias prostratus est,
 resurrexit Dominus,
ense iugulatus est
 hostis proprio;

a second Mary, different in
    her person, not in name,
she deserved to be the first
    to see him risen up.

4. Let her sing a sweeter song,
      for the Lord has risen,
    as she mingles with the rest
      of the faithful women,
    who with her proclaim the news
      to the Lord's disciples.

5. Glory be to God the Father,
      for the Lord has risen,
    health restored and victory
      to the Lord's anointed;
    equal honor through the years
      to the Holy Spirit.

Hymn 85

Goliath has been laid low

1. Goliath has been laid low,
      for the Lord has risen,
    for this foe has been dispatched,
      slain with his own sword;

cum suis submersus est
   ille Pharao.

2.   Dicant Sion filiae,
     Resurrexit Dominus,
   vero David obviae
     choros proferant,
   victori victoriae
     laudes concinant.

3.   Samson noster validus,
     resurrexit Dominus,
   circumsaeptus hostibus
     portas sustulit;
   frustratus allophylus
     stupens ingemit.

4.   Ut leonis catulus,
     resurrexit Dominus,
   quem rugitus patrius
     die tertia
   suscitat vivificus
     teste physica.

5.   Deo patri gloria,
     resurrexit Dominus,
   salus et victoria
     Christo Domini,
   par honor per saecula
     sit Spiritui.

Pharaoh with his troops was drowned
    plunged beneath the waves.

2.   Let now Zion's daughters sing,
      For the Lord has risen,
    and to greet the true David
      choruses lead out,
    then sing praises to the victor
      of his victory.

3.   Now our Samson of great might,
      for the Lord has risen,
    though surrounded by the foe,
      lifted up the gates;
    the foreigner in bafflement
      gaped and groaned aloud.

4.   Like the lion's tiny whelp,
      now the Lord has risen,
    which the Father's roaring roused
      once two days had passed,
    roaring which instilled new life,
      witness *Physica.*

5.   Glory be to God the Father,
      for the Lord has risen,
    health restored and victory
      to the Lord's anointed;
    equal honor through the years
      to the Holy Spirit.

LXXXVI

Veris grato tempore

1. Veris grato tempore,
   resurrexit Dominus,
   mundus revivescere
   cum iam incipit,
   auctorem resurgere
   mundi decuit.

2. Cunctis exsultantibus,
   resurrexit Dominus,
   herbis renascentibus,
   frondent arbores,
   odores ex floribus
   dant multiplices.

3. Transacta iam hieme,
   resurrexit Dominus
   in illa perpetuae
   vitae gaudia,
   nullius molestiae
   quae sunt conscia.

4. Qui restauret omnia,
   resurrexit Dominus;
   tamquam ista gaudia
   mundus senserit,
   cum carne dominica
   iam refloruit.

Hymn 86

In the welcome days of spring

1. In the welcome days of spring,
       for the Lord has risen,
    when the world again begins
       to resume new life,
    fittingly the world's creator
       rose up from the dead.

2. All creation leapt for joy,
       for the Lord has risen,
    and the grass sprouts up again;
       trees break into leaf,
    manifold the scents they breathe,
       issuing from their blooms.

3. Winter now at last is gone,
       for the Lord has risen,
    passing into heavenly joys
       of life that never ends,
    joys that do not apprehend
       troubles great or small.

4. Seeking to renew all things,
       now the Lord has risen;
    as if our world experienced
       all these heavenly joys,
    it has now blossomed once again
       with the Lord in flesh.

5. Deo Patri gloria,
        resurrexit Dominus,
    salus et victoria
        Christo Domini,
    par honor per saecula
        sit Spiritui.

LXXXVII

In montibus hic saliens

1. In montibus hic saliens,
    venit colles transiliens;
    sponsam vocat de montis vertice:
    "Surge, soror, et me iam sequere."

2. Ad paternum palatium,
    ad patris scandens solium,
    sponsae clamat: "Dilecta, propera,
    sede mecum in patris dextera.

3. "Omnis turba te civium,
    te regnum manet patrium,
    tuae tota cum patre curia
    praesentiae requirit gaudia.

5.   Glory be to God the Father,
      for the Lord has risen,
    health restored and victory
      to the Lord's anointed;
    equal honor through the years
      to the Holy Spirit.

Hymn 87

Leaping upon the mountain crests

1.   Leaping upon the mountain crests,
    he comes a-skipping over hills;
    he summons from the mountain peak his bride:
    "Arise, my sister, and now follow me."

2.   Mounting up to his father's palace,
    ascending to his father's throne,
    he calls unto his bride: "Beloved, haste,
    sit here with me upon my Father's right.

3.   "The entire host of citizens,
    the Father's kingdom, waits for you;
    the entire court, together with my Father,
    do seek your presence's attending joys.

4. "Quae regis sponsae congruant,
   quae reginae conveniant,
   hic intextas ex auro cyclades
   cum purpuris gemmatis indues."

5. Sit Christo summo gloria,
   qui scandens super sidera
   cum Spiritu, cum patre supera
   Deus unus regit et infera.

LXXXVIII

Quibusdam quasi saltibus

1. Quibusdam quasi saltibus
   superni patris filius
   ad terrena venit a superis,
   spoliatis nunc redit Tartaris.

2. A sinu venit patrio
   matris susceptus utero,
   in sepulcro de cruce positus
   resurrexit, per quem resurgimus.

3. Ascendentem ad aethera
   nubes excepit lucida;
   ferebatur erectis manibus
   benedicens suis astantibus.

4. "All that befits a king's betrothed,
   all that does well become a queen,
   here you will wear grand robes woven from gold
   and purple garments all with gems adorned."

5. Glory be to Christ on high,
   who, mounting high above the stars
   with the Spirit and also with the Father,
   rules as united God the heights and depths.

Hymn 88

With several successive leaps

1. With several successive leaps
   the son of the father on high
   descended to the earthly realms from heaven,
   now, having plundered hell, thither returns.

2. He came from his Father's bosom,
   was in his mother's womb received,
   though from the cross he was laid in the tomb,
   he rose, ensuring that we rise again.

3. As he rose to the sky above,
   a shining cloud received him there;
   he blessed his followers standing nearby
   with outstretched hands, and ascended on high.

4. Ascendentem cernentibus
   ac super hoc mirantibus
   astiterunt in albis angeli
   tam facie quam veste nitidi.

5. "Quid" inquiunt, "attoniti
   sic caelum intuemini?
   Quem euntem in caelum cernitis
   sic veniet in forma iudicis."

6. Sit Christo summo gloria,
   qui scandens super sidera
   cum Spiritu, cum patre supera
   Deus unus regit et infera.

LXXXIX

In terris adhuc positam

1. In terris adhuc positam
   sponsam Christus ecclesiam
   ad se rursum vocat cotidie,
   exhortatur mente conscendere.

2. Dicat haec: "Post te trahe me,
   nitenti dextram porrige.
   Super pennas ventorum evolas;
   quis sequatur, ni pennas conferas?"

4. As they watched him rising upward,
   and at this wonder marveling,
   there stood before them angels all in white,
   bright in their visage just as in their dress.

5. "Why," said they, "are you gazing thus,
   as if thunderstruck, at the sky?
   He whom you see now rising into heaven
   will come this way in the form of a judge."

6. Glory be to Christ on high,
   who, mounting high above the stars
   with the Spirit and also with the Father,
   rules as united God the heights and depths.

Hymn 89

Though she is still set on the earth

1. Though she is still set on the earth,
   Christ summons back his bride the Church
   every day back to him to return,
   urges her to mount up to him in mind.

2. Let her reply: "Draw me with you;
   as I strain, offer me your hand.
   You fly upon the feathers of the winds;
   who may follow, unless you give him wings?"

3. Columbae pennas postulet
   ut ad quietem properet.
   Alas petat potentis aquilae,
   quibus alta possit conscendere.

4. Dabit cum alis oculos,
   ut veri solis radios
   irreflexis possit obtutibus
   intueri, quo nil felicius.

5. Pennatis animantibus
   ille locus aethereus
   pro meritis virtutum congruit
   quibus alas his Deus dederit.

6. Sit Christo summo gloria,
   qui scandens super sidera
   cum Spiritu, cum patre supera
   Deus unus regit et infera.

XC

Cum in altum ascenderet

1. Cum in altum ascenderet
   et ima secum traheret
   triumphantis maiestas Domini,
   circumstabant victorem eruti.

3. Let her ask for a dove's soft wings
    to hasten forward to her rest.
    Let her seek out the sturdy eagle's wings,
    by which she may mount up unto the heights.

4. With wings he will give eyes as well,
    that she upon the true sun's rays
    may train her sight, her eyes unwavering;
    there can no greater blessing be than this.

5. That region high in heaven above
    befits creatures endowed with wings;
    these wings the God has granted here below
    to those who by their virtues merit them.

6. Glory be to Christ on high,
    who, mounting high above the stars
    with the Spirit and also with the Father,
    rules as united God the heights and depths.

Hymn 90

When unto the heights the Lord

1. When unto the heights the Lord
    mounted in majesty and triumph,
    drawing with him the lowliest of creatures,
    those he had rescued stood around the victor.

2. Superna regis civitas
   pompas educit obvias.
   "Chere" cantant victori angeli,
   et "Hosanna" salvati populi.

3. Illis tamquam quaerentibus
   et super hoc mirantibus
   hi respondent, et alternantibus
   ita cantum mulcent sermonibus.

4. Quis est iste rex gloriae,
   quid hoc decus victoriae?
   Quis est iste de Edom veniens,
   purpureo vestitu renitens?

5. Fortis et potens Dominus,
   triumphans victis hostibus;
   manu forti potens in proelio
   victor redit subacto zabulo.

6. Sit Christo summo gloria,
   qui scandens super sidera
   cum Spiritu, cum patre supera
   Deus unus regit et infera.

2.   The heavenly city of the king
     led forth processions to meet him.
     Angels sang "Greetings" to welcome the victor,
     "Hosanna" sang the people he had saved.

3.   As if they would some query make,
     the angels marveled over this;
     the people in antiphonal response
     these words did sing in tones soothing and
          sweet.

4.   Who is this monarch of glory,
     what is this famous victory?
     Who is this person who from Edom comes,
     shining so brightly in garments of purple?

5.   The Lord is strong and powerful,
     triumphing over conquered foes;
     with his strong hand so powerful in battle,
     the devil crushed, a victor he returns.

6.   Glory be to Christ on high,
     who, mounting high above the stars
     with the Spirit and also with the Father,
     rules as united God the heights and depths.

ADAM OF
SAINT VICTOR

XCI

Salve, mater Salvatoris

1. Salve, mater Salvatoris,
   vas electum, vas honoris,
       vas caelestis gratiae,
   ab aeterno vas provisum,
   vas insigne, vas excisum
       manu Sapientiae!

2. Salve, Verbi sacra parens,
   flos de spina, spina carens,
       flos spineti gloria:
   nos spinetum, nos peccati
   spina sumus cruentati,
       sed tu spinae nescia.

3. Porta clausa, fons hortorum,
   cella custos unguentorum,
       cella pigmentaria;
   cinnamomi calamum,
   myrrham, tus, et balsamum
       superas fragrantia.

4. Salve, decus virginum,
   restauratrix hominum,
       salutis puerpera!

Hymn 91

Hail, O mother of our Savior

1. Hail, O mother of our Savior,
    chosen vessel, honored vessel,
        vessel of the heavens' grace,
    vessel chosen from all ages,
    noble vessel, vessel chiseled
        by Wisdom's creative hand!

2. Hail, holy parent of the Word,
    blossom thornless on the thorn,
        thorn tree's glory and its flower:
    we the thorn tree are, we suffer
    bloodstain from our sins' thorn-pricking;
        you, however, know no thorn.

3. Fast-barred gate, and fount of gardens,
    guardian-store of fragrant ointments,
        store that houses spices sweet,
    you with fragrant smell surpass
    every shoot of cinnamon,
        myrrh and frankincense, balsam!

4. Glory of all virgins, hail,
    you who did restore mankind,
        who the world's salvation bore!

Myrtus temperantiae,
rosa patientiae,
   nardus odorifera!

5.   Tu convallis humilis,
terra non arabilis,
   quae fructum parturiit;
flos campi, convallium
singulare lilium,
   Christus ex te prodiit.

6.   Tu caelestis paradisus
Libanusque non incisus,
   vaporans dulcedinem,
tu candoris et decoris,
tu dulcoris et odoris
   habes plenitudinem.

7.   Tu thronus es Salomonis,
cui nullus par in thronis,
   arte vel materia;
ebur candens castitatis,
aurum fulvum caritatis,
   praesignant mysteria.

8.   Palmam praefers singularem,
nec in terris habes parem,
   nec in caeli curia;
laus humani generis
virtutum prae ceteris
   habes privilegia.

Myrtle tree of continence,
rose, symbol of endurance,
   nard wafting a fragrant scent!

5.   Vale of humble lowliness,
earth unsuited to the plow,
   that brought forth a noble fruit;
blossom of the plain, lily,
unique flower of every vale,
   Christ came forth from out your womb.

6.   You are heaven's blooming garden,
cedar of Lebanon inviolate,
   wafting out a dulcet warmth;
you incorporate the fullness
of all brightness and all beauty,
   of sweetness and fragrant smell.

7.   You are Solomon's throne, to whom
among all thrones there is no equal,
   in substance or craftsmanship;
chastity's ivory bright gleaming,
yellow gold of loving-kindness,
   symbolize your mysteries.

8.   Unique is the palm you flourish;
none on earth can be your equal,
   nor in heaven's court above;
you, the praise of humankind,
bear virtues' prerogatives
   more than others on the earth.

9.   Sol luna lucidior,
         et luna sideribus;
     sic Maria dignior
         creaturis omnibus.
     Lux eclipsim nesciens
         virginis est castitas;
     ardor indeficiens
         immortalis caritas.

10. Salve, mater pietatis,
     et totius Trinitatis
         nobile triclinium;
     Verbi tamen incarnati
     speciale maiestati
         praeparans hospitium.

11. O Maria, stella maris,
     dignitate singularis,
     super omnes ordinaris
         ordines caelestium.
     In supremo sita poli,
     nos commenda tuae proli,
     ne terrores sive doli
         nos supplantent hostium.

12. In procinctu constituti
     te tuente simus tuti;
     pervicacis et versuti
     tuae cedat vis virtuti,
         dolus providentiae.

9.   As the sun outshines the moon,
         and the moon in turn the stars,
     so is Mary worthier
         than all creatures everywhere.
     Light that suffers no eclipse
         is the virgin's chastity;
     her immortal charity
         is a never-failing heat.

10. Hail, dear mother so devoted,
     noble couch upon whose cushion
         rests the entire Trinity;
     you prepared a special lodging
     for the majesty so glorious
         of the Word which was made flesh.

11. O Mary, star of the ocean,
     you are one unique in merit;
     your position is exalted
         over all ranks in heaven above.
     Stationed in the peak of heaven,
     to your offspring recommend us,
     lest our enemies' fright or cunning
         make us stumble in our course.

12. As we gird ourselves for battle
     be we safe in your defenses;
     may the obstinate and crafty
     Satan's force yield to your power,
         his guile to your providence.

Iesu, Verbum summi Patris,
serva servos tuae matris,
solve reos, salva gratis,
et nos tuae claritatis
   configura gloriae.

Jesus, Word of the highest Father,
save the servants of your mother,
guilty, free us, save us gratis,
and, conforming to the glory
   of your brightness, give us shape.

PHILIP THE CHANCELLOR

XCII

Pange, lingua

1.   Pange, lingua, Magdalenae
     lacrimas et gaudium,
  sonent voces laude plenae
     de concentu cordium,
  et concordet philomenae
     turturis suspirium.

2.   Iesum quaerens convivarum
     turbas non erubuit;
  pedes unxit, lacrimarum
     fluvio quos abluit;
  crine tersit, et culparum
     lavacrum promeruit.

3.   Suum lavit mundatorem,
     rivo fons immaduit,
  pium fudit fons liquorem
     et in ipsum refluit,
  caelum terrae dedit rorem,
     terra caelum compluit.

Hymn 92

Sing, my tongue

1. Sing, my tongue, of Magdalena's
   weeping interfused with joy,
   let our voices ring with praises
   from the harmony of our hearts,
   and the turtledove's sweet sighing
   mingle with the nightingale's.

2. When she sought out Jesus' presence,
   crowds of guests did not deter;
   for his feet she there anointed,
   which she washed with floods of tears;
   with her hair she dried them, thereby
   gaining cleansing of her sins.

3. So she washed the one who cleansed her,
   with its stream the source grew wet;
   forth her source poured loving water
   and then ebbed back on himself;
   heaven its dew to earth imparted,
   earth with rain the heavens drenched.

4.   In praedulci mixtione
      nardum ferens pisticum,
  in unguenti fusione
      typum gessit mysticum;
  ut sanetur unctione
      unxit aegra medicum.

5.   Pie Christus hanc respexit
      speciali gratia;
  quia multum hunc dilexit,
      dimittuntur omnia.
  Christi quando resurrexit
      facta est praenuntia.

6.   Gloria et honor Deo,
      qui paschalis hostia,
  agnus mente, pugna leo,
      victor die tertia,
  resurrexit cum tropaeo
      mortis ferens spolia.

4.   In the mingling of such sweetness
            bringing forth the costly nard,
        by the pouring of that ointment
            she performed a mystic sign;
        sick, she anointed her physician,
            by that oiling to be healed.

5.   Christ looked on her with devotion,
            granting her a special grace,
        and because she loved him greatly,
            her sins were forgiven all.
        Of Christ's later resurrection
            she became the harbinger.

6.   Glory be to God and honor,
            saving victim in the Pasch,
        lamb in mind, in combat lion,
            victorious on that third day,
        who did rise up with the trophy,
            bearing all the spoils of death.

BONAVENTURE

XCIII

In passione Domini

1. In passione Domini,
   qua datur salus homini,
   sit nostrum refrigerium
   et cordis desiderium.

2. Portemus in memoria
   et poenas et opprobria
   Christi, coronam spineam,
   crucem, claves, et lanceam,

3. Et plagas sacratissimas,
   omni laude dignissimas,
   acetum, fel, arundinem,
   mortis amaritudinem.

4. Haec omnia nos satient
   et dulciter inebrient;
   nos repleant virtutibus
   et gloriosis fructibus.

5. Te crucifixum colimus
   et toto corde poscimus
   ut nos sanctorum coetibus
   coniungas in caelestibus.

Hymn 93

In the passion of the Lord

1. In the passion of the Lord,
   by which salvation is given to men,
   may we find our sweet refreshment
   and the desiring of our hearts.

2. In our remembering let us bear
   the punishment and hostile taunts
   of Christ, so too the crown of thorns,
   the cross and nails and lancet-thrust,

3. The hallowed wounds that he endured,
   which are deserving of all praise,
   the vinegar and gall and reed,
   the bitter misery of death.

4. From all these let us take our fill,
   and let them sweetly make us drunk;
   may they with virtues us infuse
   and with the fruits most glorious.

5. We worship you upon the cross,
   and beg of you with all our hearts
   that you may find a place for us
   amongst the heavenly ranks of saints.

6. Laus honor Christo vendito
    et sine causa prodito,
    passo mortem pro populo
    in aspero patibulo.

6. Praise and all honor be to Christ,
   sold and betrayed, though innocent,
   who suffered death for all mankind
   on that harsh gibbet of the cross.

[STEPHEN LANGTON]

XCIV

Veni, sancte Spiritus

1.   Veni, sancte Spiritus,
   et emitte caelitus
   lucis tuae radium.

2.   Veni, pauper pauperum,
   veni, dator munerum,
   veni, lumen cordium.

3.   Consolator optime,
   dulcis hospes animae,
   dulce refrigerium!

4.   In labore requies,
   in aestu temperies,
   in fletu solacium.

5.   O lux beatissima,
   reple cordis intima
   tuorum fidelium.

6.   Sine tuo numine
   nihil est in lumine,
   nihil est innoxium.

Hymn 94

Holy Spirit, come

1. Holy Spirit, come!
    Down from heaven send
    the beam of your light.

2. Come, poor among poor,
    come, bestower of gifts,
    come, O light of hearts!

3. Best of comforters,
    sweet guest of the soul,
    sweet refreshing source!

4. You are rest in toil,
    cooling breeze in heat,
    consoling in grief.

5. O most blessed light,
    fill up the hearts' depths
    of your faithful ones.

6. If your power be gone,
    nothing is lent light,
    nothing without harm.

7. Lava quod est sordidum,
   riga quod est aridum,
   sana quod est saucium,

8. Flecte quod est rigidum,
   fove quod est frigidum,
   rege quod est devium.

9. Da tuis fidelibus
   in te confitentibus
   sacrum septenarium.

10. Da virtutis meritum,
    da salutis exitum,
    da perenne gaudium.

7. Wash what is befouled,
   water what is parched,
   heal what is impaired,

8. Bend what is stiff,
   warm what is cold,
   sway what is perverse.

9. Grant to your faithful
   who confess in you
   your sacred sevenfold.

10. Grant reward of virtue,
    grant salvation's outcome,
    grant joy long-enduring.

[THOMAS OF CELANO]

XCV

Dies irae

1. Dies irae, dies illa
   solvet saeclum in favilla,
   teste David cum Sibylla.

2. Quantus tremor est futurus
   quando iudex est venturus,
   cuncta stricte discussurus!

3. Tuba mirum sparget sonum
   per sepulcra regionum,
   coget omnes ante thronum.

4. Mors stupebit et natura
   cum resurget creatura
   iudicanti responsura.

5. Liber scriptus proferetur
   in quo totum continetur
   unde mundus iudicetur.

6. Iudex ergo cum censebit,
   quidquid latet apparebit;
   nil inultum remanebit.

Hymn 95

Day of fury

1. Day of fury, that sad day
   will reduce the world to dust,
   as claim David and the Sibyl.

2. What a trembling there will be
   when the judge is to appear
   all things harshly to review!

3. Wondrous sound the horn will blare
   through the tombs of every land,
   usher all before the throne.

4. Death and nature will be stunned
   when creation shall again
   rise to answer to the judge.

5. Forth the written book will come,
   in which are all things contained
   by which will the world be judged.

6. When the judge appraises us,
   hidden things will be made plain;
   nothing will be unavenged.

7.   Quid sum miser tunc dicturus,
quem patronum rogaturus,
dum vix iustus sit securus?

8.   Rex tremendae maiestatis,
qui salvandos salvas gratis,
salva me, fons pietatis.

9.   Recordare, Iesu pie,
quod sum causa tuae viae;
ne me perdas illa die.

10.   Quaerens me sedisti lassus,
redemisti crucem passus;
tantus labor non sit cassus.

11.   Iuste iudex ultionis,
donum fac remissionis
ante diem rationis.

12.   Ingemisco tamquam reus,
culpa rubet vultus meus;
supplicanti parce, Deus.

13.   Qui Mariam absolvisti
et latronem exaudisti,
mihi quoque spem dedisti.

14.   Preces meae non sunt dignae,
sed tu bonus fac benigne
ne perenni cremer igne.

15.   Inter oves locum praesta,
et ab haedis me sequestra,
statuens in parte dextra.

7. What will I, poor wretch, then say,
   what defender then invoke,
   when the just are scarcely safe?

8. King of fearful majesty,
   saving freely those to be saved,
   save me, source of fondest love.

9. Pious Jesus, call to mind
   that for my sake you descended;
   on that day destroy me not.

10. Seeking me, you rested flagged,
    suffering the cross, redeemed me;
    let such toil not be in vain.

11. Judge, who are in vengeance just,
    grant to me your pardon's gift,
    ere the day of reckoning comes.

12. As a guilty one I groan,
    sinning makes me blush with shame;
    God, show mercy to my plea.

13. You who pardoned Magdalene,
    hearkened to the penitent thief,
    to me too have given hope.

14. Undeserving are my prayers,
    but save me, being good and kind,
    from the burns of lasting fire.

15. With the sheep secure my place,
    and set me apart from goats,
    setting me on your right hand.

16. Confutatis maledictis,
    flammis acribus addictis,
    voca me cum benedictis.

17. Oro supplex et acclinis;
    cor contritum quasi cinis;
    gere curam mei finis.

    [Lacrimosa dies illa,
    qua resurget ex favilla
    iudicandus homo reus.
    Huic ergo parce, Deus;

    Pie Iesu Domine,
    dona eis requiem.]

16.   Once the accursed are condemned,
and to piercing flames consigned,
call me with the blessed ones.

17.   Suppliant, bent low, I pray;
my heart is ground down like ash;
concern yourself with my last end.

[Tearful will be that last day,
when from ashes man will rise
indicted and to be judged.
Therefore pity him, O God;

O devoted Jesus, Lord,
grant them everlasting rest.]

SAINT THOMAS
AQUINAS

XCVI

Lauda, Sion, Salvatorem

1.   Lauda, Sion, Salvatorem,
lauda ducem et pastorem,
    in hymnis et canticis.
Quantum potes, tantum aude,
quia maior omni laude,
    nec laudare sufficis.

2.   Laudis thema specialis,
panis vivus et vitalis,
    hodie proponitur.
Quem in sacrae mensa cenae
turbae fratrum duodenae
    datum non ambigitur.

3.   Sit laus plena, sit sonora,
sit iucunda, sit decora,
    mentis iubilatio;
dies enim sollemnis agitur
in qua mensae prima recolitur
    huius institutio.

4.   In hac mensa novi regis
novum Pascha novae legis
    Phase vetus terminat;

Hymn 96

Zion, send the Savior praises

1.   Zion, send the Savior praises,
     praise our leader and our shepherd,
          in both hymns and canticles.
     Strain your efforts to the utmost,
     for he transcends all our praises,
          and your praise will not suffice.

2.   As the theme for special praising,
     living bread that is our life's bread
          lies before us on this day.
     Beyond question this was given
     to the gathering of twelve brethren
          at the sacred supper's board.

3.   Praise be full, and praise resounding,
     let our mental celebration
          be both sweet and dignified;
     for today this solemn feast day
     now recalls the inauguration
          of this table's sacred meal.

4.   At this table of our new king
     the new Pasch of this our new law
          ends the Pasch of ancient days;

vetustatem novitas,
umbram fugat veritas,
    noctem lux eliminat.

5. Quod in cena Christus gessit
faciendum hoc expressit
    in sui memoriam;
docti sacris institutis,
panem, vinum in salutis
    consecramus hostiam.

6. Dogma datur Christianis
quod in carnem transit panis,
    et vinum in sanguinem;
quod non capis, quod non vides,
animosa firmat fides
    praeter rerum ordinem.

7. Sub diversis speciebus,
signis tantum et non rebus,
    latent res eximiae;
caro cibus, sanguis potus,
manet tamen Christus totus
    sub utraque specie.

8. A sumente non concisus,
non contractus, non divisus,
    integer accipitur;
sumit unus, sumit mille,
quantum isti, tantum ille,
    nec sumptus consumitur.

this new age supplants the old,
truth all shadows puts to flight,
  light dispenses with the night.

5. Christ's enactment at that supper
stipulated what we must do
    to recall his memory;
by these sacred rules instructed,
bread and wine we consecrate now
    as salvation's sacrifice.

6. On Christians is urged the teaching
that the bread becomes his body,
    and the wine becomes his blood;
what you fail to grasp, to witness,
faith of spirit holds as certain,
    past nature's usual course.

7. Under so diverse appearance,
merest signs, not reality,
    hidden lie outstanding things;
food his flesh, as drink his blood is,
Christ remains entire, however,
    under both appearances.

8. He who takes the Christ, unbroken,
unfragmented, undivided,
    takes Him in entirety;
one takes of Him, now a thousand,
one obtains as much as many:
    taken and yet unconsumed.

9.   Sumunt boni, sumunt mali,
sorte tamen inaequali
    vitae vel interitus;
mors est malis, vita bonis:
vide paris sumptionis
    quam sit dispar exitus.

10.   Fracto demum sacramento,
ne vacilles, sed memento
tantum esse sub fragmento
    quantum toto tegitur;
nulla rei fit scissura,
signi tantum fit fractura,
qua nec status nec statura
    signati minuitur.

11.   Ecce: panis angelorum
factus cibus viatorum;
vere panis filiorum
    non mittendus canibus:
In figuris praesignatur
cum Isaac immolatur,
agnus Paschae deputatur,
    datur manna patribus.

12.   Bone pastor, panis vere,
Iesu, nostri miserere,
tu nos pasce, nos tuere,
tu nos bona fac videre
    in terra viventium.

9. Good and wicked both receive him,
   but their lot thereafter differs:
       they inherit life or death;
   death for wicked, life for good men:
   note how different is the outcome,
       though reception is the same.

10. When the sacrament is broken,
    do not waver, but remember:
    all exists within each fragment
        that is hidden in the whole;
    not the thing itself is broken,
    sign alone becomes fragmented;
    what it stands for is not lessened
        in its status or its size.

11. Mark how here the bread of angels
    is made food for us wayfarers;
    what is truly bread for children
        to the dogs must not be thrown:
    it was in figures presaged, when
    Isaac as sacrifice was offered,
    paschal lamb sent to replace him,
        manna to the fathers came.

12. Goodly shepherd, bread most truly,
    O Jesus, have pity on us,
    do you feed us, give protection,
    do you help us see our blessings
        in the land of living souls.

Tu, qui cuncta scis et vales,
qui nos pascis hic mortales,
tu nos ibi commensales
coheredes et sodales
    fac sanctorum civium.

XCVII

Verbum supernum prodiens

1.   Verbum supernum prodiens,
nec Patris linquens dexteram,
ad opus suum exiens
venit ad vitae vesperam,

2.   In mortem a discipulo
suis tradendus aemulis,
prius in vitae ferculo
se tradidit discipulis.

3.   Quibus sub bina specie
carnem dedit et sanguinem,
ut duplicis substantiae
totum cibaret hominem.

4.   Se nascens dedit socium,
convescens in edulium;
se moriens in pretium,
se regnans dat in praemium.

You, who know and can do all things,
you who here feed us poor mortals,
see to it that we share table,
as their coheirs and their comrades,
    With the saints, heaven's citizens.

Hymn 97

The Word, emerging from on high

1.   The Word, emerging from on high,
     yet quitting not his Father's side,
     came forth for his appointed task,
     and reached the evening of his life;

2.   He was to be consigned to death
     by his disciple to his foes,
     but first his flesh as feast of life
     he unto his disciples gave.

3.   To them beneath the twofold form
     his flesh he granted and his blood,
     imparting his whole person thus,
     its double substance, as their food.

4.   At birth he gave himself as friend,
     at table he became our food;
     by dying he did ransom us,
     as king, rewards us with himself.

5.   O salutaris hostia,
       quae caeli pandis ostium,
       bella premunt hostilia;
       da robur, fer auxilium.

6.   Uni trinoque Domino
       sit sempiterna gloria,
       qui vitam sine termino
       nobis donet in patria.

XCVIII

Pange, lingua

1.   Pange, lingua, gloriosi
       corporis mysterium,
       sanguinisque pretiosi
       quem in mundi pretium,
       fructus ventris generosi,
       rex effudit gentium.

2.   Nobis datus, nobis natus
       ex Maria virgine,
       et in mundo conversatus
       sparso verbi semine,
       sui moras incolatus
       miro clausit ordine.

5. O saving victim, opening wide
    the gates of heaven by your death,
    we are oppressed by hostile wars;
    bestow your strength, grant us your aid.

6. To the single and threefold Lord
    may there be glory for all time;
    may he bestow life without end
    to us within our native land.

Hymn 98

Tell, my tongue, the sacrament

1. Tell, my tongue, the sacrament
        of glorious body and precious blood
    poured out by the king of nations,
        by the fruit of a noble womb;
    by which means he paid the ransom
        to redeem the world from sin.

2. To us given, for us begotten
        from the virgin Mary's womb,
    and in the world's confines abiding,
        having scattered the word's seed,
    he his term of dwelling with us
        closed with wondrous ordering.

3. In supernae nocte cenae
        recumbens cum fratribus,
    observata lege plene
        cibis in legalibus,
    cibus turbae duodenae
        se dat suis manibus.

4. Verbum caro panem verum
        verbo carnem efficit,
    fitque sanguis Christi merum,
        et, si sensus deficit,
    ad firmandum cor sincerum
        sola fides sufficit.

5. Tantum ergo sacramentum
        veneremur cernui,
    et antiquum documentum
        novo cedat ritui.
    Praestet fides supplementum
        sensuum defectui.

6. Genitori genitoque
        laus et iubilatio,
    salus, honor, virtus quoque
        sit et benedictio.
    Procedenti ab utroque
        compar sit laudatio.

3. On the night of the last supper,
      with his brothers he reclined,
    and observed the law in fullness
      with foods by the law ordained;
    as food he to his band twelvefold
      gave himself with his own hands.

4. Word-made-flesh transforms the true bread
      by the word into his flesh;
    wine is changed into the Christ's blood;
      and, if sense fails to discern,
    faith alone is found sufficient
      to strengthen devoted hearts.

5. We this sacrament of greatness
      will revere on bended knee,
    and the observance of the ancients
      yield to a new form of rite.
    Let faith make its own addition
      to our senses' failing powers.

6. To the Father and Son likewise
      praise and exultation,
    faith, honor, and power also
      be, and benediction.
    To the one from both proceeding
      equal be laudation.

XCIX

Adoro devote,
latens veritas

1. Adoro devote, latens veritas,
   te quae sub his formis vere latitas;
   tibi se cor meum totum subicit,
   quia te contemplans totum deficit,

2. Visus tactus gustus in te fallitur,
   sed solus auditus tute creditur.
   Credo quidquid dixit Dei filius,
   nihil veritatis verbo verius.

3. In cruce latebat sola deitas;
   sed hic latet simul et humanitas.
   Ambo tamen credens atque confitens,
   peto quod petivit latro paenitens.

4. Plagas, sicut Thomas, non intueor,
   meum tamen Deum te confiteor.
   Fac me tibi semper magis credere,
   in te spem habere, te diligere.

Hymn 99

Devotedly I worship,
truth who are concealed

1. Devotedly I worship, truth who are concealed,
    under these appearances truly lying hid.
    My heart subjects itself entirely to you,
    for, contemplating you, it wholly faints away.

2. The sight, the touch, the taste are all in you
        deceived;
    but to my ears alone I safely lend belief.
    All that the son of God has said, I do believe;
    nothing is truer than the word of truth himself.

3. Only his divinity on the cross lay hid;
    but his humanity lies hidden here as well.
    I believe and proclaim that both are present
        here;
    I make the same request as the repentant thief.

4. Your wounds I do not look on as Saint Thomas
        did;
    nevertheless I do proclaim you as my God.
    So grant me ever to believe in you the more,
    to rest my hope in you, to offer you my love.

5. O memoriale mortis Domini,
   panis veram vitam praestans homini,
   praesta meae menti de te vivere,
   et te semper illi dulce sapere.

6. Pie pellicane, Iesu Domine,
   me immundum munda tuo sanguine,
   cuius una stilla salvum facere
   totum mundum posset omni scelere.

7. Iesu, quem velatum nunc aspicio,
   quando fiet illud quod tam cupio,
   ut te revelata cernens facie
   visu sim beatus tuae gloriae?

5.　O sacred offering, recalling the Lord's death,
the bread affording true life to the world of men,
grant me that my mind may seek its life in you,
and that it ever know the sweetness of your
　　taste.

6.　O my Lord Jesus, you devoted pelican,
cleanse me of impurity with the blood you shed,
for of it one small droplet could salvation bring,
and could make free the whole world of its every
　　sin.

7.　Jesus, whom I now behold all veiled up,
when will I be granted what I so desire,
to openly behold you, with your face unveiled,
and be truly blessed, seeing your glory?

C

Stabat mater dolorosa

1. Stabat mater dolorosa
   iuxta crucem lacrimosa
      dum pendebat filius.
   Cuius animam gementem
   contristatam et dolentem
      pertransivit gladius.

2. O quam tristis et afflicta
   fuit illa benedicta
      mater unigeniti!
   Quae maerebat et dolebat,
   et tremebat, cum videbat
      nati poenas incliti.

3. Quis est homo qui non fleret,
   matrem Christi si videret
      in tanto supplicio?
   Quis non posset contristari
   piam matrem contemplari
      dolentem cum filio?

4. Pro peccatis suae gentis
   fessum vidit in tormentis,
      et flagellis subditum;

Hymn 100

Stood the mother full of grieving

1. Stood the mother full of grieving
    by the cross, bitterly weeping,
        for her son was hanging there.
    Her soul, groaning lamentations,
    racked with sadness and with sorrow,
        had been pierced through by a sword.

2. O how saddened and afflicted
    was that woman, highly blessed,
        mother of her sole-born son!
    She did mourn and she did sorrow,
    and she trembled, as she witnessed
        the anguish of her famous son.

3. What man would restrain his weeping,
    if Christ's mother there he witnessed
        suffering so monstrously?
    Who would not be filled with sorrow
    to see that devoted mother
        sharing suffering with her son?

4. She beheld him weary, tortured,
    and subjected to the scourges,
        for the sins of all his race;

vidit suum dulcem natum
morientem, desolatum,
   cum emisit spiritum.

5.   Eia, mater, fons amoris,
me sentire vim doloris
   fac, ut tecum lugeam;
fac ut ardeat cor meum
in amando Christum Deum,
   ut sibi complaceam.

6.   Sancta mater, illud agas,
crucifixi fige plagas
   cordi meo valide;
tui nati vulnerati,
tam dignati pro me pati,
   poenas mecum divide.

7.   Fac me vere tecum flere,
crucifixo condolere,
   donec ego vixero;
iuxta crucem tecum stare,
te libenter sociare
   in planctu desidero.

8.   Virgo virginum praeclara
mihi iam non sis amara;
   fac me tecum plangere:
fac ut portem Christi mortem,
passionis eius sortem
   et plagas recolere.

she beheld her own sweet son there
on the point of death, forsaken,
    as he breathed his final breath.

5.   Come, mother, who are love's wellspring,
make me feel the pain of grieving,
    so that I may mourn with you;
make my heart to burn ardently
in loving of Christ God, so that
    I may be pleasing to him.

6.   Holy mother, do this for me:
in my heart do implant firmly
    wounds of your son crucified;
share them with me, all those sufferings
that your son endured while wounded,
    deigned to bear so much for me.

7.   Let me truly shed tears with you,
with him crucified share mourning,
    for as long as I shall live;
by the cross to stand beside you,
be your comrade there with gladness,
    this I long for in my grief.

8.   Virgin so renowned of virgins,
do not now be harsh unto me;
    make me share your grief with you:
make me bear Christ's death, so make me
constantly recall the suffering
    and the blows that were his lot.

9.   Fac me plagis vulnerari,
      cruce hac inebriari
         ob amorem filii;
      inflammatus et accensus
      per te, virgo, sim defensus
         in die iudicii.

10.   Fac me cruce custodiri,
      morte Christi praemuniri,
         confoveri gratia;
      quando corpus morietur,
      fac ut animae donetur
         Paradisi gloria.

9. By those blows make me sore wounded,
   by this cross intoxicated,
       out of love felt for your son;
   licked with flames and set to blazing,
   may I enjoy your protection,
       virgin, on the judgment day.

10. Make me by the cross be shielded,
    by the death of Christ protected,
        and so cherished by his grace;
    when my body death encounters,
    grant that my soul then be given
        glorious life in Paradise.

Note on the Texts

Because of the eclectic nature of the texts presented in this volume, there is not one single recent source where critical editions of all of them may be found together. The reader is directed to the critical editions listed beneath each hymn in the Notes to the Texts and Translations and collected in the Bibliography. Departures from the text of these editions are few, and those of greater importance are noted in the notes where relevant. Capitalization of *Pater/Father, Filius/Son, Verbum/Word, Dominus/Lord,* and such spellings as *praemium/ proemium,* etc., are silently regularized across all texts, and punctuation silently edited.

Abbreviations

ACW = *Ancient Christian Writers.* New York: Paulist Press, 1946–.

AH = *Analecta Hymnica.* Leipzig: Fues's Verlag (R. Reisland), 1886–1920?.

CCL = *Corpus Christianorum. Series Latina.* Turnhout: Brepols, 1953–.

CIL = *Corpus inscriptionum Latinarum.* Berlin: G. Reimer, 1846–.

CLP = Raby, *A History of Christian-Latin Poetry from the Beginnings to the Close of the Middle Ages,* 2nd ed. Oxford: Clarendon, 1953.

CSEL = *Corpus scriptorum ecclesiasticorum Latinorum.* Vienna: Akademie der Wissenschaften Wien, 1866–.

LSJ = Liddell and Scott. *Greek-English Lexicon,* 9th ed., rev. H. Stuart Jones, 1996; Suppl. by E. A. Barber and others. Oxford: Clarendon, 1968.

MGH = *Monumenta Germaniae Historica.*

ODCC = *The Oxford Dictionary of the Christian Church,* 3rd ed. rev. Oxford: Oxford University Press, 2005.

OLD = *Oxford Latin Dictionary.* Oxford: Clarendon, 1996.

PL = Migne. *Patrologiae Cursus, series Latina.* Paris, 1844–1864.

PLRE = *Prosopography of the Later Roman Empire.* 3 vols. Cambridge: Cambridge University Press, 1971–1992.

RAC = *Reallexikon für Antike und Christentum.* Stuttgart: Hiersemann, 1941–.

TLL = *Thesaurus Linguae Latinae.* Leipzig: Teubner, 1900–.

Notes to the Texts and Translations

AMBROSE

1. *Aeterne rerum conditor*

This hymn is certainly Ambrose's, for Augustine (*Retract.* 1.21) cites lines 15–16 "ex versibus beatissimi Ambrosii" (from the verses of the most blessed Ambrose). Moreover, Ambrose repeats many of the motifs at *Hexaemeron* 5.88. The hymn is specified as a *hymnus nocturnalis* in Ambrosian manuscripts. Caesarius of Arles appointed it to be sung at the Second Nocturn as an appropriate composition with which to greet the dawn. The poem is structured round the two interconnected themes of the cock as herald of the dawn and of the repentance it inspired in Peter after his triple denial of Christ.

1.4   *ut alleves:* That is, to alleviate weariness by alternating (most relevantly for this hymn) night and day.

2.4   *a nocte noctem segregans:* Isidore, *Orig.* 5.30, suggests that the cock crows at midnight, but the more obvious sense is that his crowing separates the dark hour before the dawn from the earlier night hours.

3.1   *lucifer:* "The morning star," not, of course, itself dissipating the darkness, but signaling the dawn. Walpole understood it as the sun.

3.3   *errorum:* Walpole rightly defends this reading against the "correction" *erronum* ("truant slaves"). *Errorum* (= *errantium*), the abstract word for the concrete, appropriately registers the sense of "vagrant demons."

4.1–3   *nauta . . . petra:* These motifs are developed at *Hex.* 5.88, where
         Ambrose likewise writes *ipse petra.* For Peter's denials, the cock
         crows, and Peter's bitter tears, see Mt 26:69–75, Lk 22:56–62.

5.4   *negantes arguit:* The Arian Monophysites who deny Christ's di-
         vinity are visualized as heirs to Peter's denial.

7.1   *labantes respice:* As Christ did to Peter (Lk 22:61). The connection
         is made more explicitly at *Hex.* 5.88.

7.4   *fletuque . . . solvitur:* We thus imitate the repentant Peter.

See further Walpole, 27–34; Fontaine, 143–75.

2. *Splendor paternae gloriae*

The ascription of this hymn to Ambrose is attested by Fulgentius (468–
533), bishop of Ruspe, who cites the first line and two others (*Ep.* 14.10,
CCL 91). There are numerous echoes of the hymn in other works of Ambrose. Bishop Aurelian, successor of Caesarius at Arles, ordered the hymn
to be sung at Matins, between dawn and sunrise. The hymn exploits the
onset of day to reflect on the light of the Trinity; the Father's light issues
in the Son, and Christ as true Sun directs the Spirit's rays. The imagery
of Christ as true Sun derives in part from biblical sources (Mal 4:2, "Sun
of justice"; Is 9:2, "A great light"), partly from Platonist philosophy, partly
from pagan religious tradition (the Greek cult of Helios taken over by the
Roman state religion when the emperor Aurelian pronounced Sol Invictus
as the supreme deity of the empire in 274 CE). See Rahner, *Greek Myths
and Christian Mystery*, ch. 4.

1.1   *Splendor paternae gloriae:* As often, the hymn begins with a scrip-
         tural reminiscence. See Hbr 1:3: "Qui cum sit splendor gloriae
         et figura substantiae eius" ([The Son] being the brightness of
         [God's] glory and the figure of his substance [i.e., the imprint of
         his being]).

1.2   *de luce lucem:* So *lumen de lumine* in the Nicene Creed (325 CE).

2.1   *inlabere:* (Imperative of the deponent.) Perhaps evoking Aeneas's
         prayer to Apollo in Virgil, *Aen.* 3.89: *animis inlabere nostris.*

3.1–4   *vocemus . . . releget:* Paratactic, omitting *ut* ("Let us call . . . let him
         banish").

5.4   *fraudis venena:* Referring to doctrines of the Arian heresy.

6.1–2   *Christusque . . . fides:* Here Ambrose alludes to the two species in the Eucharist. In the exordium to his *De sacramentis,* he insists that faith must precede reception of the Eucharist. At *Ep.* 47.5 he writes: "The good food of all men is Christ; the good food is faith *(bonus cibus est fides).*"

6.3–4   *sobriam ebrietatem Spiritus:* The paradoxical image is developed from Eph 5:18: "Et nolite inebriari vino, . . . sed implemini Spiritu sancto" (Be not drunk with wine, . . . but be ye filled with the Holy Spirit).

7.2–4   *pudor . . . mens:* The poetic tricolon is striking: purity as the dawn, faith as the heat of noonday, mind knowing no darkness.

8.2   *aurora totus:* For Christ, light of the Father, as the dawn, see stanza 1 above. With the inconcinnity of *aurora totus* compare *ipse petra* at 1.4.3 above.

See further Walpole, 35–39; Fontaine, 179–204.

3. *Iam surgit hora tertia*

Augustine provides evidence for Ambrose as author of this hymn, citing (*De natura et gratia* 63) lines 7–8 as Ambrosian. Caesarius and his successor Aurelian at Arles appoint the hymn to be sung at Terce (which is the second of the "Little Hours" after Prime, appointed for prayer at the third hour). The hymn is structured in four parts: the third hour, when Christ mounted the cross (so Mk 15:25), and our appropriate response (§§ 1–2); the Redemption which that hour brought to the world (§§ 3–4); Jesus's address to Mary and John, and the mystery of the Virgin Birth (§§ 5–6); and later miracles attesting the virginal Incarnation (§§ 7–8).

1.1   *hora tertia:* So Mk 15:25. Matthew and Luke speak of the sixth to the ninth hour.

1.3   *nil insolens:* Proud thoughts are inappropriate at this supreme manifestation of Christ's humility.

2.1–4   *Qui corde Christum suscipit . . . sanctum mereri Spiritum:* Evoking Eph 3:17, 16: "habitare Christum per fidem in cordibus vestris," "ut det vobis . . . corroborari per Spiritum eius in interiore ho-mine" (That Christ may dwell by faith in your hearts, . . . that [the Father] would grant you . . . to be strengthened by his Spirit with might unto the inward man).

3.1–2   *finem . . . criminis:* The people before Christ, defaced by original sin, are now cleansed.

3.3   *mortisque regnum:* See Rom 5:14.

4.1   *Hinc iam beata tempora:* It was likewise at the third hour that the Holy Spirit descended on the apostles (Act 2:15).

4.2   *Christi gratia:* See Act 2:33. Christ's passion was the occasion for the access of new grace; so Ambrose, *In Ps.* 118:6.

5.1   *triumphi:* For the cross as triumphant over Satan and death, see Paul at Col 2:14–15.

5.2   *loquebatur:* So John 19:26–27.

6.1   *nuptae foedera:* "The pact of the bride." Mary's marriage to Joseph was "drawn over" (*praetenta,* that is, spread so as to conceal) the mystery of the Virgin Birth. Mary's continuing status as virgin did not prevent her exercising the role of mother.

7.1   *Cui:* The relative pronoun refers to the Virgin Birth; the subsequent miracles attest Christ's divinity thus signaled.

7.4   *qui credidit,* etc.: So Mk 16:16: "Qui crediderit . . . salvus erit" (He that believeth . . . shall be saved).

8.1   *Nos credimus natum Deum:* A defiant affirmation against Arianism.

8.3   *peccata qui mundi tulit:* Compare John 1:29: "Qui tollit peccata mundi" (Who taketh away the sin of the world).

8.4   *ad dexteram . . . Patris:* Compare Mk 16:19: "sedit a dextris Dei" ([Jesus] sitteth on the right hand of God).

See further Walpole, 39–44; Fontaine, 179–228.

4. *Deus, creator omnium*

This hymn consoled Augustine at his mother's death: "I remembered the very true verses of your Ambrose . . ." The first two stanzas then follow (*Conf.* 9.12.32). He recalled that earlier his mother had quoted the final line at Cassiciacum (*De beata vita* 35). At Arles, Caesarius prescribed it as an evening hymn. It is structured with a fourfold division: invocation to the Creator, who grants the night for necessary rest (§§ 1–2); thanksgiving for the day now past (§§ 3–4); prayer for faith to sustain us in sleep (§§ 5–6); and entreaty to the Trinity to repel the devil's guile in the night hours (§§ 7–8).

1.1   *Deus, creator omnium:* The scriptural exordium is from the prayer of Nehemiah at 2 Mcc 1:24: "Domine Deus, omnium Creator . . ." (O Lord God, Creator of all things . . .).

2.1–2   *solutos . . . reddat:* As often in Latin, there is a combination of participle and finite verb where English prefers two finite verbs.

3.1–2   *Grates . . . preces:* The elegant chiasmic order should be noted. The thanks are for the blessings of the past day, and the prayers for the coming night.

3.3   *voti reos:* A Virgilian phrase (*Aen.* 5.237: "voti reus"), expressing the notion of obligation to fulfill a vow, here specified in the stanzas following.

4.4   *mens . . . sobria:* Not with the suggestion of drinking to be avoided, but an exhortation to adopt the serious demeanor appropriate to prayer.

5.2–3   *caligo . . . fides:* As often, Ambrose contrasts the physical darkness with the shining faith to which we aspire.

6.1   *Dormire mentem:* Suggestive of spiritual lethargy, as at 1 Corinthians 11:30: "Ideo inter vos multi infirmes et inbecilles, et dormiunt multi" (Therefore are there many infirm and weak among you, and many sleep).

6.4   *somni vaporem:* The heat of sexual arousal is perhaps implied, as in hymn 23.2.4 below, "ne polluantur corpora." Faith here cools as elsewhere it heats.

8.1–2   *Christum . . . Patrem . . . Spiritum:* This plea to the Trinity can be regarded as an anticipation of the doxology glorifying the Trinity with which hymns later close.

See further Walpole 44–49; Fontaine 241–61.

5. Intende, qui regis Israel

Several near contemporaries of Ambrose cite this hymn. Augustine quotes from it on two occasions (*De symbolo* 4.4.4; *Tract. in evang. Ioan.* 59.3), without ascribing it to Ambrose. But Celestine, bishop of Rome 422–432, cites and attributes to Ambrose the second stanza (*PL* 53.289B). Two other fifth-century bishops, Faustus of Riez and Facundus of Hermiana, quote sections of it and likewise attribute them to Ambrose, as does Cassiodorus, *In Ps. 8 Conclusio* (*ACW* 51, 116).

As we have noted, the first four hymns form part of daily worship at fixed hours; this fifth composition celebrates the nativity of the Lord. Ambrose himself was probably instrumental in establishing December 25 as the feast day at Milan; at Rome it had earlier supplanted the feast of Sol Invictus on that day.

1.1   *Intende,* etc.: The whole stanza adapts, almost word for word, part of Ps 79:2–4, which is interpreted as prophecy of Christ's coming: "Qui regis Israhel, intende, . . . Qui sedes super cherubin, manifestare coram Efraim . . . Excita potentiam tuam, et veni ut salvos facias nos" (Give ear, O thou that rulest Israel, . . . Thou that sittest upon [i.e., art enthroned upon] the cherubims, shine forth before Ephraim . . . Stir up thy might, and come to save us).

1.3   *Ephrem coram:* Ambrose interprets the Old Testament prophet as the personification of Israel; thus stanza 1 signals Christ's coming to the Jews, and stanza 2 his coming to the Gentiles.

2.4   *talis . . . partus:* The miraculous birth befits the Son of God.

3.2   *mystico spiramine:* The adjective bears the twin senses of mysterious and sacramental.

3.3   *Verbum . . . caro:* So John 1:14: "Et Verbum caro factum est" (And the Word was made flesh).

3.4   *fructusque ventris:* Elizabeth's greeting to the Virgin Mary at Lk 1:42, "Benedictus fructus ventris tui" (Blessed is the fruit of thy womb), echoes the verses, regarded as prophetic, in Ps 126:3, 131:11.

4.2   *claustrum pudoris:* In Christian Latin *pudor* bears the sense of "virginity." Ambrose implies that the hymen remained unruptured not merely at conception (as Ambrose argues at *Inst. Virg.* 8.52) but also at birth. See also his Letter 42 to Damasus; Augustine, *De haeresibus* 82; Jerome, *Against the Pelagians* 2.4.

4.3   *vexilla virtutum:* The virtues thus emblazoned are Mary's virginal chastity *(pudor)*, modesty *(verecundia)*, and faith *(fides)*. See *Inst. Virg.* 5.35; *De virginibus* 2.2.15.

4.4   *in templo:* For Mary as God's temple, see Ambrose, *De spiritu sancto* 3.80; *In Ps.* 45.13.

5.1–4   *Procedat,* etc.: This stanza and the next are a reworking of Ps 18:6–7, interpreted as prophecy of Christ's coming: "Ipse tamquam sponsus procedens de thalamo suo exultavit ut gigans ad currendam viam. A summo caeli egressio eius, et occursus eius usque ad summum eius." (He as a bridegroom coming out of his bride chamber hath rejoiced as a giant to run the way. His going out is from the end of heaven, and his circuit even to the end thereof.)

5.2   *pudoris aula regia:* Mary's womb is virginal as the court from which the bridegroom comes.

5.3   *geminae gigas substantiae:* Christ is a giant in his twin natures, divine and human.

6.3   *excursus usque ad inferos:* Compare Ambrose, *In Ps.* 43:86: "The Lord descended to hell so that those dwelling there too could be loosed from their everlasting bonds." The word *excursus* is apt for a liberating sally.

7.1   *Aequalis aeterno Patri:* Christ's divinity is stressed as a riposte to Arianism.

7.2   *carnis tropaeo:* The flesh is a trophy because Christ gains the human race in his struggle with Satan and death. For Christ's resurrected flesh as a trophy, see Mohrmann, "A propos de deux mots controversés de la latinité chrétienne," 158.

8.2–4   *lumen ... novum ... fide iugi luceat:* For Christ as a new light, see hymn 2.1. The "constant faith" is probably Christ's fidelity to us, rather than ours to him.

See further Walpole, 50–57; Fontaine, 265–301.

6. *Amore Christi nobilis*

The ascription of this hymn to Ambrose depends on its presence in Ambrosian MSS, and on its characteristic content and style. It should also be noted that its antiquity is guaranteed by the basilica built at Ravenna by

Galla Placidia only thirty years after Ambrose's death; the first two lines of the hymn are inscribed there (*CIL* 11.276).

It is appropriate that this hymn commemorating Christ's beloved disciple should follow immediately after the nativity hymn; John's feast day has traditionally been celebrated two days later, on December 27. The hymn can be read as a minibiography of the apostle, beginning from his life as a fisherman and passing first to his transformation into a fisher of men, thereafter to his role as evangelist, and finally to his role as witness to the faith.

1.2	*filius tonitrui:* So Mk 3:17: "Et Jacobum . . . et Iohannem . . . et inposuit eis nomina Boanerges, quod est Filii Tonitrui" (And James . . . and John . . . and he named them Boanerges, which is The Sons of Thunder).
1.3	*arcana . . . Dei:* With particular reference to the prologue of his gospel, in which he identifies Christ with the Word of God made flesh.
2.2	*patris senectam pascere:* The gospels offer no evidence of this. Matthew merely states that his father, Zebedee, was working with his sons in the boat when they were called by Christ (4:21).
3.2	*piscatus est verbum Dei:* At *Hex.* 5.17 Ambrose writes: "The gospel is the sea in which the apostles fish, and into which they cast their net." Here he suggests that John's catch was the knowledge that Christ was the son of God.
3.4	*vitam . . . omnium:* So John 6:55: "Qui manducat meam carnem et bibit meum sanguinem habet vitam aeternam" (He that eateth my flesh and drinketh my blood hath everlasting life).
4.1–4	*fides . . . locuta:* John is here initially depicted as catching the goodly fish of faith, and then as Faith personified uttering the prologue of the gospel. For his reclining on Jesus's breast, see John 13:23.
5.1–4	*In principio,* etc.: From here to the beginning of stanza 6, Ambrose cites John 1:1–3 word for word, taking necessary liberties with the meter.
6.2	*Sic . . . sic:* I offer this bold solution to the textual difficulty. For the confusion in the MSS, see Walpole's critical apparatus. Walpole and Fontaine both read *se laudet ipse, se sonet* ("Let him praise

and trumpet himself"), but this he does not do; he praises Christ, and it is for this that he gains the crown.

7.3–4   *hoc . . . quod fecit esse martyres:* The gospel which John wrote was the cause of martyrs laying down their lives; his writings thus transcended their deaths.

8.1–4   *vinctus . . . aemuli:* Stanza 7 implies that John did not die a martyr's death, a view echoed by Augustine, *De bono coniugali* [XXI] 25. The legend that he miraculously emerged unscathed from a cauldron of boiling oil will have originated in the apocryphal *Acta Ioannis,* which sets the incident at Ephesus. Tertullian, *Praescr.* 36, transfers the scene to Rome, and the location there is later specified as the Latin Gate. But there is no firm evidence that John was ever in Rome.

See further Walpole, 57–62; Fontaine, 305–34.

7. *Illuminans altissimus*

Cassiodorus, *Exp. In Ps.* 74.9 states: "The blessed Ambrose, in his hymn for the holy Epiphany, showed wondrous eloquence with the vivid brightness of his words." He was referring to the description of water changed to wine in stanzas 4–5. The ascription to Ambrose is further indicated by a passage in his *In Luc.* 6.84–88, in which the final four stanzas of the hymn are mirrored.

The hymn is a celebration of the Epiphany, and thus follows in chronological sequence after hymns 5 and 6. The feast day on January 6 originally commemorated the Baptism of Christ and the manifestation of his divinity (hence stanza 2), but in the west the connection with Christ's baptism was lost in favor of the manifestation of Christ to the Gentiles (stanza 3). To these theophanies are appended two further epiphanies, the miracles at Cana (§§ 4–5) and at the feeding of the five thousand (§§ 6–8).

1.3   *pax . . . veritas:* Compare Eph 2:14: "Ipse est enim pax nostra" (For he is our peace); John 14:6: "Dicit ei Iesus, 'Ego sum via et veritas et vita'" (Jesus saith to him, "I am the way and the truth and the life").

2.1   *mystico baptismate:* The adjective connotes both "hidden mystery" and "sacrament" in the theological sense; at Eph 5:32, Paul's μυστήριον *(mystérion)* is rendered in the Vulgate as *sacramentum*. For the celebration of Christ's baptism on this feast day (which still continues in Eastern Christianity with the solemn blessing of water), see *ODCC*, s.v. "Epiphany," with bibliography.

2.2–3   *fluenta . . . conversa . . . tertio:* For the three occasions, see Jos 3:14–17, 4 Kings 2:8, 14.

3.1–4   *Seu stella . . . duxerit:* See Mt 2:9. With the interlinking *seu . . . seu* in this and the previous stanza, Ambrose reveals his knowledge of the differing celebrations in East and West.

3.3   *adoratum:* Supine indicating purpose ("to adore"). For the scene, see Mt 2:11.

4.1–2   *vel . . . infuderis:* See John 2:6–7. The miracle at Cana is appended as "the beginning of miracles" that "revealed his glory" (John 2:11). Ambrose elsewhere states (*PL* 57.260) that this "manifestation" was connected with the feast of the Epiphany before his day.

5.2   *inebriare:* Adapted from John 2:10.

5.3–4   *mutata elementa . . . in usus alteros:* The repetition of these phrases in Ambrose's other works (*In Ps.* 118, 19:9; *Inst. Virg.* 34) is a further indication of Ambrose's authorship of the hymn.

6.1–2   *Sic . . . dividit:* There is no evidence that this miracle (Mt 14:15–21) was commemorated on the feast of the Epiphany. Ambrose appends it as an apt addition to the miracle of the provision of wine at Cana.

8.2   *rigatur profluus:* The metaphor of solid bread "pouring forth abundantly" is less incongruous in view of the comparison with perpetually flowing springs in stanza 7.

8.4   *viris:* These are the disciples who gathered the fragments.

See further Walpole, 62–68; Fontaine, 337–59.

8. *Agnes beatae virginis*

The close correspondence between the content of this hymn and Ambrose's *De virginibus,* which incorporates a sermon delivered on the feast of Saint Agnes, sufficiently justifies the ascription of this hymn to Ambrose.

Like Damasus (*Epigr.* 37) before him, he drew upon oral accounts of the martyrdom of the saint, who was executed probably in the persecution of Diocletian in 304–5: the epigram of Damasus begins "Fama refert" (Tradition has it), and Ambrose, *De virginibus* 1.7, writes "traditur" (it is said). Already by 350 a basilica had been raised over her remains at Rome by Constantina, daughter of Constantine. Her feast day on January 21 follows chronologically after that of the Epiphany (hymn 7).

1.1–2   *Agnes . . . natalis:* Agnes is a Greek genitive, literally meaning "of the pure one." The anniversary on January 21 commemorates her birth into heaven.

2.2   *matura nondum nuptiis:* She is said to have been twelve years old, the minimum age for marriage according to Roman law. See Ambrose, *De virginibus* 1.5–7; Prudentius, *Perist.* 14.10–11.

3.1   *Metu parentes territi:* This motif of parental precautions to guard a daughter's chastity occurs in both secular and Christian literature; see for example the exemplar of Danaë in Horace, *Odes* 3.16, and Eulalia in Prudentius, *Perist.* 3.36–40.

4.1   *Prodire quis nuptum putet:* This motif too of a maiden confronting death as if she were a bride is traditional. Compare Psyche in Apuleius, *Metamorphoses* 4.34–35.

4.3   *novas viro ferens opes:* Her husband is Christ, her dowry of blood unprecedented.

5.1   *numinis:* According to Prudentius (*Perist.* 14.27) the deity was Minerva.

5.2–3   *taedis . . . faces:* These terms extend the imagery of marriage. Agnes rejects pagan deities in favor of marriage to Christ.

6.3   *Hic, hic ferite:* As in Prudentius, *Perist.* 14.77–90, she offers her breast to the sword, but there the executioner decapitates her; compare Ambrose, *De virginibus* 1.9.

7.2   *veste se totam tegens:* This concern for modesty may be modeled on Euripides' celebrated description of the sacrifice of Polyxena in *Hecuba* 568–84. Ambrose, a good Greek scholar, could have adopted the motif directly from Euripides or from Ovid's imitation at *Met.* 13.474–80; see also Seneca, *Troades* 1132–42.

See further Walpole, 69–76; Fontaine, 363–403.

9. *Hic est dies verus Dei*

This hymn is not explicitly credited to Ambrose before the ninth century, but two lines from it are cited by Caesarius of Arles in 529, and its presence in the Ambrosian MSS, together with the close connections with Ambrose's prose works, sufficiently justify the ascription. The hymn is a meditation on the passion, death, and resurrection of Christ. The redemptive act for all mankind is signaled by Christ's pardon of the Good Thief.

1.1 *Hic est dies:* The exordium, as often, incorporates a scriptural reminiscence; see Ps 117:24: "Haec est dies quam fecit Dominus" (This is the day which the Lord hath made). Christians appropriated the Day of the Sun, the day after the Sabbath, to commemorate the Resurrection by celebration of the Eucharist. Christ is frequently invoked as the true Sun (see hymn 5 above); the "holy light" in line 2 is his.

2.2 *caecosque:* Probably blind in the metaphorical sense, so that the word reinforces the message of the previous line.

2.4 *latronis absolutio:* See Lk 23:40–43.

3.2 *brevi . . . fide:* The thief's momentary gesture of faith elicited a swift response.

3.3 *praevio gradu:* This is inferred from Lk 23:43: "Hodie mecum eris in paradiso" (Today you will be with me in paradise).

4.1 *stupent et angeli:* The arresting image is echoed by Ambrose in *De fide* 4.7, 4.26: "obstupuerant angeli," "stupuerunt angeli."

4.2 *corporis:* Namely the thief's body.

5.2 *ut abluat:* The subject is *caro* (line 4).

5.3 *peccata tollat:* John 1:29.

6.2 *culpa:* With reference to the thief's earlier career.

7.1–2 *Hamum . . . nodis:* These images of death impaled on its own hook and trapped in its own snare are developments of the Pauline theme of victory over death at 1 Cor 15:55–57. Compare hymn 83.3.1.

8.1 *cum mors . . . transeat:* Compare Rom 5:12: "Sicut per unum hominem in hunc mundum peccatum intravit, et per peccatum

mors, et ita in omnes homines mors pertransiit . . ." (As by one
man sin entered into this world, and by sin death, and so death
passed upon all men . . .).

See further Walpole, 77–82; Fontaine, 407–41.

10. *Victor Nabor Felix*

As is the case with the previous hymn, the ascription to Ambrose rests on
the presence of the hymn in the Ambrosian MSS, and on the close correspondence with Ambrose's prose works. The hymn commemorates the
execution of three martyrs during the persecution under Diocletian in
304–5 CE. They are named by Ambrose in his *In Luc.* 7.178. See also Paulinus of Milan, *Vita Ambrosii* 14.

1.3   *solo hospites, Mauri genus:* (*Genus* is accusative of respect or speci-
      fication.) The men will have come to northern Italy as troops in
      the imperial army. Moorish cavalry had long served in Roman
      armies; under Diocletian the western part of their country (Tin-
      gitana) was attached to the province of Hispania.

2.1   *Torrens harena:* The emphasis on the hardships of their native
      land adds force to the panegyric of their heroism.

2.4   *nostri nominis:* That is, Roman citizenship.

3.1   *Suscepit . . . Padus:* Since Mediolanum (modern Milan) lies well to
      the north of the river Po, their unit may have been stationed at
      Lodi (see 7.3–4 below).

3.3   *sancto replevit Spiritu:* Hence they arrived in Italy as pagans and
      were converted there. Payment in blood for the hospitality they
      received was to be made later.

4.1   *coronavit:* The subject is strictly *fides,* but we may understand *ec-
      clesia* taken over from the previous stanza.

4.3   *raptos:* The implication is that after conversion they deserted,
      and made their way to Milan.

5.3   *pro rege:* On behalf of the emperor previously, but now for
      Christ.

7.1   *Scutum . . . fides:* Compare Eph 6:16: "Sumentes scutum fidei"
      (Taking the shield of faith).

7.3 *tyrannus:* The reference could be to Diocletian himself, but more probably to the local commander, named Anulinus in the *Acta Martyrum.*

7.3–4 *oppidum Laudense:* The modern Lodi, some twenty miles southeast of Milan (*nobis* meaning "us in the city"). Perhaps that was where their military unit was stationed, and they were executed there as an example to their comrades.

8.1 *reddiderunt hostias:* (The subject has to be supplied from *oppidum Laudense,* "the Laudensians.") According to the *Acta Martyrum* a married lady called Sabina buried them and later secretly conveyed their remains to Milan in her own carriage. This legend may be alluded to in *plaustri triumphalis modo.*

8.3 *in ora principum:* That is, before the civil and ecclesiastical leaders of the city, rather than, as Walpole suggests, before the persecutors, who would not have countenanced such an open display.

See further Walpole, 82–86; Fontaine, 445–83.

II. *Grates tibi, Iesu, novas*

The attribution of this hymn to Ambrose is guaranteed by its close correspondence with the bishop's letter to his sister Marcellina (*Ep.* 77), which recounts the same event. The discovery of the martyrs' remains was made in June 386, when Augustine was teaching at Milan. He describes the discovery in a sermon (286, 4) and in the *Confessions* (9.7.16). Augustine and Ambrose's biographer Paulinus suggest that the discovery occurred at the height of Ambrose's struggle with the empress Justina for possession of a basilica at Milan. In fact, that fracas occurred during Holy Week of that year; Ambrose does not himself connect the two events. Following what he calls a presentiment, he dug in the church of Saints Felix and Nabor and discovered decapitated skeletons, which he identified as Protasius and Gervasius. Later tradition dated their deaths to the mid-second century.

1.4 *cano:* The first person identifies the hymn writer with the *repertor,* who is Ambrose.

2.2 *non latebat fons sacer:* Namely of blood (compare the next line).

Likewise at *Ep.* 77.2 and 12 Ambrose states that "the mound was wet with blood." Whatever the date of the martyrdom, Ambrose implies that the blood had been flowing ever since.

2.4   *qui clamat ad Deum:* Evoking the murder of Abel at Gen 4:10: "Dixitque ad eum, . . . 'Vox sanguinis fratris tui clamat ad me'" ([The Lord] said to him, . . . "The voice of thy brother's blood crieth to me").

3.3   *nequimus esse martyres:* "We" are Christians of Ambrose's time. By 386, Ambrose indicates, the last great era of persecution (under Diocletian) was long past.

4.1   *Hic quis requirat. . . :* Perhaps uttered in reproach to the Arians, who were skeptical of the identification of the skeletons as martyrs.

4.3   *Sanatus impos mentium:* (*Impos* is here used as a noun, "one who is not in control.") Both Ambrose (*Ep.* 77) and Augustine (*Conf.* 9.7.16) state that the bishop exorcized persons possessed by evil spirits.

5.1   *Caecus recepto lumine:* In his letter to Marcellina, Ambrose reports that Arians thought this miracle, which Augustine (*Conf.* 9.7.16) records in some detail, to have been faked.

5.3   *Severus:* Ambrose cites this name also in *Letter* 77, as does Paulinus, *Vita Ambrosii* 4. They make it clear that the official had resigned his imperial post by then.

7.1–2   *Soluta . . . vinculis, spiris . . . libera:* The second line explains the nature of the bonds in the first. The "serpents" are the demons that enslaved men until they were freed by the efficacy of the relics.

7.3   *totis urbibus:* The crowd had assembled from all the surrounding cities.

8.1   *Vetusta saecla:* The ages of old are the apostolic times, when such miracles were constantly witnessed.

8.2   *semicinctia:* Strictly speaking, belts or girdles; see Petronius, *Sat.* 94.8, in which Encolpius uses his to try to hang himself from a bed frame.

8.3   *umbra:* Compare Act 5:15: "Ut veniente Petro, saltim umbra illius

obumbraret quemquam eorum" (That when Peter came, his shadow at the least might overshadow any of them).
See further Walpole, 89–92; Fontaine, 487–512.

12. *Apostolorum passio*

No contemporary voice confirms this hymn as Ambrose's, but its presence in the Ambrosian MSS and echoes in the prose works have persuaded virtually all scholars to ascribe it to him. It was written to be sung on June 29, the feast day of Saints Peter and Paul.

1.2   *diem sacravit saeculi:* That is, has made what had been a "worldly" day into a holy day, when Christians abandoned their worldly tasks to make their yearly pilgrimage to Rome.

1.3–4   *Petri . . . Pauli:* For the pervasive tradition that Peter and Paul were martyred at Rome (Peter crucified and Paul beheaded) at the same period in Nero's reign, see Eusebius, *Eccl. hist.* 2.25, and the summary accounts with bibliography in *ODCC. Triumphus* and *corona* are words regularly associated with martyrdom in Patristic texts.

2.1   *aequales:* The two are equal in status as martyrs, but not as apostles, as the next stanza makes clear.

3.1   *Primus Petrus:* See Mt 16:18–19. Stanzas 4–5 are accordingly devoted to him alone.

3.3   *electionis vas:* So Act 9:15: "A vessel of my [sc. the Lord's] choosing."

4.1   *verso crucis vestigio:* The *Acts of Peter* (37–38), composed in Greek in the late second century, records this detail that Peter was crucified head down. For bibliography see *ODCC,* 1261.

4.4   *non immemor oraculi:* See Christ's words at John 21:18: "Cum autem senueris, extendes manus tuas, et alius . . . ducet quo non vis" (But when thou shalt be old, thou shalt stretch forth thy hands, and another shall . . . lead thee whither thou wouldst not).

5.1   *Praecinctus, ut dictum est:* So John 21:18: "Alius te cinget . . ." (Another shall gird thee . . .).

6.1   *Hinc:* Though the previous words are devoted to Peter alone,
       hinc refers to the martyrdom of both apostles as the foundation
       of the faith.

6.4   *vate tanto:* In view of the extensive writings of Paul, the refer-
       ence is probably to him rather than to Peter.

7.1–3 *per urbis ambitum . . . trinis . . . viis:* The shrine of Saint Peter on
       the Vatican hill would be approached by the Via Aurelia, and
       that of Saint Paul outside the walls by the Via Ostiensis. The
       third road indicated is the Via Appia; it would have led to the
       catacomb of Callistus, where Peter and Paul were commemo-
       rated together. Damasus's *Epigr.* 20 was inscribed there, includ-
       ing the words "You are to know that saints earlier dwelt here;
       you seek the names of Peter and Paul alike."

8.3–4 *electa, gentium caput:* (*Electa* is best taken as vocative.) Rome is
       identified as the chosen city where Paul, teacher of the Gentiles
       (so 1 Tim 2:7, 2 Tim 1:11), made his residence.

See further Walpole, 92–97; Fontaine, 515–46.

13. *Apostolorum supparem*

This hymn is confidently attributed to Ambrose on two grounds. First, it
was already current soon after his death, as references in Maximus of Turin
(*Homily* 74) and Petrus Chrysologus (*Serm.* 135), both writing ca. 450, tes-
tify. Secondly, the hymn closely reflects Ambrose's detailed account in his
De officiis 1.205–7, a passage which inspired Prudentius, *Perist.* 2 and Augustine *Tract. in evang. Ioan.* 27.12. See Davidson, *De officiis/Ambrose,* 2.634–37.

Lawrence was martyred in Rome in 258 CE by order of the emperor
Valerian. Earlier evidence in Cyprian, *Ep.* 80, and the *Liber pontificalis,* 155,
indicates that Pope Sixtus was not led out to crucifixion, but summarily
beheaded, so that the dramatic conversation recorded in stanza 2 (and in
Off. 1.205) is fictitious. According to Cyprian, Sixtus was executed in company with four deacons. The *Liber pontificalis* states that six deacons were
with him and that four days later the archdeacon Lawrence (together with
a subdeacon, a reader, and a doorkeeper) was similarly beheaded. The
grisly account of Lawrence's being roasted on a gridiron (also reported by
Ambrose at *Off.* 1.206), in itself improbable as a mode of Roman execu-

tion, may have arisen from earlier corruption of *passum* ("suffered") into *assum* ("burned"). See in general Nauroy, "Le martyre de Laurent," 44–82.

1.1	*supparem:* "Almost equal," an unusual term used elsewhere by Ambrose; see Walpole's note.
1.2	*archidiaconem:* Lawrence is accorded this title also in the *Liber pontificalis.*
2.1	*sequens:* In this improbable version, Lawrence follows Bishop Sixtus to the site of crucifixion outside the city.
2.2	*vatis:* Sixtus himself.
2.3	*Maerere, fili, desine:* Ambrose, *Off.* 1.205, states, "When Lawrence saw Sixtus his bishop led away to martyrdom, he began to weep, not for Sixtus's suffering, but because he was being left behind."
2.4	*post triduum:* The date conforms with that in the *Liber pontificalis* ("post tertia die") and in *Off.* 1.206.
3.2	*sanguinis:* "Of the shedding of blood."
4.3	*syngrapham:* The agreement or covenant obtained by Lawrence from the promise and bloodshed of Sixtus.
5.1–2	*iussus . . . prodere:* When Lawrence was ordered to hand over the treasures of the Church, the insolent gesture described in the next stanza was the cause of his execution.
7.3	*Avarus:* The "greedy" magistrate was the city prefect P. Cornelius Saecularis (see *PLRE* 1.795).
8.3	*Versate me,* etc.: The grim joking is recorded in more extended form in Prudentius, *Perist.* 2.401–8.

See further Walpole, 97–104; Fontaine, 549–81.

[AMBROSE]

14. *Aeterna Christi munera*

Citation by Maximus of Turin (*Serm.* 66) indicates that this hymn goes back to the time of Ambrose. Bede, *De arte metrica* 11, cautiously attributes it to "the Ambrosians." Thus the possible attribution to Ambrose himself must rest on correspondences with his prose works. Doubts have been raised against his authorship on the grounds of allegedly non-Ambrosian metrical features, but as Fontaine demonstrates, these are not decisive. However, the impersonal treatment, without mention of specific martyrs, is not characteristic of other hymns of Ambrose, and lends itself to easier imitation, so that the ascription must remain doubtful.

1.1   *Aeterna . . . munera:* The gifts are the martyrs themselves. It is possible to take *Christi* as gifts "bestowed on Christ" by Christian communities (as in Prudentius, *Perist.* 4.8), but more probably the phrase here means "gifts bestowed by Christ" in the spirit of Eph 4:8–13.

2.1   *Ecclesiarum principes:* Not necessarily bishops, but martyrs who led by example in their communities.

3.3   *compendio:* For the sense of "shortcut," see *OLD,* s.v. *compendium,* 3. Martyrdom is the "shortcut" to salvation.

4.3–4   *armata . . . ungulis . . . manus:* ("The hand of the maddened torturer, armed with claws.") The *ungula,* a metal claw, tore the flesh with the results described in the next stanza.

5.4   *gratia:* I take this in the sense of "for the sake of" rather than (literally) "by the grace of" (as Fontaine).

6.3   *perfecta Christi caritas:* "The perfect love of Christ for them"; *Christi* is subjective genitive, like *sanctorum* and *credentium.*

6.4   *mundi . . . principem:* Satan as lord of the world is a persistent theme in John's gospel. See 12:31, 14:30, 16:11.

7.1–2   *paterna gloria . . . voluntas Spiritus:* At Hbr 1:3, Christ is the *splendor gloriae* of the Father; here the martyrs are allotted this distinction. At 1 Cor 12:11 the Spirit bestows his gifts on individuals "prout vult" (according as he will).

See further Walpole, 104–8; Fontaine, 585–621.

[Nicetas of Remesiana]

15. *Te Deum laudamus*

This celebrated hymn in rhythmical prose, which still today occupies a prominent place in Christian liturgies, was earlier ascribed to Hilary or Ambrose or Augustine; but following the researches of G. Morin (*Revue Bénédictine* 11 (1894): 49–77) it has been generally ascribed to Nicetas the missionary bishop of Dacia, who is perhaps best known through visits to Paulinus at Nola. See Paulinus, *Ep.* 29.14, *Poems* 17, 27.149–340 (*ACW* 36.117–18, 40.106–13, 275–82). The name "Bishop Nicet" is inscribed as author on a dozen ancient Irish MSS. More recently, however, this ascription has been challenged; it is now regarded as deriving from a Paschal Vigil. See the Introduction, p. ix. The hymn in its original form closed at *iudex crederis esse venturus;* the petitions which follow were added at an early date. See Mohrmann, *Études sur le latin des chrétiens,* 161–62.

1.1–3   *Te ... te ... te:* The triple invocations here and in stanzas 2, 4, and 6 are a formula frequently found in pagan hymns; see Catullus, 34.13–20, Lucretius 1.6. But more probably its inclusion here is inspired by the Hebraic tradition; see, e.g., Ps 51:5–6, 64:2–3, 70:6–7, 73:13–15.

2.2   *universae potestates:* The Powers are technically the sixth order of angels, but the term is used more generally for all celestial beings exercising dominion over parts of the created world. Compare 64.2.1n.

2.3   *cherubim et seraphim:* The cherubim are frequently cited as God's attendants in the Old Testament, and are the highest of the nine orders of angels. The seraphim are cited only once (Is 6:2–7), but their role there as author of the *Sanctus* (see the next n.) encouraged Christian interpreters to group them with the cherubim, as in the Preface of the Mass.

3.1   *Sanctus,* etc.: This ancient hymn was probably sung as early as the late first century. It appears to be cited in Clement of Rome's *First Epistle to the Corinthians* (34.6–7). It is derived from Is 6:3, where the Seraphim sing: "Sanctus, sanctus, sanctus Dominus, Deus exercituum; plena est omnis terra gloria eius" (Holy, holy, holy the Lord God of hosts; all the earth is full of his glory).

3.2   *Sabaoth:* The Hebrew word, rendered in the Vulgate by *exercituum,* appears twice in the New Testament (Rom 9:29; Ja 5:4), and refers to the "armies" of angels who sing the hymn.

4.3   *candidatus:* Tertullian (*De paenitentia* 13) and later Fathers regard martyrdom as a second baptism; the white garment is therefore as appropriate for the martyr as for the catechumen. See Apc 7:14: "And [one of the ancients] said to me: 'These are they who have come out of great tribulation and have washed their robes and have made them white in the blood of the Lamb.'"

5.5   *Paraclitum:* The Greek word means "advocate," but from Ori-

PRUDENTIUS

gen onward the Fathers use it of the Holy Spirit in the sense of "Comforter," for the Spirit is sent to comfort us after Christ leaves this world (John 14:16).

6.1 *rex gloriae:* Ps 23:7, 9, 10 proclaims the coming of the king of glory, interpreted by the Fathers as Christ.

6.3 *devicto mortis aculeo:* Compare 1 Cor 15:56–57: "Stimulus autem mortis peccatum est . . . Deo autem gratias, qui dedit nobis victoriam per Dominum nostrum Iesum Christum" (Now the sting of death is sin . . . But thanks be to God, who hath given us the victory through our Lord Jesus Christ).

7.1–3 *ad dexteram dei . . . iudex . . . esse venturus:* Echoing the Nicene creed.

8.2 *pretioso sanguine:* So 1 Pt 1:18–19: "Non corruptibilibus . . . redempti estis, . . . sed pretioso sanguine . . . Christi" (You were not redeemed with corruptible things . . . but with the precious blood of Christ).

8.3–4 *aeterna . . . in gloria:* So 1 Pt 5:10: "Deus autem omnis gratiae, qui vocavit nos in aeternam suam gloriam" (The God of all grace, who hath called us into his eternal glory in Christ Jesus).

9.1–4 *salvum fac,* etc.: The whole stanza is a citation of Ps 27:9: "Salvam fac plebem tuam, Domine, et benedic hereditati tuae, et rege eos et extolle eos usque in aeternum" (Save, O Lord, thy people, and bless thy inheritance, and rule them and exalt them for ever).

10.1 *per singulos dies:* Drawing on Ps 144:2: "Per singulos dies benedicam tibi, et laudabo nomen tuum in saeculum et in saeculum saeculi" (Every day will I bless thee, and I will praise thy name for ever, yea, for ever and ever).

11.1 *isto:* Here "this."

See further Burn and Kähler.

PRUDENTIUS

16. *Ales diei nuntius*

This is the first of the twelve hymns of the *Cathemerinon* (on which, see the Introduction, pp. ix–x), a book composed for reading and recitation apposite to various hours during the day and to prominent feast days. The program thus adopts the pattern of hymns observable in those attributed to Ambrose. But whereas his predecessor's compositions are succinct and composed for communal participation, Prudentius writes at greater length for private meditation, exploiting the themes of the Ambrosian hymns to develop the allegorical significance of their content.

Thus in this initial hymn composed for cock crow, Ambrose's *Aeterne rerum conditor* provides the basis for sustained allegory. The cock crow represents the call of Christ bidding us to partake of his light; the sleep that the listener is bidden to renounce is the symbol of death; the darkness of night is an image of mortal sins, giving way to day as a devout soul seeks the light of Christ.

Stanzas 1–2, 21, and 25 were later extracted from the hymn to become part of the daily Office.

1.1–3   *Ales . . . excitator:* The cock greeting the imminent dawn symbolizes Christ's invitation to arise to live the Christian life. The beginning of Ambrose's second stanza, "Praeco diei iam sonat," lies behind Prudentius's "ales diei . . . praecinit."

2.1–2   *lectulos . . . desides:* The epithets "sick, drowsy, slothful" are transferred to the beds from their occupants.

2.3–4   *castique . . . proximus:* See 1 Pt 5:8, "Sobrii estote, et vigilate" (Be sober, and watch), and Mk 13:35, "Keep awake therefore, for you do not know when the master of the house cometh . . . at midnight, or at cock crow, or at dawn." Compare also Rom 13:11: "Nunc enim propior est nostra salus . . ." (For now our salvation is nearer); 1 Th 5:6 "Vigilemus et sobrii simus" (Let us watch and be sober).

3.4   *labori:* Here, as at 6.3 below, *labor* refers to the discipline of wakeful prayer. Compare Jerome, *Ep.* 107.9, where after detailing the monks' routine of prayer and psalmody, he adds, "Let the day pass thus, let the night find the monk toiling *(laborantem)* thus." John Cassian similarly refers to "the toil of vigils" *(vigiliarum laborem; De coen. inst.: PL* 49.145).

4.1–3   *strepunt aves . . . emicet:* The image is inspired by Virgil, *Aen.* 8.455–56: "The fostering light and the early-morning songs of the birds beneath the roof *(matutini volucrum sub culmine cantus) . . .*"

4.4   *figura:* The sense of "symbol" is found in Paul (e.g., 1 Cor 10:6, 11), and thereafter frequently in the Fathers. See *TLL* 6.734.80–737.60.

6.1   *coruscis flatibus:* The first meaning of the adjective ("moving rapidly") is more appropriate than the second ("flashing"); the image is of the breezes scattering the clouds.

6.3–4   *labore . . . ad spem luminis:* For the sense of *labore,* see 3.4n. above. Egan draws attention to the parallel thought in *Egeriae Peregrinatio* 36.5, probably composed in 381/384, a decade or so before this hymn. "The bishop addresses the people, giving them strength, since they have toiled the whole night long, and will continue to toil *(laboraverint . . . laboraturi sint)* that day, urging them not to grow weary, but to have hope in God *(spem in deo).*" (For the date of the *Egeriae Peregrinatio,* see Devos, "La date du voyage d'Égérie.")

7.1–2   *somnus . . . forma mortis:* Kindred expressions occur in classical literature (Homer, *Il.* 14.231, Plato, *Ap.* 40c–d), but the Fathers, influenced by scripture (John 11:11; 1 Cor 15:16–18, "Et qui dormierunt in Christo perierunt" [They also that are fallen asleep in Christ are perished]), advert to it more frequently.

8.1   *ab alto culmine:* Note the parallel with the birds at 4.2 above.

9.1–2   *somnus usque ad terminos vitae:* The expression suggests the notion of living death.

10.1–4   *vagantes daemonas . . . timere et cedere:* (*Daemonas* is a Greek accusative, found frequently in the Fathers.) This demonology derives from two sources. The first is biblical; demons in the New Testament are identified with Satan's fallen angels (see, e.g., Ambrose, *De Paradiso* 12.54–55 and *Ep.* 22; Augustine *C.D.* 8.22, 11.33). The second source is Middle Platonism; see especially Apuleius, *De deo Socratis* 132–56, discussed at length by Augustine, *C.D.* 8.14–22. The notion that demons shun the light is not emphasized in the Platonist tradition, but is strong in the Fathers, who connect the light with Christ; see above, Ambrose, hymn 1.3.3–4 (probably influencing Prudentius here); Augustine, *Serm.* 103: "These demons seek to seduce our souls, but at sunrise they flee."

11.1–4   *Invisa . . . satellites:* In this and the following stanza the Christian interpretation is developed further; since the daylight symbolizes Christ's saving power, the demons shun it fearfully. For their foreknowledge *(praescii)*, see Mt 8:29.

12.3   *soporis liberi:* That is, delivered from the sleep which represents spiritual death.

13.1   *vis . . . huius alitis:* Jesus's prophecy of the triple denial of Peter before cock crow is recorded in all four gospels; see Mk 14:30, Mt 26:34, Lk 22:34, John 13:38. Prudentius develops the treatment of Ambrose, hymn 1.4–6, in this denial theme.

14.1–4   *Fit . . . ferat:* The stanza is to be understood in the allegorical sense. The sinning before dawn represents mankind's sinful state before Christ's coming frees the world from sin.

15.1   *Flevit negator:* So Mk 14:72, Mt 26:75, Lk 22:62. For the varying judgments of Peter's conduct in Hilary (followed by Prudentius here), Ambrose, and Augustine, see van Assendelft, 77–80.

15.4   *animusque servaret fidem:* Compare Ambrose's treatment in hymn 1 above, where the cock crow rebukes "those who deny" (5.4), but then "faith returns to those who have slipped" (6.4). Thus Ambrose is more judgmental than Prudentius, who in the next stanza argues that Peter's lapse is a mere slip of the tongue.

17.1–4   *Inde est . . . Christum redisse: Inde* picks up *cantuque galli cognito.* As Peter's inherent fidelity reemerged with the cock crow, so are the faithful recalled by it to their belief in the resurrection of the Lord.

17.4   *redisse ex inferis:* Compare Mk 16:6, Mt 28:1–7, Lk 24:6, John 20:1–9.

18.2   *Tartari:* The use of this classical title for the underworld, found in Lucretius, Virgil, Horace, and others, makes its way into scripture in the Vulgate at 2 Pt 2:4. Prudentius, so familiar with classical literature, introduces the word *Tartarus* twenty times into his writings to depict the world of darkness below.

19.2   *culpa . . . obdormiat:* The motif is borrowed from Ambrose, hymn 4.6–7 above, and is characteristically developed by Prudentius.

20.3   *dum meta noctis clauditur: Meta* is used literally for the "turning post" of a racetrack, and so metaphorically for the turning points of dawn and dusk. So Ausonius, *Ep.* 20.17, writes, "So dawn departed, and so did the other *meta* of the day." Hence the phrase here *meta noctis clauditur* ("night's end is closed") must refer to the end of the period between cock crow and dawn.

21.1   *ciamus:* From *cio, cire* (usually *cieo, ciere*).

21.2   *flentes precantes sobrii:* The regimen of tears, prayers, and fasting is traditionally prescribed in the Old Testament, and is taken up by the Fathers. Compare Joel 2:12–13: "Be converted to me with all your heart, in fasting and in weeping and in mourning *(in ieiunio et in fletu et in planctu),*" quoted by Cyprian, *De lapsis* 29–30.

21.4   *dormire cor mundum vetat:* Similarly Ambrose, hymn 4.6.1 above, "Dormire mentem ne sinas" (Let not our minds succumb to sleep).

22.4   *vanis vagantem somniis:* Perhaps evoking Virgil, *Aen.* 10.642: "Quae sopitos deludunt somnia sensus" (Dreams that delude our sleeping senses); compare *Aen.* 6.283–84.

23.2   *mundiali gloria:* Prudentius refers to his former life (though *egimus* might have wider reference). He had practiced as a lawyer before pursuing a career in state administration as governor of a province in Spain. The sparse details of his career are drawn chiefly from the preface to his poems, published in 405. In it he laments "the frivolous wantonness and immodest indulgence" which disfigured his youth (lines 10–12).

23.4   *hic est Veritas:* See especially John 14:6. Prudentius depicts Christ as Truth here in contrast with the *falsa* mentioned above.

24.1–4   *Aurum . . . nil sunt omnia:* Some Latin Fathers in rejection of the secular world singled out wealth, high position, and pleasures as marks of that world. So Paulinus of Nola writing to Sulpicius Severus in 395 exclaims, "Let them enjoy their pleasures, their high offices, their wealth, for they prefer to have these on earth where our life ends rather than in heaven where it abides" (*Ep.* 1.7). *Fit mane,* at the close of the stanza, represents allegorically the coming of Christ and our recognition of him.

25.1   *somnum dissice:* Ambrose similarly closes his first hymn with *mentisque somnum discute* (hymn 1.8.2 above).

See further van Assendelft, 59–91; Eagan, 3–8.

17. *Nox et tenebrae et nubila*

This is the second of the hymns in Prudentius's *Cathemerinon,* written for contemplation at the hour of the morning office, the predecessor of Lauds *(Laudes matutinae).* As in the first hymn, there is sustained metaphor throughout, specifically concentrated upon the powers of light versus the powers of darkness. Thus each of the first five stanzas presents their conflict; the center of the poem (stanzas 15–23) renews the engagement between them. When whole stanzas are devoted to darkness (6, 9–11, 24), they are counterpoised by others devoted to light (7, 12–14, 25). Finally, the last three stanzas indicate that light has prevailed, for the opposition has vanished. See van Assendelft, 23–24.

This complex arrangement has presented difficulties to those who have sought to extract certain stanzas as a hymn for liturgical use. The most common arrangement consists of stanzas 1–3, 13, and 15; the dispelling of the darkness by the light of day symbolizes the dispelling of the darkness of the mind and heart by the light of Christ.

1.1   *Nox et tenebrae et nubila:* The cloudy darkness, addressed in the vocative, represents the spiritual and moral confusion besetting us.

1.3–4   *lux . . . Christus:* The sun's rising prefigures Christ's coming in the Eucharist. In *albescit* there may be an echo of Virgil, *Aen.* 4.586–87; "ut primam albescere lucem / vidit."

2.1–2   *caligo . . . percussa solis spiculo:* The diction suggests that here Lucretius's opposing sentiment is in Prudentius's mind. See Lucr. 1.146–48: "Hunc igitur terrorem animi tenebrasque necessest / non radii solis neque lucida tela diei / discutiant . . ." (This terror of the mind and darkness is not to be dispersed by the sun's rays nor the the bright shafts of day . . .).

2.3   *rebusque . . . redit:* The evocation of Lucretius is followed by a reminiscence of Virgil, *Aen.* 6.272: "Et rebus nox abstulit atra colorem" (And black night removed the color from things).

3.4   *regnante pallescit Deo: Pallescit* has strong manuscript support as against the future *pallescet,* and it aptly follows *redit* in 2.3. The verb indicates that our hearts "grow pale" in apprehensive recognition of past misdeeds. *Regnante Deo* can hardly refer to the Last Judgment (as van Assendelft); it is a continuation of the symbolism which equates the morning light with the divine presence and governance in the world.

4.1–4   *Tunc . . . prodita:* The stanza extends the sequence of thought in the previous strophe.

5.1   *Fur ante lucem:* The motif of the robber by night, a fact of real life, becomes a cliché in classical literature (e.g., Catullus 62.33–35; Virgil, *Georgics* 3.407; Juvenal 10.19–22; Apuleius, *Met.* 1.15). Its appearance in scripture (Mt 24:43–44 etc.) encourages the Fathers to equate the nocturnal thief with the devil (so, e.g., Tertullian, *Adv. Marcionem* 4.29.7).

6.4   *adulter occultus:* The adulterer exploiting darkness is likewise attested in both classical and biblical contexts; see, e.g., Horace, *Odes* 3.16.4 *(nocturnis ab adulteris),* and notably Job 24:15–16: "Oculus adulteri observat caliginem, dicens, 'Non me videbit oculus'" (The eye of the adulterer observeth [i.e., awaits] darkness, saying "No eye shall see me").

7.1–4   *Sol . . . potest:* The sustained metaphor of sun as representing Christ's risen presence is particularly powerful here; the patterned alliteration in lines 2 and (perhaps) 4 intensifies the rhetorical effect.

8.1–2   *Quis . . . non erubescit:* With the robber and the adulterer, the drinker forms a trio of representatives of the darkness of the world. The condemnation refers to nightly drinking and not (as van Assendelft, 101) to early-morning indulgence. Paul's condemnation at 1 Th 5:7–8 lies behind this stanza: "They that are drunk are drunk in the night. But let us, who are of the day, be sober . . ."

8.4   *castum . . . sapit:* The verb is used in the primary sense of "taste," and *castum* bears the meaning "upright." Together the expression contrasts with *sumptis poculis;* they now taste uprightness instead of wine.

9.4   *colorant:* The literal sense of applying makeup indicates a cover-up of the excessive drinking.

10.3–4   *miles . . . institor:* Prudentius evokes Horace, *Epode* 2.1–8 in this list of secular occupations, the first three of which represent service in the public domain, and the second three more menial tasks. *Togatus* ("civilian") is here used for "lawyer," as the following stanza indicates.

11.2   *triste . . . classicum:* The adjective suggests not merely the bugle's harsh sound but also its grim summons from sleep or into battle. Horace, *Epode* 2.5, has *classico . . . truci.*

12.1–3   *lucelli . . . arte . . . bellica:* The diminutive *lucelli* ("paltry gain") and *faenoris* ("interest") refer back to the "greedy gain" sought by merchants and countrymen in 11.3–4, *fandi* to the lawyer in 11.1, and *arte bellica* to the soldier in 11.2.

12.4   *te, Christe, solum novimus:* Compare 1 Cor 2:2: "I judged not myself to know any thing among you but Jesus Christ, and him crucified."

13.3   *curvato genu:* Scriptural evidence for Christ and Peter kneeling at prayer is seen at Lk 22:41, Act 9:40; and at Phlp 2:10 we are enjoined, "In the name of Jesus every knee should bow." Such a posture was adopted at the beginning of the day at the first prayer as a penitential gesture (so Tertullian, *De oratione* 23), but in the early Church it was the practice to pray standing on Sundays and between Easter and Pentecost.

15.1   *Intende nostris sensibus:* Echoing Ambrose, hymn 2.2.4 above: "infunde nostris sensibus."

16.3–4   *nitere . . . iusseras . . . flumine:* Since Christ himself was baptized in the Jordan, the Fathers occasionally use the phrase "dipped in Jordan's stream" to express baptism. See, e.g., Ambrose, *In Lucam* 1:37.

17.3   *rex Eoi sideris: Eoi sideris* may be taken with *rex,* as in the translation here, or with *vultu sereno* ("with the bright face of the eastern star"). "The eastern star" is the sun, or less likely the morning star; Christ is visualized as monarch of the morning light.

18.1–3   *taetram picem . . . crystallum:* Here Prudentius, with his wide knowledge of classical literature, draws on Ovid, *Pont.* 3.3.97–98:

"Sed neque mutatur nigra pice lacteus humor, / nec, quod erat candens, fit terebinthus ebur" (Milk is not changed into black pitch, nor does shining ivory become terebinth). Ovid is addressing from exile his friend Paullus Fabius Maximus, hopefully maintaining that Maximus's sentiments toward him could never change. Prudentius reverses the motif to state that Christ can achieve the impossible of turning black to white, and can thus cleanse us of our sins.

19.1–4   *Iacob . . . impar proelium:* The biblical account of Jacob's struggle with the angel is at Gen 32:24–32. The Fathers offer various explanations of the passage; see van Assendelft, 115–16. For Prudentius its significance in the context of the hymn lies in the fact that the struggle took place in darkness, symbolizing man's sinning nature. When at dawn Jacob is lamed by a blow from the angel, it makes him unable to resist the power of heaven, which is symbolized by the coming of dawn.

20.2   *lapsante claudus poplite:* In the Vulgate version of Genesis, the angel "touched the sinew of his thigh, and forthwith it shrank [i.e., was enfeebled]" (32:35).

21.2–4   *pars vilior . . . libidinem:* Thus Prudentius interprets the angel's blow as directed against sexual lust.

22.3   *si forte non cedat Deo:* In Gen 32:28 the angel tells Jacob, "If thou hast been strong against God, how much more shalt thou prevail against men!" Ambrose, *De Iacob et vita beata* 2.7.30, interprets: "For what does struggling with God mean but to engage in a contest of virtue, to struggle with one better, and to become an imitator of God superior to all others?"

23.2   *intemperans membrum:* It is tempting to interpret this as a continuation of the condemnation of sexual improprieties; more probably it includes all sinful activities eradicated by the light of Christ.

25.1–4   *serenum . . . subdolum . . . obscurum: Serenum* with its literal connotation of "bright weather" bears the metaphorical sense of shining openness of hearts, contrasting with *subdolum* and *obscurum.*

27.1–3   *speculator . . . prospicit:* The scriptural basis of this is Hbr 4:12–13: "The word of God . . . is a discerner *(discretor)* of the thoughts and intents of the heart. Neither is there any creature invisible in his sight, but all things are naked and open to his eyes to whom our speech is [i.e., to whom we must render an account]." When Tertullian (*Apol.* 45), Minucius Felix (32), Lactantius (*Div. inst.* 6.18), and Ambrose (*De bono mortis* 5.18) take up the notion, they all cite God as *speculator* as here.

28.1–4   *testis . . . iudicem:* The Lactantius passage above describes God as "the greatest and most just judge."

See further van Assendelft, 92–125; Eagan, 8–14.

18. *Deus, ignee fons animarum*

After the two morning hymns, the next four are devoted to later hours of the day, and they are followed by four others for particular situations *(For Those Fasting, After Fasting, For Every Hour, For Burial of the Dead)*. The two final hymns were written for Christmas Day and for the Epiphany.

This hymn for the burial of the dead extends to 172 lines. It forms a Christian *consolatio,* but it differs from the other examples of the genre, like those of Cyprian, Ambrose, Jerome, Augustine in prose, and that of Paulinus of Nola in verse (on these, see Favez, *La consolation latine chrétienne*), in that it is not addressed to the death of a particular individual. By contrast with the uncertainty of pagans concerning life after death, it hymns the certainty of eternal blessedness. Beginning with an expression of the Platonist dualism of body and soul, shackled together by God in this earthly life (stanzas 1–7) and reunited at the Parousia (8–11), the hymn stresses the need to treat the corpse with due respect in view of its future resurrection (12–17), as Tobit reverently did (18–22). The blessings of death are next enumerated (23–28), with criticism of the cult of mourning (29–31). The grave must safeguard the body, but even if the remains are scattered, God will restore them at the due time (31–37). Meanwhile the soul will await reunification with the body while reclining at rest in the bosom of Abraham (38–43).

1.1–2   *ignee fons animarum . . . socians elementa:* Throughout these initial stanzas, Prudentius "Christianizes" the Platonist dualism as formulated, e.g., by Cicero, *Tusc.* 1.40–41, where we read that the fiery *(ignea)* and airy elements occupy the heavenly region, and "the soul, on leaving the body, is borne aloft" to the element of fire to which it belongs. Cicero had earlier translated the *Timaeus* of Plato, in which the demiurge or Craftsman (δημιουργός, *dēmiourgós*) had entrusted to the lesser gods the task of welding together bodies with preexisting souls (so *Timaeus* 41a–c).

2.1–4   *Tua sunt . . . servit:* In this process of Christianization, the Fathers lay great stress on God as both creator and lord: see, e.g., Tertullian, *Apol.* 48.

3.1–4.4   Bergman, the *CSEL* editor, opts for the version of manuscript A, because it is the oldest, in these two stanzas, but there is a good case for arguing, with Dressel in his Leipzig (1860) edition, that there were two versions both dating from Prudentius's own day. The content of the two is in any case similar.

4.1–2   *cuncta creata necesse est . . . senescere:* The language is reminiscent of Lucretius, 2.1173–74: "All things gradually waste away and reach their end, wearied by old age."

4.3   *compactaque dissociari:* This argument that all things are mortal because they eventually break up into their component parts is a traditional motif in Greek philosophy.

5.3–4   *iter inviolabile . . . quo perdita membra resurgant:* Earlier Fathers from Tertullian onward had devoted treatises to bodily resurrection. Prudentius's treatment is probably influenced most by Ambrose, *De excessu Satyri* (*CSEL* 73.7.209–325; see Homes Dudden, *Life and Times of St. Ambrose,* 665–68.)

6.2   *ceu carcere clausa:* The Platonist cliché of the body as prison of the soul (here alliteratively expressed) is found in Cicero at *Tusc.* 1.74 and *Rep.* 6.14; Seneca, *Ben.* 3.20.

7.1   *terrea voluntas:* Seneca was the first to devote extended attention to the concept of the will as distinct from the intellect (see Rist, *Stoic Philosophy,* ch. 12.). The will manifests moral character, which in later Stoicism is contrasted with the degrading tendencies of the flesh. This is the contrast behind this and the next stanza: the will that associates with the element of the earth, and that (to which the soul belongs) which seeks the fiery element in nature. Horace, *Sat.* 2.2.77–79, is evoked in this stanza.

8.1   *ignis:* Here identified with the soul; see 1.1–2n.

8.3   *vehit hospita viscera secum:* See Ambrose, *De excessu Satyri* 2.88: "Since the entire course of our life is fellowship of body and soul, and the resurrection embodies either reward for good deeds or punishment of wicked acts, it is necessary that the body . . . should rise again."

9.2–4   *vacuum sine mente . . . conlegia sensus:* Prudentius here makes no distinction between mind and soul. In the Stoic system, the soul extends throughout the body; the mind as center of command (ἡγεμονικόν, *hēgemonikón*) is lodged in the heart, controlling thought and reason. Sensation (*sensus,* line 4) results when the control center sends out a "breath" to one of the sense organs. See Sandbach, *The Stoics,* 82–85. Thus Prudentius here envisages the mind reuniting with the body and reinvigorating the senses.

10.2   *socius calor:* The native heat of the body, its "comrade," returns as the soul courses through the body, its "previous dwelling." The expression was perhaps in Prudentius's mind because of Virgil, *Aen.* 9.475, where the mother of Euryalus hears the news of her son's death, and "of a sudden the heat left the bones (*calor ossa reliquit*) of the poor wretch."

12.1   *Hinc maxima cura:* Hinc suggests that the reason why Christians devote such care to burial is because the corpse is to rise to life again; see stanza 15 and Augustine, *C.D.* 1.13.

13.3–4   *myrrha Sabaeo . . . medicamine:* The Sabaeans occupied the area of southwest Arabia. They were most famous for their myrrh (*flos Sabaeus*) and frankincense (*tus*), both aromatic gums which were popular as perfumes. In Seneca's play *Hercules Oetaeus,* the hero's hair is said to drip with "Sabaean myrrh (*Sabaea myrrha*)" (376). Tertullian, *Apol.* 42.7, states that Sabaean perfumes were used at Christian burials: "We do not buy incense at all. Let the Sabaeans know that their merchandise is expended more widely and at greater cost at burials of Christians than in incensing their gods." The word *medicamen* indicates fragment ointment smeared on corpses to make them sweet smelling.

14.1–2   *saxa cavata . . . monumenta:* Like the pagan Romans before them, Christians of substance buried their relatives in stone coffins or sarcophagi. They are differentiated by being adorned frequently with relief sculptures depicting biblical scenes. For details, see Gough, *Early Christians,* 172–78.

14.2   *volunt:* Here "to have as their purpose" (*OLD,* s.v. *volo,* 16).

15.4   *gelidus sopor urget:* The phrase is inspired by Horace, *Odes* 1.24.5–6, where the poet, lamenting the death of his friend Quintilius, asks, "Does sleep without end lie heavy on Quintilius *(perpetuus sopor urget)?*"

16.3–4   *opus exhibet . . . Christo:* The sentiment is in the spirit of Mt 25:40: "As long as you did it to one of these my least brethren, you did it to me."

18.1   *sator ille Tobiae:* The book of Tobit, one of the apocryphal books of the Old Testament, records the many works of mercy performed by Tobit during his captivity at Nineveh. On a feast day his son Tobias was asked to invite some Israelites to a banquet but reported that one of them lay slain in the streets. Tobit immediately abandoned the feast to hide the body from the Assyrians, and to bury it after sundown (Tb 2:1–4).

18.3   *iam rite paratis:* An echo of Virgil, *Aen.* 4.555, where Aeneas prepares to abandon Dido, *rebus iam rite paratis.*

20.1   *Veniunt mox praemia caelo:* Tobit continued to bury slain Israelites until exhaustion set in, and as he slept, some dung fell on his eyes from a swallow's nest and blinded him. His son Tobias gained help from the angel Raphael to deliver his father of his blindness.

20.4   *inlita felle:* When in danger from a huge fish, Tobias was instructed by Raphael to drag it to land, to extract its gall, and to apply it to his father's eyes. This cured the blindness (11:13–15).

21.3   *mordax et amara medela:* Tobit as a latter-day Job was a just man tried by the Lord to be an example of patience under suffering (2:12). On being healed, Tobit prayed, "I bless thee, Lord God of Israel, because thou hast chastised me and hast saved me" (11:17).

21.4   *lux . . . nova:* The light regained by Tobit symbolizes the light of Christ bestowed on the world.

22.1   *prius:* To be taken with *quam* in 22.3.

22.3   *nocte et vulnere tristi:* Referring to Tobit's blindness.

23.1   *Mors ipsa beatior:* See Ambrose, *De bono mortis* 4.15.

23.4   *ad astra . . . itur:* The phrase is taken from Virgil, *Aen.* 9.641: "sic itur ad astra."

24.3–4 *nec . . . compago fatiscere novit:* The combination of body and soul, unstable on earth, will now know no weariness. Ambrose, building on 1 Cor 15:53 ("For this corruptible [body] must put on incorruptibility, and this mortal [body] must put on immortality"), argues that our bodies, like Christ's, will be raised to incorruption, glory, and power (*Apol. David* 22).

26.4   *suco . . . adeso: Sucus* is the vital juice essential to bodily vigor. Ovid in exile complains, "You could scarcely recognize my features on seeing them; you would ask what has become of my earlier color. Little juice *(sucus)* pervades my feeble limbs" (*Pont.* 1.10.25–28).

27.1–28.4 *Morbus . . . dolores:* In these two stanzas Prudentius's flight of fancy descends into bathos. There will be no sickness in heaven, and Morbus (personified as in Virgil, *Aen.* 6.275, where diseases and other privations gather round hell's threshold) will be shackled and tortured beneath the gaze of immortal bodies in heaven.

29.1–2 *Quid . . . miscet:* This condemnation of excessive mourning is a frequent feature of Christian consolation literature. So Jerome rebukes Paula for her grief at Blesilla's death (*Ep.* 39.6: "Excessive piety to kin shows impiety to God"). And though Paulinus of Nola's consolatory letter to Pneumatius and Fidelis on the death of their young son Celsus is more compassionate, a similar point is made (*Poem* 31.43–50).

29.3   *tam bene condita iura:* That is, God's ordinance that death is the gateway to new life (see the next stanza).

30.1–4 *Iam maesta,* etc.: The liturgical hymn formed from ten stanzas of the long poem begins with this stanza as exordium.

30.3   *sua pignora:* So Prudentius thinks especially of the pathos of the death of young children. Reassurance to grieving parents is a frequent motif in such consolation literature, as in Paulinus of Nola, *Poem* 31.

31.1   *semina sicca virescunt:* This analogy from the world of nature, that like seeds dormant in the ground we shall spring up to new life, is a familiar feature in Christian apologetic literature, inspired by scripture (1 Cor 15:36–37). See, e.g., Tertullian, *De resurrectione carnis* 52; Minucius Felix, 34.11. Prudentius probably drew on Ambrose, *De excessu Satyri* 2.54–59, as did Paulinus of Nola, *Poem* 31.231–338.

32.2   *gremioque . . . concipe:* Perhaps evoking Virgil, *Aen.* 5.30–31: "[The earth] embraces the bones of my father Anchises in its bosom *(gremio complectitur)*."

33.4   *sapientia principe Christo:* Christ is wisdom incarnate (1 Cor 1:24, "Christum . . . Dei sapientiam"), from whom all human wisdom derives.

34.4   *aenigmata:* From its sense of "obscure saying" or riddle, *aenigma* develops the meaning of "obscure representation" as at 1 Cor 13:12: "Now we see in a mirror in a dark manner *(in enigmate),*" i.e., "darkly."

35.1   *Veniant modo:* Choice between the readings *veniant* and *venient* is difficult, especially as Ambrose repeatedly suggests that the end of the world is near (*De excessu Satyri* 1.30; *Expos. Luc.* 10.2, 10.15).

36.1   *cariosa vetustas:* Compare Ovid, *Amores* 1.12.29, "cariosa senectus."

36.2–37.3   *dissolverit ossa favillis . . . cum pulvere nervos:* Ambrose (*De excessu Satyri* 2.69) suggests that the scattered particles unite and are consolidated into the previously existing bodies. Paulinus of Nola, *Poem* 31.311–14, cites Ezekiel as witness of this (Ez 37). Compare hymn 64.19.7–8n.

39.1   *Gremio senis . . . sancti:* For Lazarus reposing in the bosom of Abraham, see Lk 16:22 ("portaretur in sinum Abrahae"). Ambrose, *De bono mortis* 12.52, states that after death "we will go to where holy Abraham opens his bosom to receive the poor, as he also received Lazarus"; similarly *De excessu Satyri* 2.101. "The bosom of Abraham" is a metaphor for heaven.

39.4   *dives procul adspicit ardens:* So Lk 16:23: "Elevans autem oculos suos cum esset in tormentis, videbat . . ." (And lifting up his eyes when he was in torments, he saw . . .).

40.3–4   *tua per vestigia . . . ire latronem:* Compare Lk 23:43, where Christ says to the good thief, "Amen I say to thee, this day thou shalt be with me in paradise."

41.4   *quod ademerat anguis:* See Gen 3.

42.3   *genitali in sede:* See stanza 1.1–2n.

43.4   *liquido . . . odore:* Horace, *Odes* 1.5.2, uses the phrase in descrip-
        tion of Pyrrha's sleek young lover.

See further Raby, *CLP* 45–47; Eagan, 69–77.

SEDULIUS

19. *A solis ortus cardine*

Little is known of the fifth-century writer of this hymn, other than that he
was a priest, a convert from paganism who lived in a community presided
over by a certain Macedonius. His study of the scriptures at Rome resulted
in his composition of the *Paschale Carmen,* a biblical epic in five books. The
first was devoted to marvels in the Old Testament, and the other four to
the life of Christ, again with emphasis on the miracles.

This hymn is one of two written by Sedulius which have survived. It
records notable incidents in the life of Christ that demonstrate his two
natures, divine and human. Following the example of Hilary and Augustine, he exploits the alphabetic form inherited from the Hebrew tradition,
as in several psalms (e.g., 110, 111, 118) and in the book of Lamentations.
The full hymn accordingly comprises twenty-three stanzas. Nowadays the
first seven are sung at Lauds from the Nativity to the Epiphany, and stanzas 8, 9, 11, and 13 form the hymn sung at Vespers from the Epiphany to the
Baptism of Our Lord. The simple, unpretentious style of the hymn has
won many admirers in subsequent ages.

1.1   *A solis ortus cardine:* "From the hinge of the rising of the sun" de-
       scribes the eastern horizon. Sedulius evokes Ps 112:3: "A solis
       ortu usque ad occasum, laudabile nomen Domini" (From the ris-
       ing of the sun unto the going down of the same, the name of the
       Lord is worthy of praise).

2.2   *servile corpus:* Echoing Phlp 2.7: "formam servi accipiens" (taking
       the form of a servant [i.e., slave]).

2.3   *carne carnem liberans:* Compare Col 1:22: "Nunc autem reconcili-
       avit in corpore carnis eius" (Now he hath reconciled [you] in the
       body of his flesh).

3.1   *Clausae:* The emphasis here and in stanza 4 on the virginity of Mary, already underlined by Ambrose (above, hymn 5.4.2), is also made by Sedulius in *Paschale Carmen* 2.44–47.

3.4   *secreta quae non noverat:* Augustine, *De sancta virginitate* 4, similarly comments: "She dedicated her virginity to God while as yet unaware of what she was to conceive."

4.3–4   *intacta . . . verbo concepit:* Compare Lk 1:34, 38: "How shall this become, because I know not man *(virum non cognosco)?* . . . Be it done to me according to thy word *(secundum verbum tuum)."*

5.1   *puerpera:* "She, in childbirth . . ."

5.2–4   *quem Gabriel . . . quem . . . Ioannes senserat:* See Lk 1:35, 44.

6.1   *Faeno:* "Hay."

6.2   *praesepe:* Compare Lk 2:7 *(reclinavit eum in praesepio),* 16 *(infantem positum in praesepio).*

6.4   *nec ales:* So Lk 12:6, "not one [sparrow] is forgotten before God," harking back to Ps 146:9: "[He] giveth to beasts their food and to the young ravens that call upon him."

7.1   *Gaudet,* etc.: See Lk 2:13–20.

8.1–2   *Herodes . . . quid times?:* So Mt 2:3: "King Herod, hearing this, was troubled *(turbatus est)* . . ."

9.1–2   *qua venerant . . . praeviam:* "Following as guide the star by which they had come." Compare Mt 2:2; 2:9: "stella . . . anteedebat eos" (the star . . . went before them).

9.4   *munere:* So Mt 2:11: "They offered him gifts *(munera):* gold, frankincense, and myrrh."

10.1   *Katerva,* etc.: So spelled to maintain the alphabetic sequence (though the spelling *ka-* became quite common). For the mourning, see Mt 2:18.

10.3   *milia:* The account of Mt 2:16, "Herod . . . killed all the menchildren that were in Bethlehem and in all the borders thereof from two years old and under," gave rise to such exaggeration here and earlier in Prudentius, *Perist.* 10.737.

11.1–2   *Lavacra . . . attigit:* For Jesus's baptism at the Jordan, see Mt 3:13–15. *Puri* may indicate that Christ's presence in the river cleansed it, or alternatively it may suggest that it purified all baptized there.

11.2–3   *caelestis agnus . . . peccata qui mundi tulit:* See the words of the Baptist at John 1:29: "Ecce agnus Dei, ecce qui tollit peccatum mundi" (Behold the lamb of God, behold him who taketh away the sin of the world).

11.4   *sustulit:* Walpole renders "raised us up," but more probably *peccata* is to be understood as object: "He removed them by washing us clean."

13.2   *aquae rubescunt hydriae:* So John 2:6–9: "Six water pots of stone *(lapideae hydriae)* . . . the water made wine."

14.1–4   *Orat . . . febrium:* So Mt 8:5–13, but with no mention of genuflection. For *ardor plurimus,* see Jesus's words at Mt 8:10: "I have not found so great faith *(tantam fidem)* in Israel."

15.1–4   *Petrus . . . semitam:* See Mt 14:29–33: "And Peter, going down out of the boat, walked upon the water *(ambulavit super aquam)* . . . he was afraid, and when he began to sink, he cried out . . . immediately Jesus, stretching forth his hand, took hold of him . . ." But Peter does not manifest the faith suggested by the final line; Jesus says, "O thou of little faith, why didst thou doubt?"

16.1   *Quarta die iam fetidus:* (*Dies* is usually masculine, but feminine when denoting a fixed day.) See John 11:39, where Martha says, "Domine, iam fetet, quadriduanus enim est" (Lord, by this time he stinketh, for he is now of four days [i.e., has been dead for four days]).

16.3   *mortisque liber vinculis:* See John 11:44: "He that had been dead came forth, bound feet and hands with winding-strips . . . Jesus said to them, 'Loose him.'"

17.1–4   *Rivos . . . sanguinis:* So Mt 9:20: "And behold: a woman who was troubled with an issue of blood [i.e., hemorrhages; *sanguinis fluxum*] . . . touched the fringe of his cloak *(tetigit fimbrim vestimenti eius)*." The gospel does not mention the woman's tears.

18.1–4   *Solutus . . . lectulum:* See Mt 9:2–7, and the more dramatic account in Lk 5:18–26. *Vicissim* marks the change of action: "on his own feet, for a change."

19.1–4   *Iudas carnifex . . . pectore:* Mt 26:49 states, "And forthwith coming to Jesus, he said, 'Hail, Rabbi!' And he kissed him *(osculatus est eum*)." As Ambrose, *In Ps.* 39:17, states, "the kiss is the mark of sacred peace." *Carnifex* here probably means no more than that Judas caused Christ's death, though the word had had use in colloquial Latin as a term of abuse, in for example Plautus and Terence.

20.1–2   *Verax . . . pium:* Clearly a reference to John 18:37–38, where Jesus says, "Everyone that is of the truth *(ex veritate)* heareth my voice"; to which Pilate replies, "What is truth? *(Quid est veritas?)*" before handing him over to the Jews to be crucified (John 19:16). For the scourging, see John 19:1.

20.3–4   *crucique . . . latronibus:* See John 19:18.

21.1–4   *Xeromyrram,* etc.: This word, otherwise unattested in Latin (and perhaps not easily understood here), is used to maintain the alphabetic sequence; there is a Greek form ξηρόμυρον *(xērómuron)* (see *LSJ*). There is no mention of such perfumed plants in Mt 28:1–7. The word *compares* ("comrades," "equals") is a surprising (and touching) one with which to describe the two Marys. The angel says to them, "He is not here, for he is risen, as he said" (Mt 28:6).

22.1   *Ymnis:* The letters *y* and *z* were added to the Latin alphabet in Cicero's time to accommodate Greek words. Since no Latin words begin with *y,* the aspirate is (by no means unusually) here dropped from *hymnis* to fit the acrostic.

22.2–3   *subditum Christi triumpho Tartarum:* Educated Christians such as Prudentius and Sedulius adopt this pagan title for the underworld to denote hell. The tradition of the harrowing of hell has its basis in Mt 27:52, 1 Pt 3:18–20, but it becomes canonical only when incorporated into the Apostles' Creed about 390 CE.

23.1–2   *draconis . . . leonis:* The crushing of Satan so depicted derives from Ps 90:13: "You will tread underfoot the lion and the serpent *(leonem et draconem)*." In the New Testament see 2 Cor 11:3 *(serpens),* 1 Pt 5:8 *(leo).*

See further Walpole, 149–58; Raby, *CLP* 109–10.

Venantius Fortunatus

20. *Pange, lingua*

On Venantius Fortunatus, see the Introduction, pp. x–xi. This hymn and the next were composed to celebrate the triumphant arrival at Poitiers of a relic of the true cross from Constantinople. The meter, trochaic tetrameters catalectic, was that used by victorious armies when celebrating triumphs at Rome. In the Roman breviary, stanzas 1–4 and 6 form the hymn sung at the Office of Readings from Sunday to Friday in Holy Week; stanzas 7–10 are sung at Lauds during the same period.

1.1 *Pange, lingua, gloriosi,* etc.: This exordium is echoed by Aquinas in his eucharistic hymn (98 below).

1.3–4 *super crucis . . . triumphum nobilem:* Perhaps evoking Virgil, *Aen.* 11.5–11, where Aeneas sets up an oak on which his slain foe's armor is mounted as a trophy.

1.6 *immolatus vicerit:* The paradox is a favorite with the Fathers; e.g., Augustine, *Conf.* 10.43.69: "ideo victor quia victima" (therefore the victor, because the victim).

2.1–2 *protoplasti fraude:* The reference is to Satan's hoodwinking of Adam. The Greek word *protoplasti* ("first-formed") is taken over from the Septuagint version of Wis 7:1, 10:1.

3.1 *Hoc opus:* That is, the role of the cross.

3.3 *multiformis perditoris:* For the images of Satan as serpent and lion, see hymn 19.23.1–2n.

3.5–6 *medelam . . . inde hostis unde laeserat:* The contrast of the tree of the cross with the tree of knowledge, as here and in the previous stanza, is a frequent motif in the Fathers; see, e.g., Ambrose, *In Lucam* 10.114; Sedulius, *Carmen Paschale* 2.16.

4.1–4 *Quando . . . venit . . . plenitudo temporis, missus est . . . natus,* etc.: So Gal 4:4: "At ubi venit plenitudo temporis, misit Deus filium suum, factum ex muliere" (But when the fullness of the time was come, God sent his son, made of a woman).

4.4 *orbis conditor:* So John 1:3: "All things were made by him, and without him was made nothing that was made."

5.1　　　*Vagit:* Scripture does not record such wailing, but earlier Fathers (Hilary, Cyprian, Ambrose; see Walpole, 169–70) exploit it to underline Christ's humanity. Similarly *pannis* ("rags") emphasizes his poverty voluntarily embraced.

5.6　　　*pingit:* "Adorns," the word contrasting with the meanness of the coverings.

6.1　　　*Lustra sex:* This estimate of Christ's age at death (*lustrum* = five years) is based on Luke's "quasi annorum triginta" (3:23) when adverting to the beginning of his ministry.

6.5–6　　*agnus . . . immolandus:* A conflation of John 1:29: "Ecce agnus Dei" (Behold the lamb of God), and 1 Cor 5:7: "Pascha nostrum immolatum est Christus" (Christ, our Pasch, has been sacrificed).

7.1–2　　*acetum . . . lancea:* The catalog of indignities is assembled from Mt 27:30 *(harundinem),* 34 *(felle),* 48 *(aceto),* and John 19:34 *(lancea),* 20:25 *(clavorum).*

7.5–6　　*Terra . . . lavantur flumine:* Compare Col 1:20: "Through him [God was pleased] to reconcile all things unto himself, making peace through the blood of his cross, both as to the things on earth and the things that are in heaven."

8.1　　　*Crux fidelis:* "Faithful" in the sense that it carried out its allotted task, and perhaps also implying "on which our faith depends."

8.4　　　*flore, fronde, germine:* Referring symbolically to the martyrs inspired by the crucifixion. Compare hymns 21.7.3n., 22.9–10n.

8.5　　　*dulce clavo:* Fortunatus occasionally forms ablatives of adjectives in *-e* when the meter demands a short syllable; compare *mite* in § 9.6 below.

9.1–4　　*Flecte . . . nativitas:* The personification of the cross reaches its noble climax in the apostrophe in this and the next stanza. Note especially the references to its *viscera* ("inner parts") and its *nativitas* ("birth, nature").

10.3　　　*portum praeparare:* "To pave the way for the harbor" of heaven, which the shipwrecked world attains through Christ's death on the cross. The personification of the cross continues here; *nauta* ("sailor") extends the symbolism of the attainment of salvation in the barque of the Church under the mast that is the cross. For the popularity of this motif in the Fathers, see Rahner, *Greek Myths and Christian Mystery,* 346–53, 371–86.

See further Walpole, 164–73; Raby, *CLP* 90–91.

21. *Vexilla regis prodeunt*

This hymn, like the previous one composed to celebrate the arrival of the relic of the true cross at Poitiers about 567, is elegantly constructed in two parts. The first four stanzas describe the Crucifixion, and the second four are devoted to the cross itself. Stanzas 1, 3, 5–6, and 8 form the hymn sung at Vespers in Holy Week.

1.1   *Vexilla:* Like the trochaic meter in the previous hymn, the imagery of *vexilla,* the military standards in the Roman army, signifies the triumphal procession.

2.1   *viscera:* Fortunatus on occasion uses this word for the body generally, though in the previous hymn at 9.2 the sense of "inward parts" seems appropriate.

3.1   *insuper:* The lance-thrust is "in addition" to the wounds inflicted by the nails.

3.3   *crimine:* A stronger word than *peccatum,* connoting serious sin.

3.4   *et:* The retention of this word is one of this edition's few departures from Walpole. See the *Note on the Text.*

4.1–4 *quae concinit . . . "Regnavit a ligno Deus":* Like Tertullian before him, Fortunatus assumes that the words *a ligno* formed part of Ps 95:10. Justin Martyr, *Apol.* 1.41, likewise includes the Greek equivalent ἀπὸ τοῦ ξύλου *(apò toû xúlou).* But the Vulgate has merly "Dicite in Gentibus quia Dominus regnavit." The addition was presumably made to the Septuagint as a Christian gloss, and this was carried over into the early Latin translations as prophetic of the Crucifixion.

5.2   *regis purpura:* The purple of the king is the blood of Christ; similarly at Paulinus of Nola, *Poem* 27.89.

6.2   *pretium saeculi:* The phrase, denoting the Crucifixion as the ransom paid for freeing the world from sin, is used also in hymn 20.10.2.

6.3   *Statera:* The image of the cross as balance (the crossbeam set on the vertical) may indicate that Christ's death on the cross is weighed against Adam's plundering of the tree of knowledge.

6.4 *praedam . . . Tartari:* Referring to the souls in hell awaiting Christ's coming; see hymns 16.18.2n., 19.22.2–3n., 65.9.1n.

7.3 *fructu fertili:* The fruitful harvest connotes the martyrs; see hymns 20.8.4n., 22.9–10n.

7.4 *plaudis:* The image of the tree clapping its hands evokes Is 55:12: "All the trees of the country shall clap their hands *(plaudent manu)*."

8.3 *vita:* Life personified in Christ; compare John 11:25, 14:6.
See further Walpole, 173–77; Raby, *CLP* 88–89.

22. *Crux benedicta nitet*

Like the previous two hymns, this composition celebrates the arrival of the relic of the true cross at Poitiers. The reversion to the more traditional metrical form (the elegiac couplet of dactylic hexameter and pentameter) is perhaps designed to appeal to the more learned. The imagery conveys an aura of mysticism even more profound and intense than in the earlier hymns.

1 *Crux benedicta nitet:* The relic had been sent to Poitiers from Constantinople by the emperor Justin II and his wife; the verb perhaps alludes in part to the casing in which it was enclosed.

2 *lavit:* Fortunatus's ignorance of (or indifference to) classical quantities shortens the long syllable. The perfect indicative follows logically after *pependit,* denoting the historical occasion of the Crucifixion, so that Leo's emendation to *lavat* is otiose.

4 *lupi . . . agnus oves:* The literary conceit of the lamb rescuing the sheep from the wolf, which is Satan, is a favorite image of Fortunatus.

5 *ubi:* That is, on the cross; likewise *qua* in line 4.

6 *suo clausit funere mortis iter:* This is a second example of Christian paradox concerning Christ's death, following that in line 4.

8 *quae eripuit Paulum . . . Petrum:* Christ did not lay his own hand on Paul, but at Act 9:10–12 the disciple Ananias is instructed to do

so in Paul's vision. Peter was rescued from drowning by Christ's helping hand when he walked on the water (Mt 14:31).

9–10   *Fertilitate potens . . . tam nova poma:* Referring, as in the two previous hymns (20.8.4, 21.7.3), to the martyrs inspired by Christ's example.

11   *defuncta cadavera surgunt:* So Mt 27:52: "Et monumenta aperta sunt et multa corpora sanctorum qui dormierant surrexerunt" (And the graves were opened, and many bodies of the saints that had slept arose).

13–14   *Nullum uret . . . neque meridie:* (The short first syllable in *mĕrīdiē* is lengthened here, and the long *ī* shortened.) The two lines are an evocation of Ps 120:6: "Per diem sol non uret te, neque luna per noctem" (The sun shall not burn thee by day, nor the moon by night). See Boylan, *The Psalms* 2:285: "Parallel with the smiting of the sun is that of the moon . . . The Babylonians ascribed to moon-rays the power of causing leprosy, and the modern Arabs believe that the moon-rays cause blindness."

15   *Tu plantata . . . aquarum:* This line echoes Ps 1:3: "Erit tamquam lignum quod plantatum est secus decursus aquarum" (He shall be like a tree which is planted near the running [or: streams of] waters).

16   *spargis . . . comas:* An alternative rendering could be "You shower your leaves, adorned with fresh blossoms" (so Walpole). But this is less appropriate, since the foliage is required to ward off the heat of sun and moon.

17–18   *Appensa est . . . rubore fluunt:* The powerful image with which the hymn ends envisages Christ as the true vine (so John 15:1, "vitis vera") hanging between the arms of the cross, yielding his blood as the wine which invigorates human life.

See further Walpole, 178–81; Raby, *CLP,* 88–89.

The Old Hymnal

23. *Te lucis ante terminum*

This ancient hymn goes back to the period of the Old Hymnal (see the Introduction, pp. xi–xii), and has ever since been sung at the office of

Compline, which marks the close of the day. Originally it consisted only of two stanzas; the third was added later, as the clumsy prosody indicates, in order to provide what had become the conventional doxology at the close of a hymn. In the modern Roman breviary, the robust second stanza with its veiled allusion to nocturnal pollution has been replaced by two more emollient stanzas.

1.3   *pro tua clementia:* This is Cassander's happy emendation of *sŏlita clementia,* which is retained in the modern Roman breviary, but is metrically improbable, necessitating the lengthening of the first syllable of *solita.*

2.4   *ne polluantur corpora:* The prayer to avoid "wet dreams" is anticipated in Ambrose's hymn *Deus, creator omnium* (hymn 4 above), stanzas 6–7.

3   The scansion demands the lengthening of the second syllable of *Pater,* the second syllable of *perpetuum,* and the first syllable of *Dominum; omnipotens* does not have the requisite first short syllable or second long syllable; and a hiatus is forced between *tecum* and *in.*

See further Walpole, 298–99.

24. Iam lucis orto sidere

As the content indicates, the hymn was composed to be sung at Prime, the first hour of the liturgical day. Prime no longer has a place in the daily office; the hymn is sung at Lauds (now the first office of the day) on Thursdays. It will be noted that rhyme becomes increasingly prominent in the iambic dimeter.

1.1   *lucis . . . sidere:* The sun. This exordium is often echoed in later morning hymns.

2.1   *Linguam refrenans:* Observing the injunction in James 1:26: "If any man think himself to be religious, not bridling his tongue *(non refrenans linguam suam),* . . . this man's religion is vain."

2.3–4   *visum . . . contegat ne vanitates hauriat:* Compare Ps 118:37: "Averte oculos meos ne videant vanitatem" (Turn away my eyes that they may not behold vanity).

3.2   *vecordia:* Such "madness" or "folly" leads to impurity of thought or deed. Compare Prov 7:7, where a young man without sense *(vecors)* seeks to be seduced by a wanton woman.

4.2   *sors:* "The usual apportionment."

4.3   *mundi:* Walpole takes this as an adjective, "cleansed by our abstinence," but more probably it is the genitive of *mundus,* "by taking no part in (the things of) the world." Compare *saeculi* in hymn 25.4.3.

See further Walpole, 293–94.

25. *Aeterne lucis conditor*

Like the previous hymn, this was composed to be sung at Prime, but since Vatican II is now sung at Wednesday Lauds in Week 2.

1.1   *Aeterne lucis conditor:* This exordium clearly exploits that of Ambrose in hymn 1 above, "Aeterne rerum conditor."

1.3–4   *noctem nec ullam sentiens,* etc.: See 1 John 1:7: "But if we walk in the light, as he also is in the light . . ."

2.4   *clarus lucifer:* Here the sun, since it overshadows the other heavenly bodies.

3.3   *quod caecam noctem vicerit:* The sun's conquest of the night is the reflection in nature of Christ's victory over the darkness of death.

4.3   *dolis . . . saeculi:* See hymn 24.4.3n.

5.1   *Ira ne rixam provocet:* Evoking Prov 15:18: "A passionate [i.e., hot-tempered; *iracundus*] man stirreth up strifes *(rixas);* he that is patient appeaseth those that are stirred up."

5.3   *opum . . . famis: Famis* is an alternative form of *fames* in Late Latin. The author may have in mind Virgil, *Aen.* 3.56–57: "Accursed hunger for gold *(auri sacra fames),* to what do you not drive the hearts of men?"

6.1   *sobrii:* See Hymn 2.6.3–4n.

6.4   *Christo:* Walpole prints *Christe.* See the *Note on the Text.*

See further Walpole, 226–28.

26. *Fulgentis auctor aetheris*

This further hymn for the morning liturgy was appointed by Caesarius of
Arles to be sung at Prime; nowadays it is sung at Wednesday Lauds. It
makes no explicit comparison between the light of day and Christ the true
Sun, but exhorts men to greet the day as an opportunity of praising the
Creator and of embracing virtue.

2.4   *dulces in actus:* With particular reference to the daily office as described in the following stanza.

3.4   *serenat:* The word connotes both brightness and serenity.

4.1   *Vitemus omne lubricum:* Similarly at hymn 2.3.4 above.

5.2–4   *fides . . . spes . . . caritas:* The exhortation to embrace the three
theological virtues is a frequent feature in these hymns; see, e.g.,
hymn 14.6 above.

See further Walpole, 229–30.

27. *Deus, qui caeli lumen es*

This further hymn for morning is a more original composition than the
previous ones. The author has incorporated a more imaginative range of
images to describe the dawn in stanzas 2–3; in 4, he brings together the sun
of nature and Christ the true Sun; and in 5 he celebrates the Christ who
wields the power of the Trinity, before closing the hymn with the conventional doxology.

1.1–2   *caeli lumen . . . satorque lucis:* Compare Apc 21:23: "The glory of
God hath enlightened [the city], and its lamp is the lamb
thereof."

1.3   *paterno fultum bracchio:* The expression "arm of God" is pervasive
throughout the Old Testament. Especially relevant here is Jer
27:5: "I made the earth . . . by my great power and my stretched
out arm *(in brachio meo extento)*." See also Jer 32:17 *(in brachio tuo
extento)*.

1.4   *pandis:* "You open" the sky to release the light of day.

2.2   *rubrum sustollens gurgitem:* A striking image of the dawn raising its ruddy flood from the eastern ocean, perhaps inspired by Virgil, *Aen.* 12.114–15: "The horses of the sun now first rise from the waters of the deep *(alto gurgite)*."

3.1   *Phosphorus:* The Greek title ("Light-bringer") is used as variation for the Latin *lucifer,* employed in the following stanza. The sun is clearly indicated throughout.

4.3   *typusque Christi lucifer:* For the sun as symbol of Christ, see hymn 2.2.1 and Ambrose, *Hex.* 4.1.2: "When you see [the sun], think of its author . . . If the sun, as partner and partaker in creation, is so pleasing, how lovely must the great Sun of righteousness be!"

5.1   *Dies dierum hagius:* In hymn 2.1.4 above, Ambrose addresses Christ as *dies dierum inluminans.* Here a second Greek touch is introduced with *hagius;* the Greek ἅγιος *(hágios,* holy) was familiar from the liturgy of Good Friday, when the hymn *Hagios ho theos* was sung at the veneration of the cross.

5.2   *lucisque lumen:* See hymn 2.1.3 above and note.

5.3–4   *unum potens . . . in unum Trinitas:* Christ as the second Person of the Trinity is invested with its full power.

6.1–4   *Te nunc,* etc.: The doxology is part of the original hymn.
See further Walpole, 219–21.

28. *Mediae noctis tempus est*

This hymn was written in the late fifth or early sixth century; it closely follows Ambrose, *In Ps. 118,* 8:45–52, and is prescribed for singing at First Nocturn (hence midnight) by Caesarius of Arles, who became bishop in 502. As Walpole observes, the rules for prosody observed by Ambrose and Prudentius in the iambic dimeter are ignored; the writer is content merely to allot eight syllables to each line, which suggests a later rather than an earlier date of composition. In the revised Roman Breviary, stanzas 1–6 and 13 are sung at the Sunday Office of Readings in Week 2. The hymn celebrates the importance of the midnight hour in the history of Israel (stanzas 3–5), linked with the need for vigilance by the new Israel (6–10), and in the liberation from prison of Paul and Silas (11), linked with our need to be liberated from the prison of sin (12). The hymn is unusual in having a doxology at both beginning and end.

1.2   *prophetica vox:* Compare Ps 118:62: "Media nocte surgebam ad confitendum tibi" (I rose at midnight to give praise to thee), and hymn 38 below.

2.3   *uniusque substantiae:* See Augustine, *De Trinitate* 1.4: "All Catholic interpreters before us who have written about the Trinity had this purpose, to teach in accordance with the scriptures that Father, Son, and Holy Spirit constitute a divine unity of one and the same substance."

3.1   *Terrorem tempus hoc habet:* See Ex 12. At 12:23 the avenging angel is called in the Vulgate *percussor.*

3.4   *delevit primogenita:* Ex 12:29: "In noctis medio percussit Dominus omne primogenitum in terra Aegypti" (At midnight the Lord slew every firstborn in the land of Egypt).

4.4   *signum formidans sanguinis:* Ex 12:13: "Erit autem sanguinis vobis in signum . . . videbo sanguinem ac transibo vos" (The blood shall be unto you for a sign . . . I shall see the blood and shall pass over you).

5.1–2   *flebat fortiter . . . funera:* Ex 12:30: "There arose a great cry in Egypt, for there was not a house wherein there lay not one dead."

6.1   *verus Israhel:* Paul insists vehemently on this: see Rom 9:4–8, 11:1; Gal 6:16.

6.3–4   *hostem . . . sanguine:* As Israel was protected by the blood of the lamb, so Christians are protected from Satan by the blood of Christ.

7.2   *voce evangelica:* See Mt 25:6: "Media autem nocte clamor factus est: 'Ecce: sponsus venit'" (At midnight there was a cry made: "Behold: the bridegroom cometh").

9.2   *stinctas:* Though rarer than its compound *exstinguo* (the Vulgate has *extinguntur* at Mt 25:8), the simple verb fits more smoothly into the rhythm of the line.

9.3   *frustra pulsantes ianuam:* So Mt 25:11–12.

10.1   *vigilemus sobrie:* Compare Mt 25:13: "Watch ye therefore [i.e., keep awake; *vigilate*], because you know not the day nor the hour."

10.2   *mentes:* These are our lamps, so to say, which we must keep lit to await the Lord's coming.

11.1–2   *Noctisque mediae . . . Paulus . . . et Sileas:* So Act 16:25–26: "At midnight Paul and Silas praying praised God . . . Suddenly there was a great earthquake . . . All the doors were opened, and every one's bands were loosed."

13.1   *hagie:* Compare hymns 27.5.1, 48.6.1, and notes.

See further Walpole, 205–11.

29. *Aurora lucis rutilat*

The antiquity of this hymn is guaranteed by its presence both in ancient Irish hymnaries and in the old Frankish hymnal. As its content indicates, it was composed for singing at Eastertide; in the revised Breviary, stanzas 1–4, supplemented by two stanzas of later date, form the hymn sung at Lauds on Easter Sunday. The patterning of rhymes within each stanza should be noted; the fact that it is incomplete perhaps suggests a date in the fifth century, when the rhyming technique was still in its infancy. The hymn faithfully summarizes the gospel accounts of the Resurrection.

2.1–4   *Cum rex . . . miseros:* The stanza specifies the reason for the distress of the nether world in stanza 1. The later tradition incorporated Christ's descent into hell into the Apostles' Creed about 390. For *Tartara* see hymn 19.22.2–3, where this classical title for the underworld is also adopted.

3.1–2   *clausus lapide custoditur sub milite:* See Mt 27:65–66: "Munierunt sepulchrum, signantes lapidem cum custodibus" (They made the sepulchre sure, sealing the stone and setting guards).

3.3   *pompa nobili:* (Some MSS read *nobile,* which would fit the rhyme, but several stanzas avoid the rhyme in the third line.) Perhaps *pompa* refers to Mt 28:2–3, the earthquake and the appearance of the angel ("his countenance as lightning, and his raiment as snow,") who rolled back the stone.

4.3   *quia surrexit Dominus:* So Mt 28:6: "Non est hic, surrexit enim"
        (He is not here, for he is risen).

5.1   *Tristes erant apostoli:* So Mk 16:10: "lugentibus et flentibus"
        (mourning and weeping).

5.4   *servi:* Perhaps with reference to Judas, but more generally to the
        Jews.

6.1–2   *angelus praedixit,* etc.: So Mt 28:7: "Tell ye his disciples, . . . 'He
        will go before you into Galilee; there you shall see him *(ibi eum
        videbitis).* Lo: I have foretold it to you *(praedixi vobis)*.'"

6.4   *quantocius: = quanto ocius,* "all the more swiftly," "at once."

7.4   *osculant pedes domini:* Compare Mt 28:9: "Tenuerunt pedes eius et
        adoraverunt eum" (They . . . took hold of his feet and adored
        him).

8.3   *pergunt videre faciem:* So Mt 28:16–17.

9.2   *mundo:* This could be either an adjective with *radio* ("with spot-
        less rays") or dative of the noun ("on the world"). An implicit
        correspondence is being made between the sun in nature and
        Christ the true Sun.

10.1   *Ostensa . . . vulnera:* Cf. John 20:20: "He showed them *(ostendit eis)*
        his hands and his side."

See further Walpole, 356–59.

30. *Diei luce reddita*

The revised Breviary remains faithful to the rubric in an early MS which
prescribes this morning hymn for Saturdays. (Stanzas 1–3 and 10 form the
hymn at Lauds on Saturday in Week 4.) The conventional exordium (stanzas 1–3) greets the light of day as symbolic of the light of Christ; the rest of
the hymn catalogs the sins which are the moral darkness of the world and
begs the light of Christ to preserve us from the failings spotlighted especially in the letters of Saint Paul.

2.1–2   *Per quem . . . condidit:* Compare John 1:3, "Omnia per ipsum
        facta sunt" (All things were made by him [sc. the Word =
        Christ]).

3.2   *lex veterna:* Not the Old Testament, but the "ancient law" of al-
        ternation of light and darkness in the world of nature. As of-

ten in these hymns, nature's daylight is symbolic of Christ the true Light (so here *vera lux*).

5.1–4   *non cogitemus,* etc.: Compare hymn 26.4.

5.4   *vincamus in bono malum:* So Rom 12:21: "Vince in bono malum" (Overcome evil by good).

6.3–4   *avaritia, malorum radix omnium:* So 1 Tim 6:10: "Radix enim omnium malorum est cupiditas" (The desire of money is the root of all evils).

7.1–2   *Vinum . . . perdita:* Compare Eph 5:18: "Be not drunk with wine, wherein is luxury [i.e., debauchery], but be ye filled with the Holy Spirit."

7.4   *tuum . . . poculum:* Compare Mt 20:22: "Can you drink of the chalice that I shall drink?"

8.1–2   *conservet pacis foedera . . . caritas:* So Eph 4:2–3: "Subportantes invicem in caritate, solliciti servare unitatem Spiritus in vinculo pacis" (Supporting one another in charity [= loving-kindness], careful to keep the unity of the Spirit in the bond of peace).

8.3–4   *illibata castitas credulitate:* Compare 1 Tim 1:5: "Charity from a pure heart and a good conscience and an unfeigned faith."

9.2   *malesuada famis:* A Virgilian phrase; compare *Aen.* 6.276: "malesuada Fames."

9.4   *prophetae . . . psalmus:* Compare Ps 61:11: "If riches abound *(divitiae si affluant),* set not your heart on them."

10.1–4   *Praesta,* etc.: In the closing doxology, which becomes increasingly the norm, the phrase *sancto repleti Spiritu* again evokes Eph 5:18 as at § 7.2 above.

See further Walpole, 238–40.

31. *Certum tenentes ordinem*

This short hymn, as the early MSS and 1.3 indicate, was sung at Terce, and today in the revised Breviary it is prescribed for Terce in Advent, the three stanzas being supplemented with a fourth as doxology.

1.1   *Certum . . . ordinem:* The three hours of Terce, Sext, and None had long been observed in both east and west, and the *Apostolic Constitutions* in the later fourth century added morning and evening prayers. It is uncertain whether at the date of composition of this hymn Benedict's further prescription of Compline had been added to the monastic day.

2.1   *Ut simus habitaculum:* Compare Eph 2:22: "In whom [i.e., Christ as cornerstone] you also are built together into a habitation *(habitaculum)* of God."

2.2   *illi . . . Spiritui:* I render *illi* as "of Pentecost" in view of the lines which follow.

2.4   *hac hora:* See Act 2:15: "seeing it is but the third hour of the day."

3.2–4 *ornavit . . . praemiis:* The reward was promised not for mere adherence to the routine of the divine office, but for thereby witnessing to belief in Christ. Compare John 3:15: "Whosoever believeth in him may not perish but may have life everlasting."

See further Walpole, 242–43.

32. *Dei fide, qua vivimus*

This hymn was traditionally sung at Terce in Lent, and has the same role in the revised Breviary today, again with an appended fourth stanza as doxology.

1.1–3 *fide . . . spe . . . caritatis:* For the motif of the three theological virtues (compare 1 Cor 13:13), traditional in these hymns, see hymns 14.6, 26.5.

2.1   *hora tertia:* So Mk 15:25: "And it was the third hour, and they crucified him." Mt 27:45 speaks of the sixth hour, when darkness covered the world, but the crucifixion had taken place by then.

2.4   *ovem . . . perditam:* Presumably with reference to the penitent thief (Lk 23:43), though it is possible to take *ovem* as a collective singular.

3.3   *ut eruat a saeculo:* For *a saeculo* compare hymn 25.4.

3.4   *a chirographo:* This was a signed bond. See Col 2:14: "Blotting out the handwriting of the decree *(chirographum decreti)* that was against us." The bond by which "we" were bound was the bond of sin inherited from Adam.

See further Walpole, 330–31.

33. *Dicamus laudes Domino*

This hymn from the Old Hymnal is in the revised Breviary prescribed for Sext in the week before the nativity of the Lord, and again in the period between the Epiphany and the Baptism of the Lord.

1.3   *hora voluta sexies:* This indicates that the hymn was sung at Sext.

2.1   *in hac* (sc. *hora*): Compare John 19:14: "It was the day of Preparation for the Passover, about the sixth hour *(hora quasi sexta)*."

2.4   *virtute:* Here "power," as often in later and medieval Latin.

3.2   *meridies:* That is, the hour of Sext, at which Pilate consigned Jesus to the Jews for execution.

See further Walpole, 243–44.

34. *Deus, qui claro lumine*

According to the rubric in the early MSS, this hymn was sung at Vespers on Sundays. In the revised Roman Breviary it is now appointed for Vespers on Thursday in Week 2.

1.1–3   *claro lumine . . . tuam . . . gloriam:* An implicit comparison is made between the brilliance of created light and the splendor of the Creator.

2.1   *urgente Vespero:* Vesper is Venus as the evening star, more usually given its Greek title, Hesperus.

3.1   *tu:* Emendation to *te* would avoid a strained anacoluthon.

4.1–2   *Ut . . . saeculi:* The hymn implores the Creator not to allow the darkness of the material world *(saeculi)* to shroud our minds as well as our bodies.

4.4   *lucem prosperam:* The implicit notion here is that if our minds are not darkened by sin, we can greet the coming day having successfully overcome the temptations of the night.

See further Walpole, 254–55.

35. *Sator principesque temporum*

This traditional hymn for Vespers is in the revised Breviary now allocated to Tuesday Vespers in Week 2, but with the omission of stanzas 3 and 5.

2.2–4   *obscura ne silentia . . . telis patescant invidi:* Compare Eph 6:16: "The shield of faith, with which you will be able to quench all the flaming darts *(tela)* of the evil one"; Wis 2:24: "invidia diaboli" (by the envy of the devil). As Walpole notes, *obscura silentia* should be understood by metonymy as "we in the dark and silent night."

3.1   *spiritus:* The soul, the living breath, is visualized as keeping guard over the body.

3.4   *fallax . . . gaudium:* The joy is "deceitful" because the devil deceives us with wanton pleasures, a motif frequent in hymns for Vespers and Compline. The theme is resumed in stanza 4.

4.2   *faces:* The word is already widespread in classical Latin to denote the heat of lust; see *OLD*, s.v. *fax*, 7.

See further Walpole, 253–54.

THE NEW HYMNAL

36. *Rector potens, verax Deus*

This short hymn and the next are found in both the Canterbury and the Durham hymnals, and appear to have been the work of the same author. Walpole speculated that it was Ambrose, even though all the hymns indubitably his contain eight stanzas. The revised Breviary allots this hymn to the hour of Sext between Christmas and Epiphany. This hymn, like many others, compares the powers of nature with men's moral lives; here the heat of the sun at midday corresponds with the emotions of anger and lust.

1.3   *splendore mane instruis:* Ambrose would probably not have tolerated a hiatus between *mane* and *instruis*. Walpole inserts *qui* between the two words to lend credence to his speculation that Ambrose is the author, but more probably the hymn is to be assigned to a later date when authors become more indifferent to the "rule" of elision.

2.1   *flammas:* Note the deliberate play between the *ignes* of the noon-day sun and the *flammae* and *calor* which Christ is begged to dowse.

See further Walpole, 110–11; Wieland, 30–31; Milfull, 131–32.

437

37. *Rerum deus tenax vigor*

This fine hymn is a meditation on the shortness of life on earth followed by eternity. Just as the close of each day is followed by a sequence of other days, so our lives at eventide look forward to enduring glory. In the revised Breviary this hymn follows directly after the previous one, being assigned to the hour of None between Christmas and Epiphany.

1.1   *Rerum Deus tenax vigor:* As often in these hymns, God is first visualized in his philosophical role as the power animating nature.

1.2   *immotus in te permanens:* The notion of God's unchangeability goes back on the one hand to scripture (Ps 101:27: "Ipsi peribunt, tu autem permanes" (They [sc. the heavens] shall perish, but thou remainest); Ja 1:17: "Father of lights, with whom there is no change nor shadow of alteration"), and on the other to Neoplatonism mediated through Augustine (e.g., at *Conf.* 1.6.9–10).

2.1   *Largire clarum vespere:* The prayer for clear skies in the evening is a metaphor for lucidity of mind at the close of life, to enable us to prepare for a holy death.

See further Walpole, 111–12; Wieland, 31; Milfull, 132–33.

38. *Primo dierum omnium*

This hymn, as its content indicates, was sung at Sunday Nocturns. In the Canterbury hymnal four further stanzas are added, but as Blume and Walpole have argued, they form a separate hymn addressed to Christ *(Iam nunc, paterna claritas),* whereas this hymn is an exhortation to monastic communities.

1.2   *quo mundus exstat conditus:* That is, the seventh day of creation (Gen 2:2). *Exstat* means no more than *est.*

1.3   *vel:* "And."

1.4   *morte victa:* Compare 1 Cor 15:54: "When this mortal hath put on immortality . . . 'Death is swallowed up in victory *(absorpta est mors in victoria).*'"

2.3–4   *nocte quaeramus pium, sicut prophetam novimus:* See Ps 118:62, "I rose at midnight to give praise to thee," and Ps 133:1–3, "Bless the Lord, all you servants of the Lord, who stand in the house of the Lord . . . In the nights lift up your hands . . . and bless ye the Lord."

4.1–2   *sacratissimo . . . tempore:* As noted above, the hymn was sung on Sundays (the rubric in the Canterbury hymnal prescribes it between November and Easter).

4.3   *horis quietis:* Because sung at Nocturns.

See further Walpole, 262–63; Wieland, 24–25; Milfull, 115–19.

39. *Summae Deus clementiae*

This hymn, in earlier days appointed to be sung at Nocturns on Saturdays, is in the revised Breviary allotted to the Office of Readings on Saturdays in Week 1, "when the Office of Readings is said at night or at break of day." Note at stanza 3 the revision in the Breviary to offer a less guilt-ridden message.

1.2   *mundi . . . machinae:* God is visualized from the two perspectives of personal father concerned for his children and of creator of the universe. The phrase *machina mundi* is found earlier in Lucretius 5.96.

1.3–4   *unus potentialiter trinusque personaliter:* The thought is possibly inspired by Ambrose, above in hymn 4.8.3, "unum potens per omnia."

2.3–4   *corda . . . perfruamur: Corda* can possibly be taken as nominative, identified with "we" as subject of *perfruamur,* but more probably it is a bold internal accusative.

3.1–2   *Lumbos . . . congruo:* The revised Breviary tones down the sexual implication by reading *lumbos adure congruis / tu caritatis ignibus.*

3.3   *accincti ut:* Note the hiatus as an indication of later composition. The Breviary avoids it by reading *adsint* for *sint.*

4.3   *patriae:* For heaven as homeland, see Hbr 11:14 and 16.

See further Walpole, 274–75; Wieland, 52; Milfull, 171–73.

40. *Consors paterni luminis*

This hymn, traditionally sung at Nocturns on Tuesdays, retains this role in the revised Breviary when the Office of Readings is held during the night or early morning. It has often been ascribed to Ambrose, but its absence from Ambrosian manuscripts and its brevity both argue against it.

1.1–2   *Consors . . . dies:* See hymns 25.1, 27.1 above, of which this hymn is a partial echo, deriving ultimately from *lumen de lumine* in the Creed.

2.1   *tenebras mentium:* With a play on the darkness of the night.

4.1–4   *Praesta,* etc.: This doxology, which is appended to many later hymns, is found in all manuscripts containing this hymn.

See Walpole, 268–69; Wieland, 40–41; Milfull, 147–48.

41. *Somno refectis artubus*

In keeping with the traditional practice of singing this hymn at Monday Nocturns, the revised Breviary allots it to the Office of Readings on Monday of Week 1 when conducted at night or at first light. The claim of Hincmar in the Carolingian age that Ambrose is the author is perhaps to be discounted on the grounds of pervasive use of rhymes and the brevity of the poem.

1.1   *Somno refectis artubus:* The hymn was clearly composed to be sung shortly before dawn.

2.1   *Te . . . primum:* Compare hymn 1.8.3, "Your name our voice must first proclaim" *(Te nostra vox primum sonet),* that is, before embarking on the daily tasks.

3.2   *diurno sideri:* The sun is meant here. Throughout the stanza Christ as the true light and sin as the darkness shrouding the earth are symbolized.

3.4   *labescat:* Literally "totter," a learned word perhaps reflecting the author's acquaintance with Lucretius (1.537, 4.1285).

See further Walpole, 266–68; Wieland, 37–38; Milfull, 140–41.

42. *Aeterna caeli gloria*

This hymn was traditionally sung on Fridays at Lauds, as is the practice today. The alphabetic form line-by-line (note repetition of *c* in stanza 1, *hortus* for *ortus* in 3.1 and *kadit* for *cadit* in 3.3, omission of letters after *t*) is earlier found in the psalms (110, 111, 118) and is exploited by earlier hymn writers, in particular Hilary, Augustine, and Sedulius (see hymn 19 above, though the alphabetic form there is stanza-by-stanza).

1.1   *caeli gloria:* Since the following line refers to the hope of men, the phrase probably denotes praises sung by angels.

1.3   *celsitonantis:* Such compound forms are favored particularly by poets of the Carolingian age. This epithet for the Father was used by Hrabanus Maurus and by Theodulf of Orléans. The simple form *Tonans* is commonly used by classical poets for Jupiter, a usage taken over to describe the Christian God by Lactantius, Prudentius, and others. Note that *c* is repeated; the palatalized *c* of *ce-* is perhaps regarded as a different entity from velar *ca-* in the next line.

2.2   *mens sobria:* Echoing Ambrose; see hymn 4.4.4.

3.1   *Hortus: Ortus* is aspirated in the interests of the alphabetic scheme. The tendency to aspirate was mocked as rustic by classical writers (see Catullus 84), but becomes more common in Late and Medieval Latin.

3.3   *kadit:* For *cadit,* to maintain the alphabetic sequence.

3.4   *lux sancta:* Christ, the light of the world.

4.2   *noctem . . . saeculi:* Symbolizing sin.

5.1–4   *fides . . . spes . . . caritas:* As noted earlier, the motif of the three theological virtues is pervasive in these hymns; see 14.6, 26.5, 32.1.

See further Walpole, 276–79; Wieland, 50; Milfull, 167–69.

43. *Lucis creator optime*

The following five hymns, presumably composed by the same hand, draw their inspiration from the account in Genesis of the first five days of creation. This first of the five is nowadays allotted to its traditional place in Sunday Vespers.

1.2   *lucem dierum,* etc.: See Gen 1:3: "And God said, 'Be light made.' And light was made."

2.2   *diem vocari:* Gen 1:5: "And [God] called the light day."

2.3   *taetrum chaos:* When "the earth was void and empty, and darkness was upon the face of the deep" (Gen 1:2). Chaos is found in both secular and Christian poets as an image of night. Just as at the Creation darkness followed God's creation of the day, so darkness has fallen when this hymn is sung at Vespers. Its plea is that the darkness of sin may not shroud the hearts of the singers.

4.1   *pulset:* The subject is *mens* in the previous stanza. Compare Mt 7:7: "Knock, and it shall be opened to you."

See Walpole, 280–81; Wieland, 32; Milfull, 138–39.

44. *Immense caeli conditor*

This is the second of this sequence of hymns for Vespers, all drawing on the Creation myth in Genesis, and the theme here is God's creation on the second day; hence its traditional place in Vespers on Monday, the second day of the week.

1.2–4   *mixta . . . dedisti limitem:* Compare Gen 1:7: "So God made a firmament and divided the waters that were under the firmament from those that were above the firmament." The author of Genesis visualizes the firmament of heaven as solid mass, with waters coursing above it as well as below on the earth.

2.3   *flammas temperet:* That is, the fire of the sun, which the waters in the universe restrain from scorching the earth.

2.4   *solum ne dissipet:* Compare Gen 9:11: "Neither shall there be from henceforth a flood to waste the earth *(dissipans terram)*."

3.3–4   *fraudis novae . . . error . . . vetus:* "Fresh" deceit because the ancient sin of Adam was instigated by Satan's earlier wiles.

4.1–2   *lucem . . . luminis iubar:* The gift of grace in 3.2 is visualized as the light that God instituted at the Creation.

4.3–4   *haec . . . hanc:* As Walpole suggests, the first refers to *lux,* the sec-
         ond to *fides* (as reflected in the translation); but the two are here
         virtually identical.
See further Walpole, 281–82; Wieland, 39–40; Milfull, 145–47.

45. *Telluris ingens conditor*

The third day in the account of Creation in Genesis becomes the theme
for Tuesday Vespers in the revised Breviary as in the earlier tradition.

1.2–4   *mundi solum . . . terram dedisti immobilem:* Compare Gen 1:9: "Let
         the waters . . . be gathered together into one place, and let the
         dry land appear."
2.1–4   *Ut germen,* etc.: So Gen 1:12: "And the earth brought forth the
         green herb *(et protulit terra herbam virentem)* and such as yieldeth
         seed according to its kind and the tree that beareth fruit having
         seed."
3.1–2   *perustae . . . viroris gratia:* Comparison is made between parched
         minds and parched creation; the grace brings spiritual greenness
         to our minds as the Creator fertilizes the earth.
3.3   *ut . . . diluat:* The subject is *gratia,* or possibly *mens.*
4.1–4   *obtemperet,* etc.: The subject of the four verbs is *mens* understood
         from *mentis* at 3.1.
4.4   *mortis actum:* The deeds that bring eternal death.
See further Walpole, 283–84; Wieland, 42; Milfull, 151–52.

46. *Caeli deus sanctissime*

For Wednesday Vespers this hymn continues to exploit Genesis, compar-
ing the creation of sun, moon, and stars, which illumine the world, with
the light of Christ, the true Sun that shines upon our hearts and minds.

1.2–4   *lucidum centrum . . . decoro lumine:* The "shining center" of the sky
         refers to the position of the sun. For its creation, see Gen 1:14.
2.2–4   *solis . . . lunae . . . siderum:* Gen 1:16: "God made two great lights—
         a greater light to rule the day and a lesser light to rule the night—
         and the stars." The author of the hymn interprets the later part

of the passage as meaning that moon and stars together rule the night.

2.4   *vagos recursus siderum:* Referring to the five known planets. The strict sense of *recursus* is "returning courses"; the author of the hymn may be drawing here on Cicero, *Nat. D.* 2.52–53, where estimates of the varying times taken by the five to complete their circuits are given.

3.3–4   *primordiis et mensium signum:* The hymn writer glosses on the account in Genesis to explain the moon's waxing and waning.

4.1   *Illumina cor hominum:* Christ the true Sun is begged to pour his light into men's hearts, as sun and moon enlighten the world. Augustine's celebrated doctrine of illumination may be in the mind of the hymn writer here; for the texts in Augustine, see Copleston, *A History of Philosophy,* vol. 2, pt. 1, 77–82.

See further Walpole, 284–86; Wieland, 45; Milfull, 157–59.

47. *Magnae Deus potentiae*

The hymn for Thursday Vespers takes as its starting point the creation of the lower animals.

1.2   *qui ex aquis,* etc.: Gen 1:21: "So God created . . . every living and moving creature which the waters brought forth according to their kinds and every winged fowl according to its kind." The hymn interprets this as meaning that the birds were also brought forth from the waters.

3.2   *unda sanguinis:* Walpole regards *sanguinis* as a rogue nominative, to mean "whom blood and water cleanse," echoing John 19:34, "At once blood and water came forth." But *sanguinis* for *sanguis* is not attested elsewhere, and *unda* is used of liquids other than water. The hymn writer may have had in mind Hbr 4:14: "sanguis Christi . . . emundabit."

3.4   *mortis taedium:* The weariness of everlasting death in hell.

4.3–4   *elisa . . . corruat:* A reminiscence of Ps 144:14: "The Lord lifteth up all that fall *(corruunt)* and setteth up all that are cast down *(elisos)*."

See further Walpole, 286–87; Wieland, 48; Milfull, 163–64.

48. *Conditor alme siderum*

This hymn is appropriately allocated to the season of Advent in view of stanza 3, and to Vespers in view of the references to the evening of the world and to the setting sun in stanzas 3 and 5. In the revised Breviary, stanza 5 is omitted as in some MSS, and the doxology is changed to lend greater prominence to Christ. The recurrent rhyming indicates a date of composition well after the fourth century.

2.1–2   *interitu mortis:* "In the extinction of death," the moral death incurred by Adam's sin.

3.1   *Vergente mundi vespere:* The coming of Christ is visualized as the end of the old world and the beginning of the new. See Hbr 9:26: "He has appeared once for all at the end of the age *(in consummatione saeculorum)* to remove sin by the sacrifice of himself."

3.2   *uti sponsus de thalamo:* This evocation of Ps 18:6, "tamquam sponsus procedens de thalamo suo" (as a bridegroom coming out of his bridechamber), had already been famously exploited by Ambrose in hymn 5.5 above.

3.4   *clausula:* The word is not elsewhere attested in the sense of "womb"; the connection with *clausus,* "closed," "inaccessible," points to Mary's virginity.

4.2   *genu curvantur omnia:* So Phlp 2:10–11: "Ut in nomine Iesu omne genu flectat caelestium, terrestrium et infernorum, et omnis lingua confiteatur quia Dominus Iesus Christus in gloria est Dei Patris" (That in the name of Jesus every knee should bow of those that are in heaven, on earth and under the earth, and that every tongue should confess that the Lord Jesus Christ is in the glory of God the Father).

5.1–3   *sol . . . luna . . . astris:* For the worship of God by the inanimate forces of nature, compare Ps 103:19–33, etc.

6.1   *hagie:* For the Greek invocation, see above, hymns 27.5, 28.13 and notes.

7.3   *Paraclito:* The Greek word means "Advocate," but the Fathers from Origen onward interpret it in John 14:16 and 26 ("The Paraclete, the Holy Ghost, whom the Father will send in my name") as "the Comforter."

See further Walpole, 299–302; Wieland, 56–57; Milfull, 181–84.

49. *O lux beata Trinitas*

Hincmar, followed by some modern scholars, ascribes this hymn to Ambrose, but its absence from the Ambrosian MSS, the pervasive rhyme, and the brevity of the hymn all tell against an early date. In the revised Breviary it is appointed for Second Vespers on Sundays in Week 2.

1.1	*beata:* The adjective is perhaps juxtaposed between the two nouns to be taken with both.
1.2	*principalis:* The sense of "primal" or "sovereign" seems more appropriate than Walpole's "princely."
2.1–2	*laudum . . . vespere:* The words make reference to the offices of Lauds and Vespers.
2.2	*deprecamur:* A contrast with *laudum* is intended; hence "we plead for pardon." Some MSS offer the alternative reading *deprecemur* as a subjunctive parallel with *laudet,* but the indicative is more natural.

See further Walpole, 288–91; Wieland, 55; Milfull, 109–11.

50. *Christe, redemptor omnium*

The hymns earlier composed commemorating Christ's nativity (see hymns 5 and 19 as examples) dominate the Christmas liturgy, but this hymn has an honored place at Vespers on Christmas Day. Earlier it was sung at various hours on this feast day.

1.2	*ex Patre, Patris unice:* The line evokes the Nicene Creed: "filium dei unigenitum. Et ex patre natum . . ."
1.3–4	*ante principium natus:* Compare Prov 8:22–23: "The Lord possessed me [sc. Wisdom] in the beginning of his ways before he made any thing from the beginning. I was set up from eternity . . ."
2.1	*Tu lumen, tu splendor Patris:* The words echo Ambrose's hymn (2.1 above).
3.1	*salutis auctor:* So Hbr 2:10: "auctorem salutis."
3.3	*illibata:* "Intact" in the sexual sense.
4.3–4	*solus . . . salus:* So Act 4:12: "Neither is there salvation in any other

(non est in alio aliquo salus). For there is no other name under heaven given to men whereby we must be saved." Note the play on *solus/salus.*

5.1   *Hunc caelum, terra,* etc.: *Hunc* refers to Christ. Ps 95:11–13 is evoked here as celebrating the Lord's coming: "Laetentur caeli, et exultet terra; commoveatur mare et plenitudo eius" (Let the heavens rejoice, and let the earth be glad; let the sea be moved and the fulness thereof).

See further Walpole, 306–8; Wieland, 60–61; Milfull, 190–93.

51. *Ex more docti mystico*

This hymn composed for the Lenten season was assigned to different days and hours in earlier hymnals. In the revised Breviary the first four stanzas, with an appended doxology, are assigned to the Office of Readings on Sundays. Mone, *Lateinische hymnen,* 1.94–95, notes the close parallels of content with the works of Gregory the Great, and ascribes the hymn to him, but the ascription must remain uncertain.

1.1   *Ex more . . . mystico:* The number of days in Lent has mystical significance because the number forty is often associated with cleansing and purifying (so states Cassiodorus in his *Commentary on Psalm 40 (ACW* 51, p. 407), instancing the days of the Flood, the period of Moses's fasting to merit converse with God, Elijah's similarly lengthy abstention from food, and Jesus's period of fasting.)

2.1–3   *Lex et prophetae . . . Christus sacravit:* See Gen 7:12, Ex 34:28, 3 Kings 19:8, Mk 1:13. It is likely that Cassiodorus inspired this stanza.

3.1   *Utamur ergo parcius,* etc.: Benedict, *Rule* 49, similarly specifies for Lent greater abstention from food, drink, sleep, conversation, and scurrilous joking.

4.3–4   *nullumque . . . locum:* Compare Eph 4:27: "Nolite locum dare diabolo" (Give not place to the devil).

5.1   *Dicamus:* That is, in our prayers.

7.2   *caduci plasmatis:* The Greek word πλάσμα *(plásma),* earlier connoting anything fashioned, such as a statue, is taken over in Christian Latin to describe the human body "fashioned" by the Creator.

7.3–4   *ne des honorem . . . alteri:* Evoking Is 48:11: "Gloriam meam alteri non dabo" (I shall not give my glory to another). God makes this promise to the Israelites; the composer of the hymn begs God likewise not to abandon the sinners of the new Israel.

See further Walpole, 321–23; Wieland 78. Milfull indicates that the Durham hymnary divides the hymn into two: stanzas 1–4 as 56^1 and 5–8 as 56^2.

52. *Audi, benigne conditor*

This hymn, with minor changes, is in the revised Breviary allotted to Vespers from Ash Wednesday until the end of Week 5 in Lent. Earlier it was sung at various hours during Lent. The similarity to the previous hymn encourages (but is far from proving) the view that both are from the same pen, identified as Gregory's by Mone, *Lateinische hymnen,* 1.95–96. But this is speculative.

2.1   *Scrutator . . . cordium:* Compare Rom 8:27: "[God,] that searches the hearts *(scrutatur corda)* . . ."

4.3–4   *ieiunet ut . . . a labe:* The striking image underlines the contrast between body and mind. By afflicting our bodies with fasting, we starve our minds from committing sin.

5.4   *ieiuniorum munera:* The "tasks" or "duties" of fasting.

See further Walpole, 320–21; Wieland, 75–76; Milfull, 238–41.

53. *Iesu, nostra redemptio*

It could be argued that this hymn more appropriately belongs to Holy Week (it was earlier appointed for Nocturns at Easter) than to Ascension Thursday, to which the revised Breviary allots it for First Vespers.

1.4   *in fine temporum:* See hymn 48.3.1n. for Christ's advent as the close of the old era.

2.2–4   *ut ferres nostra crimina . . . ut nos a morte tolleres:* For Christ prefigured as suffering servant, see Is 53:4. 1 Pt 2:24 takes up the theme: "Qui peccata nostra ipse pertulit in corpore suo super lignum, ut, peccatis mortui, iustitiae viveremus" (Who his own self bore our sins in his body upon the tree, that we, being dead to sins, should live to justice).

3.1–2   *Inferni . . . redimens:* The doctrine of the harrowing of hell is developed from scriptural passages, notably Mt 27:52–54, and is eventually incorporated into the Apostles' Creed.

4.4   *tuo vultu saties:* Compare Ps 16:15: "Ego autem in iustitia apparebo conspectui tuo; satiabor cum apparuerit gloria tua" (But as for me, I will appear before thy sight in justice; I shall be satisfied when thy glory shall appear).

5.3   *sit nostra in te gloria:* Compare 2 Cor 10:17: "Qui autem gloriatur, in Domino glorietur" (But he that glorieth, let him glory in the Lord).

See further Walpole, 364–65; Wieland, 88–89; Milfull, 287–89.

54. *Aeterne rex altissime*

This hymn, the antiquity of which is demonstrated by its presence in Carolingian MSS, is in the revised Breviary appointed for the Office of Readings on the feast of the Ascension.

1.1   *altissime:* The word is frequently used of God in the Old Testament, as at Ps 9:3: "I will sing to thy name, O thou Most High (*Altissime*)."

1.4   *triumphus gratiae:* That is, the grace to triumph over sin and death.

2.1   *Scandens:* This is to be regarded as a continuation of the invocation, and is therefore vocative.

2.3–4   *caelitus . . . humanitus:* Both adverbs are found in classical Latin.

3.1   *machina:* Often "structure" or "fabric," especially, since Lucretius, of the universe. *OLD,* s.v. *machina,* 6.

3.2–3   *caelestium, terrestrium, et infernorum,* etc.: So Phlp 2:10: "Ut in nomine Iesu omne genu flectat caelestium et terrestrium et infernorum" (That in the name of Jesus every knee should bow of those that are in heaven, on earth and under the earth).

4.1   *Tremunt videntes angeli:* The motif is borrowed from Ambrose; see hymn 9.4.

5.2   *Olympo:* Mount Olympus is constantly cited as the abode of the gods in classical literature, and some Christian poets adopt it as a title of heaven. The revised Breviary avoids it by recasting the line to "manens perenne praemium" (enduring and eternal prize).

6.3   *corda sursum subleva:* See the Preface of the Mass, "sursum corda."

7.1   *cum repente:* See Mt 24:30: "And they will see the Son of Man coming on the clouds of heaven *(in nubibus caeli)* . . ."; likewise Mk 13:26. The difficulty in the phrase *cum repente coeperis* has led to the alternative reading *rubente* ("on a crimson cloud") for *repente,* and this is adopted in the revised Breviary. But in Late Latin the force of *coepi* is often weakened, so that the sense is virtually "when you suddenly gleam bright."

See further Walpole, 361–64; Milfull, 301–4.

55. *Optatus votis omnium*

Like the previous two hymns, this is appropriately assigned to the feast of the Ascension. In the revised Breviary, stanzas 1 and 3–7 (with minor variations of text and an appended doxology) form the hymn for Lauds on the feast day.

1.3   *mundi spes:* So 1 Tim. 1:1: "Christi Iesu, spei nostrae" (Christ Jesus, our hope).

1.4   *caelos:* The masculine form is used here as in classical Latin in preference to the neuter plural *caela.*

2.1–2   *Ascendens . . . remeans:* The awkward syntax (apparent nominative absolutes), together with the crude prosody, presumably prompted the decision to exclude this stanza from the version in the revised Breviary. Compare Eph 4:8: "Ascendens in caelum, captivam duxit captivitatem" (Ascending on high, he led captivity captive), echoing Ps 67:19 ("Ascendisti in altum; cepisti captivitatem").

3.2 *mundi perempto principe:* Compare John 12:31: "Nunc princeps huius mundi eicietur foras" (Now shall the prince of this world be cast out). Also John 16:11.

4.1 *Est elevatus in nubibus:* Compare Act 1:9: "Elevatus est, et nubes suscepit eum" (He was raised up, and a cloud received him).

4.4 *protoplasti:* For the Greek form, see hymn 20.2.1–2n.

5.2 *nostrae virginis:* "The virgin of our race."

6.3 *nostrum . . . vexerit:* That is, by raising in his own person our human flesh to heaven, he has paved the way for us to follow.

See Walpole, 359–61; Wieland, 93–94.

56. *Iam Christus astra ascenderat*

This hymn for Pentecost was earlier divided into sections to be sung at Terce, Sext, and None; in the Durham hymnary only the first three stanzas appear. The revised Breviary has stanzas 1, 3, 4, followed by two appended stanzas.

1.2 *regressus unde venerat:* Compare John 16:28: "I came forth from the Father . . . and I go to the Father."

1.3 *promisso Patris munere:* See Lk 24:49: "And I send the promise of my Father *(promissum Patris mei)* upon you."

2.2–3 *mystico septemplici . . . septies: Mysticus* connotes both "hidden mystery" and "sacrament." The number seven was sacramental, since the Creation was completed in seven days, the gifts of the Spirit are seven, the theological and cardinal virtues combined are seven, and so forth. The period from the Resurrection to Pentecost, consisting of seven times seven days, is thus depicted as sacramental.

3.1 *hora . . . tertia:* So Peter states at Act 2:15: "Seeing as it is but the third hour of the day."

3.2 *repente . . . intonat:* Compare Act 2:2: "Factus est repente de caelo sonus . . ." (Suddenly there came a sound from heaven . . .).

4.2 *ignis almus:* In classical poetry deities are often dignified with this adjective. The fire can be so described because it is the Holy Spirit.

4.3   *fida Christi:* "Trusting in Christ"; *Christi* is objective genitive af-
        ter the adjective, which bears a participial sense.

5.3–4   *voces diversae . . . magnalia:* The voices are those of both apostles
        ("They began to speak with divers tongues," Act 2:4) and the by-
        standers ("They were all amazed and wondered, saying, . . . 'We
        have heard them speak in our own tongues the wonderful works
        of God,'" Act 2:7 and 11). *Magnalia* translates New Testament
        Greek τὰ μεγαλεῖα (*tà megaleîa,* "great deeds").

6.2   *Graecus Latinus barbarus:* They are specified in greater detail at
        Act 2:9–11.

7.1   *Iudaea . . . incredula:* So Act 2:13: "But others sneered and said:
        They are filled with new wine *(musto)*."

7.3   *ructare musti crapulam:* ". . . that they are belching forth the in-
        toxication of new wine."

8.4   *Iohele teste:* So Peter at Act 2:16–21, citing Joel 2:28–32.
See further Walpole, 368–71; Wieland, 94–96; Milfull, 311–13.

57. Beata nobis gaudia

This second hymn for Pentecost is closely parallel to that which precedes.
In the revised Breviary it is appointed for Lauds on Whit Sunday.

1.3   *Spiritus Paraclitus:* For *Paraclitus,* see hymn 48.7.3n.

2.2   *linguae figuram:* So Act 2:3: "Dispertitae linguae tamquam ignis"
        (Divided tongues as of fire).

3.3   *musto madere:* See hymn 56.7.3n.

4.1   *mystice:* For the sense, see hymn 56.2.2n., with reference to the
        mystical number of seven times seven days since the Resurrec-
        tion.

4.4   *lege fit remissio:* Under the Old Law (Lv 25:10: "Thou shalt hallow
        the fiftieth year, and thou shalt proclaim liberty to all the inhab-
        itants of thy land . . ."), the year of Jubilee was proclaimed every
        fifty years. Slaves gained their freedom and lands reverted to
        their former owners (see bibliography in *ODCC* (3rd ed.), s.v.
        "Jubilee, Year of"). The fifty days after the Resurrection simi-
        larly denote the Christian deliverance from enslavement to sin.

5.4   *dona Spiritus:* See Act 2:4: "They were all filled with the Holy

Ghost, and they began to speak with diverse tongues, according as the Holy Ghost gave them to speak."

See further Walpole, 365–67; Wieland, 97–98; Milfull, 307–9.

58. *Rex gloriose martyrum*

This hymn and the next, devoted to praise of martyrs, are so similar in content and style that they appear to have been written by the same hand. They point the contrast between the heroism of martyrs of the past and the deficiencies of the confessors of the present, who acknowledge their sins and plead for pardon for them. In the revised Breviary this hymn is prescribed for the Office of Readings when more than one martyr is being celebrated.

1.1–2   *martyrum . . . confitentium:* In this stanza martyrs of the past are grouped with confessors of the present (both are witnesses to the faith), as the tense of *perducis* in line 4 indicates.

2.3   *tropaea sacra:* The "sacred trophies" are the butchered bodies of the martyrs. Just as Christ's body was a trophy commemorating his victory over Satan and death (see hymn 5.7 above), so the bodies of those who died to witness to him are a further mark of that victory.

3.2   *parcendo confitentibus:* This line is better taken with what follows than with what precedes. Those who sing this hymn emulate the martyrs by confessing Christ, but without manifesting a similar heroism.

See further Walpole, 384–85; Wieland, 123–24; Milfull, 391–92.

59. *Deus, tuorum militum*

In the revised Breviary this hymn is sung at Vespers on the feast of the Common of a single martyr. Additional stanzas have been added after § 1 and § 4, together with a conventional doxology.

1.2   *sors:* For God as our "portion," see Ps 72:26: "Pars mea Deus in aeternum" (God . . . is my portion for ever).

3.1   *Poenas cucurrit:* The martyr endures the pains with the steadfast endurance of the marathon runner.

4.3   *in hoc triumpho:* Literally "on this triumph"; perhaps "on this
        commemoration of the martyr's triumph."
See further Walpole, 386; Wieland, 122–23; Milfull, 397–99.

60. *Iesu, corona virginum*

This hymn composed for the Common of Virgins is speculatively attributed to Ambrose by Walpole and Wieland. But its absence from the Ambrosian corpus, its brevity, and the frequent rhymes all suggest a later date
of composition. It is possible that Augustine's treatise *De sancta virginitate*
(ed. with *De bono coniugali* by P. G. Walsh, Oxford, 2001) inspired the hymn.
In the revised Breviary it is sung at Second Vespers in the Common of Virgins.

1.1   *corona:* Here as elsewhere the inspiration for this title is Is 28:5:
        "On that day the Lord of hosts will be a crown of glory *(corona
        gloriae).*"
1.3   *quae sola virgo parturit:* Her uniqueness is emphasized by Augus-
        tine, *De sancta virginitate* 4–5.
2.1   *Qui pascis inter lilia:* An echo of Ct 2:16: "Dilectus meus mihi et
        ego illi qui pascitur inter lilia" (My beloved to me [i.e., he is
        mine] and I to him who feedeth among the lilies).
2.2   *saeptus choreis virginum:* Similarly Augustine, *De sancta virginitate*
        27.
2.3   *sponsus decorus gloria:* A reworking of Is 61:10: "quasi sponsum
        decoratum corona" (as a bridegroom decked with a crown).
3.1–2   *Quocumque pergis, virgines sequuntur:* So Apc 14:4: "Hii sequuntur
        Agnum quocumque abierit" (These follow the Lamb whitherso-
        ever he goeth). Augustine writes: "God's virgins who are blame-
        less do indeed follow the Lamb wherever he goes" (49; trans.
        Walsh, p. 137).
See further Walpole, 112–14; Wieland, 131; Milfull, 410–12.

61. *Iesu, redemptor omnium*

Walpole reasonably suggests that this hymn was composed by the same
author as 58 and 59 above. In the revised Breviary, where it is appointed for

the Office of Readings on the feast of the Common of more than one saint, an extra stanza has been inserted between § 2 and § 3, and a doxology appended.

1.2   *praesulum:* Not necessarily "bishops" here, but outstanding leaders in the Church of their day.
1.3   *in hac die: Dies* is feminine because it connotes a fixed day.
2.2   *confessor:* See Mt 10:32: "Whosoever therefore shall confess me before men, I will also confess him before my Father, who is in heaven."
3.3   *caelestibus:* The word is placed between *angelis* and *praemiis,* so that it can be understood with both.

See further Walpole, 387; Wieland, 127–28; Milfull, 405–7.

62. *Quem terra pontus aethera*

This hymn, which appears in several Carolingian manuscripts, is ascribed to Venantius Fortunatus by Walpole and others. Certainly the content and treatment are reminiscent of that poet, but the hymn does not appear in the body of his writings, so that the ascription remains no more than an attractive suggestion. In the revised Breviary it is introduced at the Office of Readings in the Common of the Blessed Virgin Mary, though it is confined there to stanzas 1–2 and 4–5, with an appended doxology.

1.3   *trinam . . . machinam:* The "triple fabric" of the world picks up the content of the first line.
1.4   *claustrum . . . baiulat:* The contrast between the majesty of God the Creator and his humility in becoming a feeble child is characteristic of the thought of Fortunatus.
2.4   *gestant puellae viscera:* This line is borrowed by the author of the seventeeth- or eighteenth-century Christmas carol *Adeste fideles.*
3.2–3 *quod angelus fert semina,* etc.: The bold poetic image visualizes the angel Gabriel bearing the seed and planting it in Mary's ear. On conception through the ear see J. H. Waszink, "Empfängnis," in *RAC* 4.1253.

4.4   *ventris sub arca:* At Apc 11:19, the ark of God's covenant appears in his temple. Mary's womb has become his temple and ark.

5.1   *Benedicta caeli nuntio:* Compare Lk 1:28: "Blessed *(benedicta)* art thou among women."

5.4   *fusus est:* "Was brought forth," perhaps suggesting an easy delivery.

7.1   *Eva:* The notion that Mary was active in the work of redemption and reversed the calamity imposed on mankind by Eve is especially prominent in the writings of Ambrose. Thereafter this reversal is often signaled in hymns by wordplay between *Eva* and *Ave,* Gabriel's initial greeting to Mary (Lk 1:28). See for example hymn 63.2.

7.4   *fenestra:* From its primary meaning of "window" or "shutter," the sense of "aperture" develops; hence here "means of entry."

8.1–2   *ianua . . . porta:* Such metaphors in descriptions of Mary appear in the *Laus Mariae,* a sixth-century poem in elegiacs possibly the work of Fortunatus, and thereafter in hymns and litanies to Our Lady, as in the Litany of Loreto.

8.2   *lucis:* That is, Christ, Light from Light.

See further Walpole, 198–200; Wieland, 82–83; Milfull, 267–71.

63. *Ave, maris stella*

This famous hymn to the Virgin Mary, dating probably from the Carolingian period, is in the revised Breviary appointed to Second Vespers on the Common of the Blessed Virgin Mary. In the Durham hymnary, stanzas 5 and 6 are transposed.

1.1   *maris stella:* The Blessed Virgin took over from pagan goddesses the protective roles assigned to them. Prominent among them was Isis, whose concern for mariners was demonstrated by the yearly festival of the *Navigium Isidis.* When associated with Mary, the title extends its sense to depict her as guiding star as men make their way through the salt surge of this world.

1.4   *felix caeli porta:* See hymn 62.8n.

2.1–4   *Ave ... Evae:* See hymn 62.7n.

3.1   *Solve vincla reis:* By this (Carolingian) date the cult of Mary had developed to such a degree that it not merely overshadowed that of other saints but threatened to arrogate the role of Christ. But in this hymn the next stanza restores the proper order of priorities.

4.2   *sumat per te precem:* Emphasizing Mary's more modest role as *mediatrix.*

5.2   *inter omnes mitis:* Mary's gentle humility is a prominent theme in the treatises of Ambrose, Jerome, and Augustine.

6.2   *iter para tutum:* "Safe" in the moral sense; as guiding star Mary lights the way to heaven.

7.4   *honor tribus unus:* The glory owed to the Holy Spirit is the common possession of the three Persons of the Trinity.

See further Wieland, 83–84; Milfull, 271–74.

COLUMBA OF IONA

64. *Altus Prosator*

This long and learned hymn, attributed though not with certainty to Columba of Iona (see the Introduction, p. xiii) is, characteristic of early Irish hymns in its alphabetic structure, heavy trochaic rhythm, frequent rhyme, and exotic diction, including occasional Graecisms and Hebraisms. Its theme is the glorification of the work of the Trinity, from the creation of the angels and the birth of the material world to the imminent end of the world and the Judgment to follow.

1. Glorification of the Trinity

1.1–2   *vetustus dierum:* So the vision of the Father in Daniel: "antiquus dierum" (7:9).

2. Creation of the angels

2.1   *bonos ... angelos:* Ps.-Dionysius in his *Celestial Hierarchies* (ca. 500) arranged the nine orders of heavenly beings into three hierarchies: cherubim, seraphim, thrones; dominations, virtues, powers; principalities, archangels, angels. In this scheme, only the last two have relations with mankind, whereas in this hymn the six choirs mentioned all serve as messengers to men.

2.9–12   *sed haberet . . . fatimine:* Construe: *sed haberet [eis] in quibus magnifice ostenderet caelestia privilegia possibili fatimine.*

3–4. The fall of Lucifer and his satellites

3.7   *apostatae angeli:* For the fall of the angels, see 2 Pt 2:4. The use of Greek words in this stanza, *apostatae* and *cenodoxia* (vainglory) is notable.

4.1   *Draco:* See Apc 12:9: "That great dragon was cast out, that old serpent, . . . and his angels were thrown down with him."

4.4   *sapientior omnibus:* So Gen 3:1: "Serpens erat callidior cunctis animantibus terrae" (The serpent was more subtle than any of the beasts of the earth).

4.12   *parasito:* From the original sense of the man who seeks a free dinner, the word comes to mean a flatterer and thereafter a deceiver.

5. The creation of the world

5.3   *caelum et terram,* etc.: The hymn follows the order of creation outlined in Genesis: sky and earth, sea and waters, heavenly bodies, lower creatures, man.

5.12   *protoplastum:* The Greek word descriptive of Adam ("first-formed") appears earlier in hymns by Fortunatus (see Hymn 20.2.1) and others.

5.12   *praesagmine:* Prophecy, with reference to God's words at Gen 1:20–30.

6. Angels praise the creation

6.1   *Factis simul sideribus:* In spite of 4.7 above ("stars" there is a metaphor for shining angels), the stars are not identical with the angels, which have already been created; the beauty of the heavens stirs them to admiring praise.

6.11–12   *arbitrio non naturae donario:* Their praise was not a condition of their existence, but freely given.

7. The fall of man, and Satan's second fall

7.3   *secundo ruit:* After the first fall, Satan was allowed to dwell as a serpent in Eden. To shield men from his evil designs, his followers are now consigned to hell: see Mt 25:41.

8. The demons confined to the earth's atmosphere

8.3   *cuius:* Modifies *satellitum.*

8.3   *aëris spatium:* Referring to the atmosphere. Late Antique and early medieval cosmography located diabolical powers there. The seventh-century Irish *Liber de ordine creaturarum* (book 8) also places Satan and the demons here. See M. Smyth, "Understanding the Universe in Seventh-Century Ireland," in *Studies in Celtic History* (Woodbridge, Eng., 1996): 185–86 and 223–24.

8.5   *invisibilium:* The demons' invisibility is providential: men cannot see their bad example and fornicate in public. See J. Stevenson, "Altus Prosator," *Celtica* 23 (1993): 349–50, on this passage and its source (Cassian, *Collationes* 8.12).

8.9–10   *nullis . . . tegentibus saeptis ac parietibus:* The ablative is to be construed with *fornicarentur,* emphasizing the potential shamelessness of human beings.

9. Climatic conditions on the earth

9.2–5   *ex fontibus . . . maris:* In this complex description of the source of rain which waters the crops, *ex fontibus* is to be taken with *maris,* and *tribus dodrantibus* is in apposition to *fontibus.* The ocean is visualized as covering three quarters of the earth's surface in three deeper expanses.

9.11   *quique:* Namely *thesauri,* though it would have been more logical (and, in fact, makes more syntactic sense, though the antecedent must be masculine) to allot the activity to the winds themselves. There is an evocation of Ps 134:7 here: "[The Lord] brings forth winds from his treasure houses *(ventos de thesauris suis).*"

10. Punishment of despotic rulers

10.5   *ecce gigantes:* These lines evoke Wis 14:6–7 ("When the proud giants perished . . . blessed is the wood by which justice cometh"),
which describes God's destruction of the corrupt inhabitants of
the world through the Flood, and the survival of human and animal life in the ark. The punishment of the "giants" echoes Job
26:5: "Ecce: gigantes gemunt sub aquis et qui habitant cum eis"
(Behold: the giants groan under the waters and they that dwell
with them).

10.9–11   *Cocytique Charybdibus . . . Scyllis:* These learned references go
back to Virgil's *Aeneid.* Cocytus is the river of lamentation in
Hades (Virgil, *Aen.* 6.132, 297), here used of hell itself. The rocks
of Scylla and the whirlpool of Charybdis were situated in the
straits of Messina (3.420–25). Here they are placed in hell as
metaphors to describe the horrors there.

11. Rain and rivers

11.1–2   *aquas . . . crebrat Dominus:* So 2 Kings 22:12: "Cribrans aquas de
nubibus caelorum" (sifting the waters from the clouds of
heaven).

11.8   *telli:* A variant form for *telluris.*

12. The foundations of the earth

12.5   *iduma:* A Hebraism for "hand." The hand of God, indicative of
his power, is ubiquitous in the Old Testament.

13. Sufferings in hell

13.4   *vermes et dirae bestiae:* Compare Sir 10:13: "When a man shall
die, he shall inherit serpents and beasts and worms *(bestias et
vermes).*"

13.8   *fletus et stridor dentium:* So Mt 8:12: "Ibi erit fletus et stridor dentium" (There shall be weeping and gnashing of teeth).

13.9   *Gehennae:* The valley of Hinnom south of Jerusalem is cited
in scripture to depict the place of punishment in hell; see Mt
5:29–30.

14. The unavailing prayers of those in hell

14.6   *librum scriptum,* etc.: So Apc 5:1: "Librum scriptum . . . signatum sigillis septem" (A book written . . . sealed with seven seals).

14.8   *de Christi monitis:* See Apc 5:6–14.

14.9–10 *resignaverat postquam victor exstiterat:* So Apc 5:5: "[He] hath prevailed to open the book and to loose the seven seals thereof."

15. The garden of Eden

15.3   *legimus in primordio:* See Gen 2:8–10.

15.5–6   *flumina quattuor:* So Gen 2:10: "A river went out of the place of pleasure . . . which from thence is divided into four heads *(quattuor capita).*"

15.8   *lignum vitae:* Gen 2:9: "Lignum etiam vitae in medio paradisi" (The tree of life also in the midst of paradise). For the association of the tree with Christ's cross, see hymn 20.2–3, and its rich fruit, 20.8.

16. Moses ascends to Mount Sinai

16.1–2   *Quis . . . ascendit:* Compare Ex 19:3–6. "Moses autem ascendit ad Deum, vocavitque eum Dominus de monte . . ." (And Moses went up to God, and the Lord called unto him from the mountain . . .).

16.3–7   *tonitrua . . . fulgura:* Ex 19:16: "Coeperunt audiri tonitrua ac micare fulgura . . . clangorque bucinae vehementius perstrepebat . . ." (Thunders began to be heard and lightning to flash . . . and the noise of the trumpet sounded exceeding loud. . .).

17–18. The day of judgment

17.3   *dies irae:* The prophecy of Zephaniah, 1:15, "Dies irae dies illa" (That day is a day of wrath), inspires the celebrated hymn of this title (95 below). The day of judgment is also prophesied in Is 34:8: "The day of the vengeance of the Lord."

17.4   *tenebrarum et nebulae:* See Mt 24:29: "The sun will be darkened, and the moon will not give its light."

18.1–2   *Stantes . . . ante tribunal:* So Apc 20:12: "Stantes in conspectu throni" (standing in the presence of the throne).

18.7–8   *librosque . . . patefactos:* Apc 20:12–13: "And the books were opened . . . and the dead were judged by those things which were written in the books, according to their works."

18.9–10   *fletus ac . . . singultus:* Compare Mt 8:12.

19. The general resurrection

19.1   *Tuba primi archangeli:* So Apc 8:7: "Et primus angelus tuba cecinit" (The first angel blew his trumpet).

19.4   *polyandria:* The Greek word (literally "great gathering of men") is used first for the dead, and thereafter for their resting places (sepulchres).

19.7–8   *conglobantibus . . . ossibus:* As often when the Fathers wish to depict the general resurrection, Ez 37 is cited. Compare 18.32.6–33 and 7n.

19.9–12   *animabus . . . mansionibus:* Acquaintance with Prudentius's account of the fusion of soul and body (see hymn 18.8–11) seems probable here.

20. The stars' courses symbolizing Christ's journey

20.1   *ex climactere:* From its initial sense of the rung of a ladder, the word here means "from its high point."

20.2–3   *Orion . . . Vergilio:* The author demonstrates his astronomical learning. *Vergiliae* (here corrupted into *Vergilius*) is the old Roman name for the Pleiades. For their proximity to Orion, see Cicero, *Nat. D.* 2.113–14.

20.5   *Thetis:* The name of the leading sea nymph is used by metonymy for the ocean itself, as in Virgil, *Ecl.* 4.32, etc.

20.9–10   *oriens post biennium Vesperugo:* Vesperugo is Venus as evening star; it takes only a year to complete the circuit of the Zodiac.

20.11–12   *sumpta . . . intellectibus:* "These, with their figurative meanings, are understood as types *(problemata)*." *Problemata,* which originally means "subjects for debate," is used here for "types" or symbols of Christ, who likewise traveled beneath the earth and rose again.

21. The second coming of Christ

21.1–12   *Xristo: Christus* is regularly spelled with an *X* to meet the needs of abecedarian verse.

21.5–12   *tectisque luminaribus,* etc.: The whole description is adapted from Apc 6:12–15: "The sun became black as sackcloth of hair, and the full moon became as blood, and the stars from heaven fell upon the earth as the fig tree casteth its green figs when it is shaken by a great wind *(stellae caeli ceciderunt super terram sicut ficus)* . . . And [everyone] . . . hid themselves in the dens and in the rocks of the mountains *(in speluncis et petris montium)* . . ."

22. Acclaim by the heavenly dwellers

22.3–4   *milibus angelorum vernantibus:* The verb ("to celebrate spring") is elsewhere used of the singing of birds.

22.5–9   *quattuorque . . . animalibus,* etc.: See Apc 4:6–8, 4:4. The twenty-four elders, two from each tribe, represent office bearers in the Church, and the four living creatures are traditionally interpreted as the evangelists ("plena oculis ante et retro" (full of eyes before and behind), Apc 4:6).

22.9   *coronas admittentibus:* So Apc 4:10: "Mittebant coronas suas ante thronum" ([The elders] cast their crowns before the throne).

22.11   *tribus vicibus:* "In triple interchange" (i.e., of angels, beasts, elders).

23. The impious condemned, the faithful rewarded

23.1–2   *Zelus ignis . . . consumet adversarios:* So Hbr 10:27: "Ignis aemulatio quae consumptura est adversarios" (The rage of a fire which shall consume the adversaries).

23.3–4   *nolentes Christum . . . venisse:* So Hbr 10:29.

23.9   *pro meritis,* etc.: Earlier Fathers interpreted the yields (thirtyfold, sixtyfold, a hundredfold in the parable of the sower, Mt 13:3–23) as depicting the scale of rewards in heaven for different kinds of saintly lives. Thus Jerome (*In Matt.* 13:23; *Contra Iov.* 1.3) allotted the hundredfold, sixtyfold, and thirtyfold to consecrated virgins, chaste widows, and married women, respectively. Augustine challenges this view in *De sancta virgini-tate* 46.

See further Atkinson, 1.66–83, 2.150–69; Clancy–Markus, 39–60; Stevenson.

THE VENERABLE BEDE

65. Laetare, caelum, desuper

This hymn, entitled *De resurrectione Domini,* is a representative example of the thirteen surviving compositions in the *Liber Hymnorum* of the Venerable Bede, though most of the others are considerably longer. All are devoted to leading feast days in the Church's calendar. Bede evokes passages of scripture and earlier hymns that had become familiar in his day.

1.1–2 *Laetare,* etc.: The exordium evokes Ps 95:11: "Laetentur caeli, et exultet terra; commoveatur mare" (Let the heavens be glad, and let the earth be glad; let the sea be moved [i.e., roused]).

2.1–2 *Iam tempus,* etc.: So 2 Cor 6:2: "Ecce: nunc est tempus acceptabile; ecce: nunc est dies salutis" (Behold: now is the acceptable time; behold: now is the day of salvation). Paul evokes Is 49:8: "In tempore placito . . . in die salutis."

2.3–4 *agni sanguine refulsit:* A bold image, analogous to Apc 7:14: "They have washed their robes and have made them white in the blood of the Lamb *(dealbaverunt eas in sanguine Agni)."*

3.2 *ligni prioris,* etc.: For the motif, compare hymn 20.2–3.

5.1 *Miretur omne saeculum:* A line borrowed from Ambrose; see hymn 5.2.3.

5.2 *mysticae:* For the double sense of "sacramental" and "of hidden power," see hymns 5.3.2, 7.2.1.

5.3 *haec signa:* Pointing forward to stanzas 6–8.

6.1–4 *Sol,* etc.: So Lk 23:44: "Now it was almost the sixth hour, and there was darkness over all the earth."

7.3–4 *errare noctem passus est:* Compare Mt 27:45: "From the sixth hour there was darkness over the whole earth."

8.1–4 *Finduntur,* etc.: So Mt 27:51–52: "Rocks were cleft, and tombs were opened, and many of the saints who had slept arose."

8.2   *saxa:* I read *saxa* for *ante,* which I cannot translate.

9.1   *Tartarus:* We have noted earlier (hymns 16.18.2n., 21.6.4n.) how Christian writers adopt this secular title for hell.

9.2   *ad se trahentis omnia:* Compare John 12:32: "Omnia traham ad me ipsum" (I . . . will draw all things to myself).

9.4   *animas sanctas:* See the citation at 8.1–4n. above.

11.4   *tantis renatis fratribus: Tantis* is often found in the sense of *tot* in Late and Medieval Latin. The reference is to the holy ones delivered from hell.

See further Fraipont, 417–18.

<h2 style="text-align:center">ANONYMOUS</h2>

<h3 style="text-align:center">66. Agnoscat omne saeculum</h3>

This hymn in celebration of the Nativity does not appear in the Old or New Hymnal. Walpole, echoing the views of earlier scholars, argues strongly in favor of Venantius Fortunatus as author, and both content and style certainly favor the ascription. He further argues that the same author composed hymn 62 above. But neither appears in the collected works of Fortunatus, so we must be content to regard these attributions as an attractive possibility. In the revised Breviary, stanzas 1–3 and 7, supplemented with an appended doxology, are appointed for Second Vespers on the feast of the Annunciation, a less appropriate occasion than the traditional feast of Christmas.

1.1   *Agnoscat omne saeculum:* The line is adapted from a line in Ambrose's Christmas hymn; see hymn 5.2.3 above.

1.2   *vitae praemium:* Christ is himself our life, bestowed as reward by the Father through the redemptive suffering of the Son.

2.1   *Esaias quae praecinit:* See Is 7:14: "Behold: a virgin shall conceive and bear a child."

2.3   *annuntiavit angelus:* See Lk 1:35.

3.2   *verbi fidelis semine:* "The faithful word" of Gabriel in his address to Mary is visualized as bearing the seed with which she is impregnated.

4.1   *Radix . . . Iesse floruit:* Jesse was the father of David; his residence

465

was at Bethlehem. Isaiah (11:1) prophesied that "a shoot shall come forth from the stock of Jesse, and a branch shall grow out of his roots" (Egredietur virga de radice Iesse, et flos de radice eius ascendet). Christian interpreters signaled this as a reference to the coming of the Messiah.

4.2–4   *virga . . . virgo:* The play on words indicates that the virgin Mary is the fruitful rod or branch which grew out of the root.

5.1   *Praesepe . . . pertulit:* An echo of Sedulius (see hymn 19.6.1–2). The contrast between the grandeur of the Creator and the humility of the Child is a favorite theme of Fortunatus.

6.4   *sub legis . . . vinculo:* The law, that is, of the human condition, not the Old Law as at Gal 4:4.

7.1–2   *Adam vetus . . . Adam novus:* For the contrast between the old Adam and the new Adam, see hymn 20.2. The scriptural basis is at Rom 5:14, 1 Cor 15:45.

See further Walpole, 193–98.

67. *Lucis largitor splendide*

"This beautiful and evidently ancient hymn" (so Walpole) does not appear in either the Old or the New Hymnal. It was composed by one of the many imitators of Ambrose, echoing many of his memorable phrases, and evoking especially hymn 2 above. In the revised Breviary, the first four stanzas with appended doxology are the hymn for Lauds in Week 2.

1.1   *Lucis largitor,* etc.: The extended exordium in stanzas 1–3 echoes a favorite theme of Ambrose; see especially hymns 1, 2, and 4 above.

2.2–4   *non is . . . lumine:* Here the light-bringer must be the morning star rather than the sun, as line 4 indicates.

3.2   *lux ipse totus et dies:* A borrowing from hymn 25.1.2.

4.1–2   *rerum conditor,* etc.: These two lines exploit the opening stanzas of hymns 1 and 2 above.

5.1–2   *plena Spiritu . . . Deum gestantia:* See 1 Cor 6:19: "Or know you not that your members [i.e., body] are the temple of the Holy Ghost, who is in you, whom you have from God?"

7.3–4   *sanctumque ... Spiritus:* See the previous note, and compare 1 Cor
         3:16.
See further Walpole, 223–26.

68. *Rerum Deus fons omnium*

This short hymn is devoted to the Creation theme, but not specifically to
any of the seven days described in Genesis. God's incessant activity in
keeping in being the wonders of Creation is to be the spur to us to be similarly active in pursuit of the virtues, and thus to win our reward at the
Judgment. Walpole tentatively suggests a Spanish origin on the basis of its
Mozarabic transmission and its scansion of *egris (aegris)*.

2.1–2   *Non ... fessus ... non saucius:* Though God shows no weariness or
         exhaustion in his labors, he is aware of our need for rest to en-
         sure that we do not succumb to physical infirmity. Clearly, then,
         this hymn was appropriately allotted to an evening hour.
4.3   *in vicem:* That is, the joy will compensate for the earlier fear.
See further Walpole, 291–93.

69. *Nunc, sancte nobis Spiritus*

The resemblance to hymns 36 and 37, at least in length and presentation,
prompted Walpole to suggest that all three are the work of the same author. But his claim that he is Ambrose has gained little support. In the revised Breviary this hymn is allotted to Terce in Advent, with an appended
doxology which seems superfluous in view of the content of the first
stanza.

1.1   *Nunc:* The hymn was composed for Terce because it was at the
         third hour that the Holy Spirit descended at Pentecost; see Act
         2:15.
2.1   *Os lingua,* etc.: The catalog is perhaps inspired by Lk 10:27: "Dili-
         ges Dominum Deum tuum ex toto corde tuo et ex tota anima
         tua et ex omnibus viribus tuis et ex omni mente tua" (Thou shalt
         love the Lord thy God with thy whole heart and with thy whole
         soul and with all thy strength and with all thy mind).

467

2.3   *flammescat igne caritas:* For *caritas* as a gift of the Spirit, see Rom 5:5: "The charity [love] of God *(caritas Dei)* is poured in our hearts by the holy Spirit who is given to us." It must blaze forth with the fire which descended at Pentecost.

2.4   *accendat ardor proximos:* As happened at Pentecost, when Peter's message attracted about three thousand to be baptized (Act 2:41).

See further Walpole, 108–10.

70. *Qua Christus hora sitiit*

The revised Breviary continues the traditional practice of allotting this hymn to Sext in Lent. The first stanza prescribes the hour at which it is to be sung.

1.1   *Qua Christus hora sitiit:* With reference not to Christ's thirst on the cross, but to his resting by Jacob's well; compare John 4:6–7: "It was about the sixth hour *(hora quasi sexta)*. There cometh a woman of Samaria to draw water. Jesus saith to her, 'Give me to drink.'"

1.2   *crucem vel in qua subiit:* So John 19:14–16: "It was . . . about the sixth hour . . . Then [Pilate] delivered him to them to be crucified."

1.4   *siti iustitiae:* Compare Mt 5:6: "Beati qui esuriunt et sitiunt iustitiam . . ." (Blessed are they that hunger and thirst after justice . . .).

2.1   *et esuries:* Continuing with the evocation of the Beatitude just cited, but here connoting hunger for Christ in the Eucharist. As he is the sun of righteousness, after receiving him we can avoid sin and seek virtue.

3.1   *Charisma sancti Spiritus:* The word *charisma* is normally applied to the special gifts bestowed on individuals in the Church (see 1 Cor 12:7–31); but it can also be used more generally to mean "grace."

See further Walpole, 332–33.

71. *Iam Christe, sol iustitiae*

Though this hymn does not appear in the Old or the New Hymnal, it has long enjoyed an honored place in the Lenten Office. In the revised Breviary it is appointed for Lenten weekdays at Lauds (with minor changes in the text).

1.1   *sol iustitiae:* See the prophecy of Malachi, interpreted as anticipating Christ's resurrection: "For you who revere my name the Sun of righteousness *(Sol iustitiae)* shall rise" (4:2).

2.1   *Das tempus acceptabile:* So 2 Cor 6:2: "Now is the acceptable time *(tempus acceptabile)* . . ." Here Lent is visualized as the acceptable time for repentance.

2.3   *convertat ut benignitas:* Compare Rom 2:4: "Knowest thou not that the benignity *(benignitas)* of God leadeth thee to penance?"

4.1   *Dies venit:* The day is Easter Sunday, the time when the blossoming in nature is in harmony with the spiritual blossoming inspired by the Resurrection.

4.3   *laetemur in hac:* Compare Ps 117:24, evoked throughout the stanza: "Haec est dies quam fecit Dominus; exultemus et laetemur in ea" (This is the day which the Lord hath made; let us be glad and rejoice therein).

5.1–2   *Tè . . . Trinitas:* The doxology is part of the original hymn.

5.4   *novum canamus canticum:* Compare Apc 14:3: "Et cantabant quasi canticum novum ante sedem" (They sang as it were a new canticle before the throne).

See further Walpole, 326–28.

72. *Tu, Trinitatis unitas*

This hymn has been attributed variously to Ambrose and Gregory, but on no firm evidence. The final stanza may not belong to the original hymn; it is addressed to Christ alone, in contrast to the exordium, which is a prayer to the Trinity. The hymn was originally composed for singing at Nocturns (see 2.1–2); in the revised Breviary it is allotted to the Office of Readings on Fridays in Week 1.

2.3 *vulnerum:* For sins as "wounds," a frequent motif in these hymns, see, e.g., 22.2, 60.4.4.

3.1 *fraude . . . daemonum:* Compare hymns 1.3.3, 40.2.2.

4.1–4 *Ne corpus,* etc.: This stanza is omitted in the revised Breviary, presumably because the first line is considered distasteful.

5.1 *Redemptor:* See the preliminary note to this hymn.

See further Walpole, 272–73.

73. *A patre unigenitus*

This exceptionally ingenious alphabetic hymn incorporating frequent rhyme is probably of Carolingian date. It has no specific point of reference such as would attach it to a particular feast, so that in the past it has been allotted variously to Christmas and to the Epiphany, and today in the revised Breviary it is sung at First Vespers on the feast of the Baptism of the Lord. For the reason for allocating it there, see the next note.

1.3 *baptisma cruce consecrans:* The revised Breviary prefers the Mozarabic version of the hymn, which has *baptismi rore consecrans* ("consecrating us with the water of baptism"). But the notion that the Cross consecrates our baptism is a traditional theme. See Ambrose, *De mysteriis* 20: "What is water without Christ's cross?" Similarly Fortunatus in hymn 20.7.3–4 above.

2.2 *excepit formam hominis:* So Phlp 2:7: "Semet ipsum exinanivit, formam servi accipiens, in similitudinem hominum factus . . ." ([He] emptied himself, taking the form of a servant [i.e., slave], being made in the likeness of men . . .).

2.3 *facturam:* For the notion of the redemption of "creation," see Sedulius in hymn 19.2.2–4 above: "He took the body of a slave, so that by liberating flesh with flesh he might preserve the world which he had founded."

3.4 *fidelibus:* I take this as anticipatory, "so that they became faithful." The Mozarabic text preferred in the revised Breviary reads *deificum,* an awkward second adjective after *klarum.*

4.1 *Mane nobiscum:* Echoing Lk 24:29: "Stay with us *(mane nobiscum),* because it is towards evening." This and the following line, "Dispel the darkness of our night," makes the hymn appropriate for Vespers.

5.3 *sceptrum . . . inclitum:* As Walpole explains, the "glorious scepter" s the new Israel, the Church; compare Jer 51:19: "Israel, the scepter of his inheritance *(sceptrum hereditatis eius)*." Lam 2:1 appends to Israel the epithet *inclitam.* (Walpole explains the apparently irregular meter of this line by supposing a pronunciation *isceptrum,* or that *tu* has dropped out before *tuum.*)

5.4 *tuo . . . clipeo:* Compare Prov 30:5: "God is a shield *(clypeus)* for those who have taken refuge in him."

6.2 *Xriste:* Compare 64.21.1, where the word is spelled *Xriste* to maintain the alphabetic sequence.

6.4 *zelum:* In the hymn of Sedulius (19 above), the final stanza of the alphabetic hymn similarly begins *Zelum draconis invidi;* envy personified is a title of Satan. Compare also 64.23.1: "Zelus ignis furibundus," where *zelus* is rather the righteous ardor of the judgment day.

See further Walpole, 309–11.

THEODULF OF ORLÉANS

74. *Gloria, laus, et honor*

For Theodulf in his Carolingian background, see the Introduction, p. xiv. The hymn in elegiacs printed here is actually the first section of a long poem of seventy-eight lines penned to celebrate Palm Sunday at Angers, where Theodulf had been imprisoned in 818. He was a prolific versifier; the poem is one of seventy-nine assembled and edited in *MGH Poetae Latini Aevi Carolini* (ed. Dümmler). Sirmond, in his edition of 1646, heads the poem "Verses to be sung by children on Palm Sunday." The lines which follow this extract are concerned with the procession and the contingents taking part in it and are accordingly less relevant to this collection. Today the first twelve lines form the hymn for the Processional on Palm Sunday; of the many translations (see Julian, *A Dictionary of Hymnology,* 426), the most celebrated is "All glory, praise and honour."

1–10   *Gloria,* etc.: The exordium evokes Ps 23:7–10. The poet may imagine the crowd in procession hymning the psalm. "Who is the king of glory? The Lord of hosts. He is the king of glory" (23:10).

2   *puerile decus prompsit hosanna pium:* Theodulf describes the earlier participation of the children in the singing at Angers.

3–4   *Davidis . . . venis:* Evoking Mt 21:9, the reaction of the crowd on Jesus's entry into Jerusalem: "Osanna Filio David! Benedictus qui venit in nomine Domini!" (Hosanna to the Son of David! Blessed is he that cometh in the name of the Lord!). This is an echo of Ps 117:26: "Benedictus qui venit in nomine Domini." Lk 19:38 is also in Theodulf's mind: Luke's version is "Blessed is the king *(rex)* who comes . . ."

16   *tĕtris:* Indifference to quantity allows Theodulf to shorten the *e;* in classical Latin the adjective is *taeter* or *tēter.*

19   *arte:* In classical Latin the *bonae artes* are the virtues which govern men's conduct; the sense of *ars* here is similar.

21–2   *Sis pius ascensor . . . urbs veneranda Dei:* Christ's instruction to his disciples to bring to him a colt (so Luke; in Matthew an ass and her colt) on which to ride into Jerusalem is happily transposed; Christians are to become the colt so that they may accompany Christ into the heavenly Jerusalem, the city of God.

See further Raby, *CLP* 171–77.

[HRABANUS MAURUS]

75. *Veni, creator Spiritus*

This famous hymn has often (but dubiously) been assigned to Hrabanus Maurus, the distinguished pupil of Alcuin at Tours, and as abbot of Fulda the teacher of Walahfrid Strabo and Lupus of Ferrières. The author composed the hymn in part to affirm the orthodoxy of the *filioque* clause in the Creed. It was initially sung at Vespers on Whit Sunday; in the revised Breviary it is appointed every day for Vespers between the Ascension and Pentecost Sunday and is sung regularly when the sacrament of Confirmation is conferred.

1.1   *creator Spiritus:* Drawing on biblical texts such as Ps 103:30, "Thou shalt send forth thy Spirit, and they [sc. earthly creatures] shall be created," the Fathers, and notably Ambrose (see *De Spiritu sancto* with Homes Dudden, *Life and Times of St. Ambrose,* 578–83) lay great stress on the Spirit as creative force.

2.1   *Paraclitus:* The Greek word means "Advocate," but as John 14:16, 16:7, where it is applied to the Holy Spirit. The Fathers from Origen onward interpret it as "Consoler" or "Comforter."

2.2   *donum Dei:* At Act 8:20, Peter rebukes Simon for his offer of money for the power of laying on hands; he describes the Spirit as *donum Dei.*

2.3   *fons vivus, ignis, caritas:* For the Spirit as living water, see John 7:38–39; as fire at Pentecost, Act 2:3; as love, Rom 5:5.

2.4   *spiritalis unctio:* See 1 John 2:20: "You have the unction [i.e., have been anointed, *unctionem habetis*] by the Holy One."

3.1   *septiformis munere:* The seven gifts of the Spirit are listed at Is 11:2: wisdom, understanding, counsel, fortitude, knowledge, piety, fear of the Lord. Compare hymn 94.2.2n.

3.2   *dextrae Dei tu digitus:* Compare Lk 11:20: "I by the finger of God cast out devils." See also Mt 12:28, where Christ claims to cast out demons by the Spirit of God. The Fathers reconcile the two passages by identifying the Spirit as the finger of God.

3.3–4   *tu rite . . . sermone ditas guttura:* With particular reference to the miracle at Pentecost (Act 2:4: "All . . . began to speak in other languages, as the Spirit empowered them"), which Peter explains by the prophecy of Joel (Act 2:16, Joel 2:28–29).

3.4   Walpole prints *ditans.* See *Note to the Text.*

4.3–4   *infirma . . . perpeti:* The couplet is borrowed from Ambrose; see hymn 5.7.3–4 above.

5.2   *protinus:* For the sense of "continually," see *OLD:* "Straight on (in continuance of a process) . . ."

6.3   *te utriusque Spiritum:* Here the author lays emphasis on the *filioque* doctrine, that the Spirit proceeds from both Father and Son. This was not part of fourth-century creeds, but under the influ-

ence of the western Fathers, especially Augustine's *De Trinitate,*
it was incorporated following the Third Council of Toledo
(589).

See further Walpole, 373–76; Lausberg.

WIPO

76. *Victimae paschali laudes*

Wipo, Swabian poet and historian, was chaplain to the emperors Conrad
II and Henry III in the first half of the eleventh century. This hymn, reflecting the role of the Sequence in transition before it attains its more
regular form a century later, is one of the most celebrated hymns of the
early Middle Ages. The dialogue form made it apposite for the stage, and
it became prominent in dramatic enactments of the visit of the disciples
to the empty tomb. In the modern Roman liturgy, it is sung as the Sequence to the Mass on Easter Sunday during the day, with the omission of
the sixth stanza out of respect for Jewish sensibilities.

1.1   *Victimae paschali:* Compare 1 Cor 5:7: "Pascha nostrum immola-
       tus est Christus" (Christ, our Pasch, is [i.e., has been] sacrificed).

1.1–2 *laudes immolent:* So Hbr 13:15: "By him [viz. Jesus] therefore let us
       offer the sacrifice of praise *(hostiam laudis)* always to God."

2.1   *Agnus redemit oves:* Evoking the *Crux benedicta nitet* of Fortunatus
       (hymn 22.3–4 above): "On which [viz. the Cross] the sacred
       Lamb in his devoted love became a victim for us, and rescued
       his sheep from the mouth of the wolf."

2.2–4 *Christus . . . peccatores:* See Rom 5:10: "If when we were enemies
       we were reconciled *(reconciliati sumus)* to God by the death of
       his Son."

3.1–2 *Mors et vita duello . . . mirando:* See 1 Cor 15:54: "Absorta est mors
       in victoria" (Death has been swallowed up in victory).

4.1–4 *Maria . . . resurgentis:* This stanza and the next, recounting Mary
       Magdalene's visit to the empty tomb, are inspired by Lk 24:2–10,
       Mt 28:1–8, John 20:11–18.

5.1   *Angelicos testes:* In Luke and John there are two angels, in Mat-
       thew and Mark only one.

5.2   *sudarium et vestes:* See John 20:7, where Peter (not Mary) sees the cloth "that had been about [Jesus's] head," and "the linen cloths."

5.4   *praecedet suos in Galilaea:* So Mt 28:7, Mk 16:7 ("praecedit vos in Galilaeam").

6.3   *turbae fallaci:* In Mt 28:12–15, Jewish elders bribed the guards of the tomb to state that the disciples had spirited the body away, "and the story is still told among the Jews."

See further Raby, *CLP* 217–19; Young, 1.273–75.

Aimar of Le Puy

77. *Salve, regina*

This antiphon, one of the four anthems of Our Lady sung at the close of Compline, is persuasively attributed to Aimar, bishop of Le Puy (1087–98). Initially it was sung on the four great feasts of the Blessed Virgin. Since 1568 it has been sung at Compline. The English translation, *Hail, holy queen,* customarily concludes the public recital of the Rosary.

2.1   *exsules filii Evae:* For the traditional view that Mary is the second Eve who restores what was lost in Eden, see hymn 63.2. We are pictured here as Eve's descendants, exiled from God's favor in this vale of tears.

3.1   *advocata nostra:* As at hymn 63.4, Mary is the intercessor for us with her son.

4.1–2   *benedictum fructum ventris tui:* So Elizabeth's greeting (Lk 1:42): "Benedictus fructus ventris tui" (Blessed is the fruit of your womb).

See further Raby, *CLP* 226–27; *ODCC* (3rd ed.), s.v. "Salve Regina," with further bibliography.

Peter Abelard

78. *O quanta qualia sunt illa sabbata*

Of the three books of Peter Abelard's *Hymnarius Paraclitensis* (see the Introduction, pp. xvi–xvii), the first is devoted to "Hymns for Night" and

"Hymns for Day." Under "Day Hymns" Peter wrote eight for Sundays and two for each of the other six days, to be sung at Lauds and Vespers. This, perhaps the most famous of all Peter's hymns, was composed for Vespers on Saturdays. As a hymn for the Sabbath, it celebrates the glory of the eternal Sabbath that mortals hope to enjoy in heaven.

1.1   *illa sabbata:* Strictly "those sabbaths"; what we on earth divide into separate days will in heaven be subsumed into one eternal day of rest.

1.3   *fessis . . . fortibus:* Joys will be shared by weary and vigorous alike.

1.4   *omnia Deus in omnibus:* So 1 Cor 15:28: ". . . ut sit Deus omnia in omnibus" (so that God may be all in all); compare Eph 1:23 ("omnia in omnibus adimpletur"), Col 3:11 ("omnia et in omnibus Christus").

2.1   *Vere Ierusalem:* For heaven as the true Jerusalem, see Apc 21:2: "Civitatem sanctam, Hierusalem novam, vidi descendentem de caelo" (I saw the holy city, the new Jerusalem, coming down out of heaven).

2.2   *cuius pax iugis est:* The meaning of Jerusalem, "Vision of Peace," is the central focus of Augustine's *City of God,* and thereafter is prominent in many hymns, beginning with the pre-Carolingian *Urbs beata Ierusalem* (Walpole's hymn 119).

4.3   *ad Ierusalem ab Babylonia:* The name of Babylon "the great, the mother of the fornications and the abominations of the earth" (Apc 17:5), was popularly rendered as "Confusion" (Augustine, *C.D.* 16.4), and was the symbol of the unregenerate world, as Jerusalem denoted the city of God. Our journey from earth to heaven is depicted as the liberation of the new Israel from its Babylonian captivity of sin, as the Israelites of old were delivered from bondage at Babylon (see 1 Ezr, book 6).

5.2   *cantica Sion:* Zion was the citadel of Jerusalem, and the name is frequently cited to denote the city itself (see, e.g., Is 1:27), and thereafter the heavenly city. See Hbr 12:22: "You are come to Mount Zion and to the city of the living God, the heavenly Jerusalem." For the songs of Zion, see Apc 14:1–3.

6.2   *sabbatizantium:* "Those celebrating the Sabbath." For the pres-

ence of this verb in the Vulgate, see Lv 25:2: "Sabbatizes sabbatum Domino" (Observe the rest of the sabbath for the Lord).

7.1–4   *Perenni Domino . . . Spiritus:* This doxology is appended by Peter
to all the hymns sung in the day.

See further Szövérffy, 76–78.

79. *Verbo Verbum*

The second book of the *Hymnarius Paraclitensis* is devoted to hymns for
feast days. Peter Abelard composed four for the celebration of the Nativity; this hymn was to be sung at First Nocturn. The emphasis throughout
is on the role of the Virgin; the impoverished circumstances of the birth
are contrasted with her noble ancestry and with the miraculous ease of the
virgin birth.

1.1–6   *Verbo Verbum virgo . . . verus . . . vera:* Note the alliterative conceit;
compare 3.2, 4.1–2nn.

1.1–2   *Verbo Verbum virgo concipiens:* Mary conceived the Word *(Verbum),* the son of God (John 1:1) by the word *(verbo)* of Gabriel
(Lk 1:31).

1.3–4   *verus . . . Oriens:* The prophecy of Zechariah in the gospel of Luke
(1:78–79) is evoked here: "Though the bowels of the mercy of
our God, in which the Orient [i.e., dawn, *oriens*] from on high
hath visited us, to enlighten them that sit in darkness."

2.1–2   *Felix dies, dierum gloria:* There is an echo of these lines in a
Sequence composed by Peter's contemporary Adam of Saint
Victor *(Salve dies, dierum gloria).*

2.7–8   *felix stella . . . solem:* For Mary as *stella,* see hymn 63 above; for
Christ as the true Sun, hymn 2.2, etc.

3.2   *puerpera:* A favorite word in hymns of praise of Mary's birth
pangs; see, for example, hymn 19.5. (Note the attractively alliterative *pauper puerpera.*)

3.6   *celsa genere:* That is, through her husband Joseph, whose descent
from priests and kings is detailed in the genealogy with which
Matthew's gospel begins. In the alternative tradition of the *Pro-
tevangelium of James* (10.1), her lineage is Davidic.

4.1–2   *Vitae viam in via:* Compare the strong alliteration with *v* in these
         lines with the opening words of the hymn. For Jesus as the way
         to life, see John 14:6. Mary bore him *in via* when en route to
         Bethlehem to be enrolled (Lk 2:6).

5.1–3   *Obstetrices ... deerant, sed angeli ... aderant:* Peter here draws upon
         a hymn composed by Notker Balbulus (842–912), the pioneer in
         regularizing the Sequence in the liturgy. In his sequence *Natus
         ante saecula dei filius* in his *Liber Hymnorum* (see Steinen, *Notker
         der Dichter*), Notker writes: "Gaude, dei genitrix, quam circum-
         stant obstetricum vice concinentes angeli gloriam Deo" (Re-
         joice, mother of God, for in place of midwives angels surround
         you singing the glory of God [Steinen, p. 12 = *PL* 131.1006]). The
         inspiration for the choir of angels is Lk 2:13–14.

6.4–7   *non erat macula ... Non est dolor ... nec scissura:* In his hymns and in
         his sermons Peter preaches that the Virgin Birth was miracu-
         lously free of the rupture of the hymen and the attendant pain.
         The notion goes back to Ambrose, *Inst. Virg.* 8 [52–57], which
         draws on earlier Greek tradition (see Clement of Alexandria,
         Stromata 7.16 [= 7.93.7]).

7.1–8   *In excelsis,* etc.: This doxology, a distillation of Lk 2:14 ("Gloria in
         altissimis Deo, et in terra pax hominibus bonae voluntatis"), is
         repeated in the other Christmas hymns.

See further Szövérffy, 81–84.

80. *Dei patris*

In this second Christmas hymn, composed to be sung at Second Nocturn,
Peter Abelard turns from Mary to the Child. The main motif throughout
is the contrast between the lowly station in which Christ chose to be born
and the majesty of his dominion over heaven and earth, a favorite theme
of Fortunatus earlier.

1.2   *unicus:* Christ is not only God's only-begotten son, but also
         Mary's only divine child.

1.5–8   *angustias ... continet:* Throughout the hymn the contrast is maintained between the humility of the son of God and his grandeur as creator. The rhymes (here *sustinet/continet*) accentuate the contrast.

2.2–4   *tugurio . . . palatio:* An effective continuation of the theme.

3.7   *super istis:* "In the matter of these things."

4.1–2   *In praesepi vagit:* Fortunatus (see hymn 20.5) is the inspiration here: "Vagit infans inter arta / conditus praesepia."

5.2–4   *pabulo . . . refectio:* The sustained contrast here continues with the fodder on which Jesus lies against his identity as the refreshment of angels, which is a reference to the Eucharist *(panis angelicus).*

5.6   *grex animalium:* He continues the contrast, with the cattle on one side and the angels on the other. It is notable that he does not refer to the ox and the ass (which do not appear in the scriptures and are first found in Pseudo-Matthew), but to "the herd of animals."

6.1–8   *In excelsis . . . hodie:* See the note on this doxology in the preceding hymn.

See further Szövérffy, 85–86.

81. *Quam beatum stratum*

In this third Christmas hymn, appointed to be sung at Third Nocturn, Peter Abelard turns the focus back on Mary, as in the first hymn. Here he lays emphasis on the uniqueness of the Virgin Birth, and on the miracle by which she delivered the divine Child without pain and fed him with her milk.

1.7–8   *cuius palmo caelum concluditur: Palma* is the more regular form for the palm of the hand, but *palmus* more specifically denotes the width of the palm as a unit of measurement, as is apt in this context. For the motif compare hymn 62.4 above.

2.2   *reginae ceterae:* Mary is frequently invoked as queen at this date. See hymn 77; other antiphons sung at this date are *Ave, regina caelorum* and *Regina caeli.*

2.8   *doloris nescius:* See hymn 79.6 and note.

3.4   *nutricum ubera:* Peter here introduces a contemporary note. As Power, *Medieval Women,* 46, remarks: "New-born children in upper classes were commonly handed over to wet nurses."

3.7–8   *clauso . . . utero:* The emphasis on the virginity of Mary in childbirth is frequent in hymns from Ambrose onward. See hymn 5.4: "Claustrum pudoris permanet"; Sedulius, hymn 19.3; etc.

5.2–4   *fortassis esurit, quae . . . reficit:* Peter may here have remodeled an idea in Sedulius, hymn 19.6 above: "He who lets no bird go hungry / With but a little milk was fed." In that hymn the Child goes hungry whilst ensuring that the meanest bird is well nourished; here the Child has his fill while his mother feels the pangs of hunger.

5.5–6   *Stupent caeli, mirantur angeli:* Ambrose has earlier exploited this motif in a different context (hymn 9.4 above).

See further Szövérffy, 87–89.

82. *Gaude, virgo*

Peter Abelard's final hymn for Christmas is appointed for Lauds. It offers striking testimony to the cult of the Virgin, for here too the spotlight is on Mary, so that in three of the four Nativity hymns she takes center stage. Here the emphasis is upon the prophetic proclamations in the Old Testament of her coming, and on her role as advocate for sinning mortals.

1.1–7   *Gaude . . . quae . . . meruisti:* The *gaude* motif becomes popular in such invocations to the Virgin, as in the Easter antiphon *Regina caeli, laetare.* Here the joy which she has deserved to bestow is the Christ-child himself.

2.1–8   *Patriarchis . . . oracula:* The "mysteries of the Law" and "the oracles of prophets" include such passages as Ct 4:12–16 ("A garden enclosed, a fountain sealed up . . . the well of living waters"), Ex 3:2 (the burning bush), Nm 17:8 (Aaron's rod), Jdg 6 (Gideon's fleece), Is 11:1 (the rod of Jesse), Ez 44:2 (the closed door). See Raby, *CLP* 368–75.

3.4–7   *suspirant . . . spes nostra . . . advocata:* These expressions echo those in the antiphon *Salve, regina* (hymn 77 above).

4.1–8   *Ad iudicis,* etc.: The entire stanza develops the theme of *advocata* ([legal] advocate) introduced at the close of the previous stanza.

5.5–6   *ut salventur servi:* Perhaps recalling John 15:15: "I will not now call you servants *(servos)* . . ." The slavery alluded to here is slavery to sin.

See further Szöverffy, 89–91.

83. *Christiani, plaudite*

Following the Christmas hymns, Peter Abelard next composed four for the Epiphany, four for Candlemas, ten for Good Friday, and six for Holy Saturday. Then, by appending four for Easter Day, he achieved a numerical balance between the ten for Good Friday and the ten for Holy Saturday and Easter Sunday. This, the first of the four Easter Sunday hymns, celebrates the harrowing of hell, and was sung at First Nocturn.

1.2   *resurrexit Dominus:* The refrain, inserted as the second line in each stanza of all four Easter Sunday hymns, accentuates the joy inspired by the Resurrection. It is claimed for Peter, perhaps wrongly, that by this innovation he paved the way for the rondeau in the secular lyrics in Medieval Latin.

1.3   *mortis principe:* Satan is accorded this title frequently in the Fathers. See, for example, Gregory, *Moralia* 19.4; Cassiodorus, *Exp. in Ps.* 8.10.

1.5   *Victori occurrite:* Following the example of the apostle Peter, who ran to the empty tomb: so Lk 24:12.

2.1   *zabulo:* = *diabolo.*

2.3   *spoliato barathro: Barathrum* ("pit") is used for Hades by classical writers (for example, Virgil, *Aen.* 8.245) and thereafter by Prudentius and later hymn writers.

2.4   *suos eruit:* See hymn 19.22.2–3 and note.

2.5–6   *Stipatus . . . rediit:* There is no scriptural account of the return of Christ from the realm of the dead. An escort of angels would be more appropriate for Christ's return to heaven. But this is not an Ascension Day hymn.

3.1   *Fraus in hamo fallitur:* Deceit personified is an image of Satan. The notion that he feeds on human flesh and is impaled on the hook which lies within (the symbol for the redeeming power of Christ) goes back to Ambrose. See hymn 9.7 above: "That Death should swallow its own hook," where Death is likewise an image of Satan impaled on Christ's hook.

4.1   *Captivatis inferis:* The *inferi* here must be the wicked angels (and not the souls of the just whom Christ has delivered), for they are taken captive; moreover, they are contrasted with the angels in heaven *(superis)* who are enriched with the accession of souls rescued from hell.

5.4   *Christo Domini: Domini,* not *Domino,* must be read to effect the rhyme with *Spiritui.*

See further Szövérffy, 127–28.

84. *Da Mariae tympanum*

For this second Easter Day hymn, which was to be sung at Second Nocturn, Peter Abelard embarks on a strikingly original theme, a comparison between the prophetess Maria (Miriam, sister of Aaron) in the Old Testament and the Maria who is Mary Magdalene in the New. The first Mary celebrates the liberation of the Jews from the yoke of the Egyptians after the crossing of the Red Sea; the second Mary celebrates the liberation of mortals from the grip of Satan following the Redemption.

1.1–4   *Da Mariae tympanum:* See Ex 15:20–21: "Then [sc. after the crossing of the Red Sea] the prophetess Miriam, Aaron's sister, took a tambourine in her hand; and all the women went out after her with tambourines and with dancing, and Miriam sang to them."

1.5–6   *Holocausta . . . Iacob immolet:* The patriarch who had gained the name Israel (Gen 32) signifies here the new Israel, which is the Church. See Augustine, *Enarr. in Ps.* 19:2, and at greater length Cassiodorus, *Exp. in Ps.* 19:2, 84:2. For a holocaust of song as opposed that of regular animal sacrifice, see Ps 50:17–18: "My mouth shall announce your praise . . . In holocausts you will not take delight."

2.1–6   *Subvertens . . . pelagus:* See Ex 14:26–28: "The waters . . . covered
. . . all the army of Pharaoh." In this stanza, the refrain *resurrexit
Dominus* is actually the main clause, rather than being syntacti-
cally independent or exclamatory, as it is in most other stanzas
of these hymns. Compare 86.3.2.

3.1   *Dicat tympanistria:* The timbrel player is Mary Magdalene. She
does not in fact sing, but as Peter states in *Sermon* 13 (*PL* 178.485),
"The one Mary (i.e., Miriam) took up an actual timbrel, the
other held a timbrel of the spirit."

3.5–6   *resurgentem merita prima cernere:* So John 20:14: "When she had
said this, . . . she saw Jesus standing there"; compare Mk 16:9:
"Surgens . . . apparuit primo Mariae Magdalenae" (He rising . . .
appeared first to Mary Magdalene). In Matthew (28:1–9) she is
accompanied by Mary the mother of James when she encoun-
ters Jesus.

4.3–4   *reliquis fidelibus . . . feminis:* In Luke (24:10) a group of women, including Mary Magdalene, sees the empty tomb and reports the
words of the angel to the apostles. This report is "the sweeter
song" that Mary Magdalene sings.

See further Szövérffy, 129–30.

85. *Golias prostratus est*

In this, the third hymn for Easter Day, which was to be sung at Third Nocturn, Peter Abelard introduces a series of Old Testament types, which
prefigure Christ's resurrection and victory over Satan.

1.1   *Golias prostratus est:* The Philistine giant felled by David and then
dispatched with his own sword becomes in Patristic exegesis a
type of Satan, just as the victor David becomes a type of Christ.
Bernard of Clairvaux ironically attached the label "Golias" or
Antichrist to Peter Abelard himself; see Walsh, "Golias and Goliardic Poetry," 1–9.

1.6   *ille Pharao:* See hymn 84.2 above. Peter here identifies the Pharaoh with Satan.

2.1   *Dicant Sion filiae:* Just as the Jewish women of old hymned the
destruction of the Egyptians in the Red Sea (hymn 84.1), so the

daughters of Zion who are the nuns in the convent of the Paraclete (Zion in Patristic exegesis often means the Church) must now acclaim the risen Christ, as the women with Mary Magdalene greeted the empty tomb (Lk 24:3).

3.1–6   *Samson:* He, like David, is a type of Christ. Following the praise of him in scripture (Hbr 11:32), the Fathers make him a figure of faith and hope. When his strong arms topple the pillars of the enemy, this is interpreted as faith overcoming Satan (so Paulinus of Nola, *Ep.* 23:17). For the incident recorded here, see Jdg 16:2–3: when Samson's foes at Gaza ambushed him at the city gate, "He took both the doors of the gate with the posts thereof and the bolt and laying them on his shoulders carried them up to the top of the hill."

3.5   *allophylus:* Literally "foreigner"; here suggests "Philistine."

4.1–6   *Ut leonis catulus:* This stanza happily combines images from scripture and from the *Physiologus,* a famous Alexandrian work on the behavior of animals (English translation by M. Curley, 1979) which was composed probably in the second century CE. At Gen 49:9, Judah is described as *catulus leonis,* and the Fathers depict him as a prefiguration of Christ (see, for example, Cassiodorus, *Exp. in Ps.* 59:9).

4.4   *die tertia:* Christ lay in the tomb for three days and was then awakened by the Father, just as in the *Physiologus* the lion rouses his whelp, which has lain senseless for three days. *Physica* in the final line of the stanza is an abbreviated title for *Physiologus.*

See further Szöverffy, 131–32.

86. *Veris grato tempore*

This final hymn for Easter Day, to be sung at Lauds, is of notable interest because of its similarity to the secular love lyric, as the exordium suggests. The *Carmina Burana* contain love poems which begin with such lines as *Veris leta facies, Veris dulcis in tempore, Vere dulci mediante.* In such secular compositions the renewal in nature is depicted as in harmony with the quickening of human love; in this religious lyric such renewal is conjoined with the Resurrection, by which Christ makes all things new.

2.6   *dant:* The subject is *arbores,* which embraces shrubs as well as trees.

3.2   *resurrexit Dominus:* Hitherto this refrain has been in parenthesis, but here and in the next stanza it becomes the main clause. Here the sense is: "The Lord has risen into never-ending joys." Compare 84.2.2.

4.1   *Qui restauret:* A purpose clause after *resurrexit:* "The Lord has risen to restore all things."

See further Szövérffy, 132–33.

87. *In montibus hic saliens*

Peter Abelard composed four hymns to celebrate the Ascension, as he did for Easter Day. In this, the first of the four, to be sung at First Nocturn, he exploits the Song of Songs and Psalm 44 to depict Christ triumphantly aloft, inviting his bride the Church to join him in the court of heaven.

1.1–2   *In montibus . . . colles transiliens:* Very close to Ct 2:8: "Ecce: iste venit saliens in montibus, transiliens colles" (Behold: he cometh leaping upon the mountains, skipping over the hills).

1.4   *Surge, soror:* So Ct 2:10: "Surge; propera, amica mea, . . . formonsa mea, et veni" (Arise; make haste, my love, . . . my beautiful one, and come). Christ summons the Church triumphant, the city of God in heaven.

2.3–4   *Dilecta, propera; sede,* etc.: Peter fuses Ct 2:10 ("propera") with Ps 109:1: "Sede a dextris meis" (Sit thou at my right hand), echoed at Mt 22:44.

4.3–4   *hic intextas . . . indues:* So Ps 44:10: "The queen stood on your right hand in gilded robes *(in vestitu deaurato)."*

5.1–4   *Sit Christo,* etc.: The same doxology is repeated in the three other hymns for the Ascension.

See further Szövérffy, 133–34.

88. *Quibusdam quasi saltibus*

In this second Ascension hymn, to be sung at Second Nocturn, Peter Abelard details the Son's round journey from heaven to earth and hell and back to heaven, paraphrasing the scriptural accounts of the final stage of the journey.

1.3–4   *ad terrena . . . redit:* This initial stanza is inspired by Ambrose's hymn *Intende, qui regis Israel* (hymn 5.5–6 above).

1.4   *Tartaris:* See hymn 65.9.1n; also 16.18.2, 21.6.4. The plural is used to achieve the rhyme.

2.1–3   *A sinu . . . utero . . . sepulcro:* Christ's pilgrimage is described in a series of confinements. For his initial lodging in the bosom of the Father, see John 1:18; his presence in the Virgin's womb, Mt 1:18; in the tomb, Mt 27:60.

3.2   *nubes excepit:* Peter now turns to Act 1:9: "While they looked on, he was raised up, and a cloud received him *(nubes suscepit eum)* out of their sight."

3.3–4   *erectis manibus benedicens:* Compare Lk 24:50–51: "Elevatis manibus suis benedixit eis. Et factum est dum benediceret illis recessit ab eis et ferebatur in caelum." (Lifting up his hands he blessed them. And it came to pass whilst he blessed them that he departed from them and was carried up to heaven.)

4.3–5.4   *astiterunt in albis angeli . . . in forma iudicis:* Compare Act 1:10–11: "Ecce: duo viri adstiterunt iuxta illos in vestibus albis, qui et dixerunt, 'Viri Galilaei, quid statis aspicientes in caelum? Hic Iesus, qui adsumptus est a vobis in caelum, sic veniet quemadmodum vidistis eum euntem in caelum.'" (Behold: two men stood by them in white garments, who also said, "Ye men of Galilee, why stand you looking up to heaven? This Jesus, who is taken up from you into heaven, shall so come as you have seen him going into heaven.")

See further Szövérffy, 135–36.

89. *In terris adhuc positam*

In this hymn for Third Nocturn, Peter Abelard returns to the theme of the first Ascension hymn, in which Christ summons the perfected Church to join him in heaven, and he urges the Church, still rooted in earthly existence, to ascend to heaven in mind. Echoes of the psalms are audible throughout.

2.1   *Post te trahe me:* Compare Ct 1:3: "Trahe me; post te curremus" (Draw me; we will run after thee).

2.2   *nitenti dextram porrige:* This is a frequent theme in the psalms. Compare 138:10: "Even there also shall thy hand lead me, and thy right hand shall hold me." See also Ps 17:36: "Thy right hand hath held me up."

2.3   *Super pennas ventorum:* Compare Ps 17:11: "Volavit super pinnas ventorum" (He flew on the wings of the winds).

3.1–2   *Columbae pennas . . . properet:* See Ps 54:7: "Who will give me the wings like a dove's, and I will fly and be at rest?"

3.3   *Alas petat . . . aquilae:* Compare Is 40:31: "But they that hope in the Lord . . . shall take wings like as eagles *(adsument pinnas sicut aquilae).*"

4.1   *Dabit . . . oculos:* In order to gaze upon the Beatific Vision without being blinded, fresh eyes are required. This motif leads on from the earlier citation of eagles, for they have proverbially sharp sight. For the desire to gaze on God, see Ps 24:15: "My eyes are ever on the Lord."

4.2   *veri solis:* For Christ as the true Sun, see hymn 2.2, etc.

See further Szövérffy, 137–38.

90. *Cum in altum ascenderet*

This final hymn for the Ascension, sung at Lauds, visualizes the reaction of the angels at Christ's rising. They enquire about the identity of the new arrival and the reason for his triumphal entry into heaven. The souls that Christ has rescued from the clutches of Satan form two choirs who answer antiphonally with words adapted from Psalm 23.

1.1–4   *Cum in altum,* etc.: See Eph 4:8: "Ascendens in altum, captivam duxit captivitatem" (Ascending on high, he led captivity captive). This evocation persists throughout the entire stanza. The use of the neuter *ima* to express creatures from below may have been inspired by Horace, *Odes* 1.34.12–13: "God can exchange high and low *(ima summis),*" which in the context refers to persons.

2.3   *Chere:* The angels say "Greetings" (χαῖρε, chaîre) to Christ in

Greek; Peter Abelard may have derived knowledge of the word from the *Hymnos Acathistos,* the sixth-century hymn in honor of the Virgin.

3.1   *Illis . . . quaerentibus:* This openmouthed inquiry by the angels (they would surely have been aware of Christ's arrival!) is echoed in Abelard's *Sermon* 26 (*PL* 178.539–41, at 539B, cited by Szövérffy, 139): "Sicut ex dictis ecclesiasticorum doctorum collegimus, Domino ascendente in coelos quidam angelorum dubitantes vel potius admirantes de tanta glorificati hominis magnificentia, ceteros assistentes non semel interrogabant, 'Quis est iste rex gloriae?'" (As we have gathered from the words of the doctors of the church, when the Lord went up into the heavens, certain of the angels, doubting, or rather wondering, at this glorified man's extreme magnificence, standing by the others asked each other several times, "Who is this king of glory?")

4.1   *Quis est iste rex gloriae?:* So Ps 23:8: "Quis est iste Rex Gloriae? Dominus fortis et potens" (Who is this King of Glory? The Lord, who is strong and mighty). (Compare stanza 5.)

4.3   *de Edom veniens:* See Is 63:1: "Quis est iste qui venit de Edom?" (Who is this that cometh from Edom?). Edom was an alternative for Esau, and was then used to specify the land of Idumaea occupied by Esau and his descendants. Later it was used for Judea generally.

4.4   *purpureo vestitu:* Christ is clad in purple or crimson garments because of the blood he shed on the cross. See also Is 63:2–3.

5.3   *potens in proelio:* The evocation of Ps 23:8 continues: "Dominus fortis et potens, Dominus potens in proelio" (. . . the Lord mighty in battle).

See further Szövérffy, 139–40.

ADAM OF SAINT VICTOR

91. *Salve, mater Salvatoris*

Adam of Saint Victor, a Breton who entered the abbey of Saint Victor in Paris about 1130, is usually credited with having brought to perfection the later ("regular") form of the Sequence. This hymn is the most famous of his compositions and was composed for the feast of the Nativity of the Virgin Mary (September 8), to whom Adam is said to have had a special devotion. The hymn assembles many of the symbolic references to the Virgin garnered from the Old Testament.

1.2   *vas electum,* etc.: The celebrated description of Paul (Act 9:15: "vas electionis") is transferred to the Virgin Mary; *vas honoris* evokes 2 Tim 2:21: "If any man therefore shall cleanse himself . . . he shall be a vessel unto honor *(vas in honorem),* sanctified and profitable to the Lord." See also Rom 9:21: "An non habet potestatem figulus luti ex eadem massa facere aliud quidem vas in honorem, aliud vero in contumeliam?" (Or hath not the potter power over the clay, of the same lump to make one vessel unto honour, and another unto dishonour?)

1.5–6   *vas excisum manu Sapientiae:* A vessel chiseled, that is, by the Son, who is the wisdom of God (Lk 11:49, 1 Cor 1:24).

2.2   *flos de spina:* Compare Ct 2:2: "Sicut lilium inter spinas, sic amica mea inter filias" (As a lily among thorns, so is my love among the daughters).

2.4   *nos spinetum:* Perhaps evoking Lk 6:44: "Unaquaeque enim arbor de fructu suo cognoscitur. Neque enim de spinis colligunt ficus neque de rubo vindemiant uvam." (For every tree is known by its fruit. For men do not gather figs from thorns, nor from a bramble bush do they gather grapes.)

3.1   *Porta clausa, fons hortorum:* She is a "closed gate" because she remained a virgin. Compare Ez 44:2: "Porta haec clausa erit; non aperietur" (This gate shall be shut; it shall not be opened). She is "the fountain of gardens," from whom Wisdom (= Christ) has poured forth; the phrase *fons hortorum* is taken from Ct 4:15.

3.2–3   *cella . . . unguentorum, cella pigmentaria:* Compare Ct 1:3: "Post te curremus in odorem unguentorum tuorum. Introduxit me rex in cellaria sua." (We shall run after thee to the odor of thy ointments. The king hath brought me into his storerooms.) *Cella pigmentaria* in classical Latin would mean "a painted room"; in Medieval Latin it can mean "a store of spices."

3.4–6   *cinnamomi . . . fragrantia:* Evoking Sir 24:20–23: "Sicut cinnamomum et balsamum aromatizans odorem dedi. Quasi murra electa dedi suavitatem odoris, . . ." (I gave a sweet smell like cinnamon and aromatical balm. I yielded a sweet odor like the best myrrh.)

4.4–6   *Myrtus . . . rosa . . . nardus:* For the myrtle, see Is 55:13: "Instead of the nettle shall come up the myrtle tree." For the rose, Sir 39:17: "Bud forth as the rose planted by the brooks of waters." For the nard, Ct 1:11: "Nardus meus dedit odorem suum" (My spikenard gave forth the odor thereof).

5.1–5   *Tu convallis . . . singulare lilium:* The inspiration for this stanza is Ct 2.1, where the maiden cries: "Ego flos campi et lilium convallium" (I am the flower of the field and the lily of the valleys). The second line, *terra non arabilis,* refers to the perpetual virginity of Mary.

6.1   *caelestis paradisus:* Compare Ct 4:13: "Emissiones tuae paradisus malorum punicorum cum pomorum fructibus" (Thy plants are a paradise of pomegranates with the fruits of the orchard).

6.2–3   *Libanusque non incisus, vaporans dulcedinem:* This is an echo of Sir 24:21: "Quasi libanus non incisus vaporavi habitationem meam" (I perfumed my dwelling as the frankincense [i.e., cedar of Lebanon] not cut). The tall cedars of Lebanon with their fragrant odor are interpreted by the Fathers as symbolic of the saints, following Ps 103:16 ("The cedars of Lebanon which [God] hath planted") and Ps 91:13 ("The just . . . shall grow up like the cedar of Lebanon").

7.1   *thronus es Salomonis:* Solomon is the epitome of wisdom, and since Christ is depicted as the wisdom of God (see § 1 above), the reference here is to Mary as the throne of Christ; she is frequently depicted in sacred art with the infant Child on her knee.

7.4–5   *ebur . . . aurum:* See 3 Kings 10:18 (= 2 Par 9:17): "King Solomon also made a great throne of ivory and overlaid it with the finest gold *(auro fulvo nimis)*."

7.6   *praesignant mysteria:* Thus the ivory is the mystic symbol of Mary's chastity, and the gold of her charity.

8.1   *Palmam praefers singularem:* Since Adam has earlier made reference to the cedar of Lebanon, Ps 91:13 is probably evoked here: "The just shall flourish like the palm tree; he shall [be multiplied] as the cedar in Lebanon." *Palmam* may thus bear a double sense: Mary both manifests the uprightness of the palm tree, and as the greatest of saints she takes the palm, as the following lines indicate.

8.6   *privilegia:* Mary has "special rights" to virtues because of her chastity and charity emphasized in stanzas 7 above and 9 below, and also because of her humility as shown in the *Magnificat.*

10.3   *nobile triclinium: Triclinium,* strictly speaking, denotes the arrangement of couches on three sides of the dining table. But each couch housed three guests, and Mary by entertaining Christ houses the Trinity, for the three are inseparable (see Augustine, *De Trinitate* 1.5, 1.8, 15.23).

11.1   *stella maris:* See hymn 63. The play on *Maria/maris* ("Mary/sea") is impossible to reproduce.

12.1   *In procinctu:* The word in classical Latin is frequently used to express "readiness for battle," here envisaged as the struggle with Satan.

12.10   *configura:* Compare Phlp 3:21: "Qui reformabit corpus humilitatis nostrae, configuratum corpori claritatis suae" ([Christ] will reform [i.e., re-form, *reformabit*] the body of our lowness, made like to the body of his glory".

On Adam and his Marian symbolism see further Raby, *CLP* 363–75.

Philip the Chancellor

92. *Pange, lingua*

Philip of Paris, Chancellor of Notre Dame 1218–1236, notorious for his authoritarian ways (he excommunicated the Masters and scholars of the University of Paris on one occasion, he was an inveterate critic of Franciscans and Dominicans, and he attacked evidences of corruption in the Roman curia), reveals a different side as a talented hymnographer. The hymns which he composed in honor of Mary Magdalene are especially felicitous, as this example demonstrates. In his day it was commonly assumed that Mary Magdalene was the sinner who anointed Jesus's feet (Lk 7:37–50). The central theme of this hymn is that she who washed Christ physically was cleansed by him spiritually.

1.1	*Pange, lingua:* The exordium of a hymn of Fortunatus (20 above) was exploited also by Aquinas (98 below).
1.1	*Magdalenae:* The woman who washed Christ's feet was commonly identified with Mary Magdalene because a few verses later in Luke's gospel (8:2) Mary is named as one of the women exorcised of evil spirits. The women then accompany Jesus.
2.3–5	*lacrimarum fluvio,* etc.: So Lk 7:38: "Lacrimis coepit rigare pedes eius et capillis capitis sui tergebat . . ." (She began to wash his feet with tears and wiped them with the hairs of her head).
2.5–6	*culparum lavacrum promeruit:* So Lk 7:47: "Many sins are forgiven her, for she hath loved much."
3.1–6	*Suum lavit mundatorem,* etc.: The stanza happily plays on the mutual cleansing. Christ cleanses the woman spiritually as she cleanses him physically.
4.2	*nardum . . . pisticum:* The original Greek sense of *pisticus* is "trustworthy." From this develops the meaning of "genuine," and thereafter "costly."
4.4	*typum . . . mysticum:* The application of the oil was an outward sign of the inner process of her own cleansing.
5.3	*quia multum . . . dilexit:* Echoing Luke's "dilexit multum" (see 2.5–6n. above).
5.6	*facta est praenuntia:* Part of the "special grace" she was granted was to report the Resurrection to the apostles (Lk 24:10–25).
6.2	*paschalis hostia:* Compare 1 Cor 5:7: "Pascha nostrum immolatus est Christus" (Christ, our Pasch, is sacrificed). The motif is resumed in *agnus mente* (6.3), for Christ is the new paschal lamb.
6.6	*mortis . . . spolia:* The "spoils" are the faithful souls which he has rescued from hell.

See further Raby, *CLP* 399.

BONAVENTURE

93. *In passione Domini*

Bonaventure (1221–74), the greatest in the line of Franciscan theologians, was also a notable writer of hymns. Like other friars in the Order founded by Francis of Assisi, he focuses on the physical sufferings of Christ in his passion and crucifixion. This hymn was one of eight composed for the Office of the feast of the Holy Cross, and was sung at Matins. It is striking in its stark simplicity.

2.3–4   *coronam spineam,* etc.: See John 19:5–34.
3.3   *acetum . . . arundinem:* See Mk 15:36, Mt 27:34, John 19:29.
4.2   *inebrient:* The metaphor is in the spirit of Eph 5:18.
6.1–2   *vendito . . . prodito:* So Mt 26:14–15 and 48. Bonaventure concludes his hymn not with the conventional doxology of the Trinity, but with praise of Christ alone.
See further Raby, *CLP* 421–25.

[Stephen Langton]

94. *Veni, sancte Spiritus*

As noted in the Introduction (p. xviii), this "Golden Sequence" has been ascribed to a variety of authors, including Stephen Langton, archbishop of Canterbury, and Pope Innocent III, both of whose authorship is attested by contemporaries (see Raby, *CLP* 343). It is, however, now considered anonymous. The hymn is, appropriately, allocated to the mass for Pentecost.

1.1   *Veni, sancte Spiritus:* The influence of hymn 75 above, *Veni, creator Spiritus,* is evident in this exordium.
2.1   *pauper pauperum:* Paul identifies the Spirit closely with Jesus, and subsequently they are regarded as virtually identical. Thus here the poverty of Christ (see 2 Cor 8:9) is transferred to the Spirit.
2.2   *dator munerum:* See Is 11:2 for the seven gifts: "The spirit of wisdom and of understanding, the spirit of counsel and of fortitude, the spirit of knowledge and of godliness. And he shall be filled with the spirit of the fear of the Lord." Paul at Gal 5:22 lists the fruits as distinct from the gifts; these are nine in number, but in the Latin Vulgate they are twelve because owing to scribal insertions three are doublets of three in Paul's list. See D. O'Connor's edition of Aquinas, *Summa Theologiae* 1a 2a, 68–70 (Blackfriars ed., vol. 24; London, 1974), app. 7. Also compare hymn 75.3.1n. above.

3.1   *Consolator:* This becomes the usual interpretation of the Greek word παράκλητος (*paráklētos,* "Paraclete"), which strictly means "advocate." Origen first proposed the sense of "consoler" to express the notion that the Holy Spirit consoles us, Christ having left the earth at the Ascension.

9.3   *sacrum septenarium:* For the seven gifts, see 2.2n. above. See further Raby, *CLP* 343–44.

[Thomas of Celano]

95. *Dies irae*

This hymn has been traditionally assigned to Thomas of Celano, contemporary and biographer of Francis of Assisi; more recently, this ascription, made by the Dominican Bartholomew of Pisa, has been challenged with the claim that Thomas merely revised a twelfth-century text of Benedictine origin and infused it with a more penitential flavor. The hymn was first composed as a *tropus* (an unauthorized meditation inserted into the liturgy), but it was soon incorporated as a Sequence in the Mass for All Souls, and subsequently in requiem masses generally, the last six lines being added for that purpose. The hymn is a scriptural meditation on the day of judgment, contrasting the Old Testament God of judgment with the New Testament Christ of mercy; so the first seven stanzas contain a stream of expressions depicting grim fear. But then in the eighth, the God of fearsome majesty makes way for the source of fatherly love, and thereafter we are instructed on the limits to which he will go to find and save us.

1.1   *Dies irae, dies illa:* As with much medieval devotional poetry, the hymn begins with scriptural evocation. The prophet Zephaniah (1:15) declaims: "Dies irae dies illa, dies tribulationis et angustiae . . ." (That day is a day of wrath, a day of tribulation and distress . . .).

1.2   *solvet saeclum in favilla:* Evoking the destruction of Sodom and Gomorrah; see Gen 19:28: "And [Abraham] saw the ashes rise up (*ascendentem favillam*) . . ."

1.3   *teste David cum Sibylla:* David was believed to be the author of all the psalms, many of which allude to the Final Judgment. See, for example, 51:7–8, 74:3–4, 95:13, 97:9. Augustine devotes a chapter

of his *City of God* (18.23) to a prophecy of the Sibyl of Erythrae, a long extract of which depicts the destruction of the world at the Last Judgment.

2.2   *quando iudex est venturus:* Mt 24–25 and Apc 20:11–15 lie behind this and what follows.

3.1   *Tuba mirum sparget sonum:* See Mt 24:31: "And he will send his angels with a trumpet *(tuba)* uttering a loud call . . ."

3.2–3   *per sepulcra . . . ante thronum:* Compare Apc 20:11–12: "And I saw a great white throne and one sitting upon it, from whose face the earth and heaven fled away, and there was no place found for them. And I saw the dead great and small, standing in the presence of the throne . . ."

5.1–3   *Liber scriptus,* etc.: See Mal 3:16; Apc 20:12, "Alius liber apertus est . . . et iudicati sunt mortui ex his quae scripta erant in libris secundum opera ipsorum" (Another book was opened . . . and the dead were judged by those things which were written in the books, according to their works).

6.1   *censebit:* This is the original reading, replaced by *sedebit* in the more modern settings of the *Dies irae.*

7.3   *dum . . . sit:* In Medieval Latin, *dum* with the subjunctive is found bearing the causal sense which in classical Latin is rendered by *cum* with the subjunctive.

8.1–3   *tremendae maiestatis . . . fons pietatis:* This is the hinge of the hymn, in which the image of the fearsome Father gives place before the devoted love of the Son.

9.2   *tuae viae:* I render "your journey" here as denoting the journey from heaven to earth, embracing the whole of Christ's life on earth, rather than merely the journey to Calvary. This interpretation is supported by the following note.

10.1   *sedisti lassus:* With reference to the meeting at the well with the Samaritan woman. Compare John 4:6: "Iesus ergo, fatigatus ex itinere, sedebat sic super fontem" (Being wearied with his journey, [Jesus] sat thus on the well). The woman represents those who receive the word beyond Israel.

13.1   *Mariam:* That is, Mary Magdalene. For her identification with the woman who washed and anointed Christ's feet and was granted pardon for her sins (Lk 7:37–50), see hymn 92.1n.

13.2   *latronem:* The Good Thief: see Lk 23:42–43.

15.1–2   *oves . . . haedis:* See Mt 25:33: "Statuet oves quidem a dextris suis, hedos autem a sinistris" (He will set the sheep on his right hand, but the goats on the left). Raby notes that the judgment scene is depicted over doorways and in windows of the cathedrals of this period (443).

16.1–2   *Confutatis . . . addictis:* See Mt 25:41: "Discedite a me, maledicti, in ignem aeternum, qui paratus est diabolo et angelis eius" (Depart from me, you cursed, into everlasting fire, which was prepared for the devil and his angels).

17.2   *cor contritum quasi cinis:* Evoking the humble posture of Abraham at Gen 18:27: "Since I am dust and ashes *(cinis)*."

17.[4–9]   *homo . . . huic:* In the appended six lines, I take *homo . . . huic* as referring to mankind in general, a sense which accords with *eis* in the final line.

See further Raby, *CLP* 443–52.

Saint Thomas Aquinas

96. *Lauda, Sion, Salvatorem*

When Pope Urban IV in 1264 established the feast of Corpus Christi, which was to be celebrated on the Thursday after Trinity Sunday, Thomas Aquinas was entrusted with the task of composing the Office and the Mass for the day. This famous (and very skillful) hymn was written as the Sequence. The theological precision of the hymn squares exactly with the explanation of the Eucharist in Aquinas's *Summa Theologiae* 3a, 73–83, composed a few years later.

1.1   *Lauda, Sion:* The citadel of Jerusalem is frequently cited as a title of the *civitas Dei,* the city of God, which is the Church in this world and heaven in the next.

2.4   *in sacrae mensa cenae:* See Mt 26:20–30.

3.4   *dies . . . sollemnis:* Corpus Christi 1264.

3.4–5   Aquinas has recourse to hypermetrical lines here to emphasize the connection between the feast and the Last Supper *(prima institutio mensae).*

4.2–3   *novum Pascha . . . vetus:* See Dt 16:2: "You shall sacrifice the *phase* to the Lord your God." The *phase* (Hebrew for "passing over" [*transitus*]) denotes (the ceremony of) the paschal lamb, the Passover; for Christ as the new Passover offering, see 1 Cor 5:7: "Pascha nostrum immolatum est Christus" (Christ, our Pasch, has been sacrificed).

4.5   *umbram . . . veritas:* The old Pasch is the foreshadowing *(umbra)* of the coming of Christ and his passion and crucifixion, the true Passover.

5.3   *in sui memoriam:* So Lk 22:19: "Hoc facite in meam commemorationem" (Do this in memory of me).

5.5–6   *in salutis . . . hostiam:* "As the victim that brings salvation."

6.1–6   *Dogma . . . ordinem:* With this whole stanza compare 98.4.

6.2–3   *in carnem . . . in sanguinem:* So Mt 26:26 and 28.

7.1   *Sub diversis speciebus:* The bread and wine are mere signs *(signa)* of the reality *(res)* of Christ's body.

8.4–9.1 *sumit unus, sumit mille . . . sumunt boni, sumunt mali:* Unless there is some other common source, the hymn here oddly seems to exploit the jingle of a twelfth-century drinking song, *In taberna quando sumus (Carmina Burana* 196): "Bibit ille, bibit illa, bibit servus cum ancilla, . . . bibit ista, bibit ille, / bibit centum, bibit mille" (He drinks, she drinks, with a maid a slave drinks, she drinks, he drinks, a hundred drink, a thousand drink).

10.1   *Fracto . . . sacramento:* During the Mass the priest breaks the consecrated bread for distribution to the congregation.

11.1   *panis angelorum:* Compare John 6:50: "Hic est panis de caelo descendens" (This is the bread which cometh down from heaven"); also 6:59.

11.4   *non mittendus canibus:* So Mt 7:6: "Nolite dare sanctum canibus" (Give not that which is holy to dogs).

11.6–8   *Isaac . . . agnus Paschae . . . manna:* See Gen 22:2–18; Ex 12:3–28, 16:4–35.

12.1   *panis vere:* Compare John 6:32: "panem . . . verum" (the true bread); also 6:35, 48: "Ego sum panis vitae" (I am the bread of life); 6:51: "panis vivus, qui de caelo descendi" (the living bread, which came down from heaven).

See further Raby, *CLP* 405–8.

97. *Verbum supernum prodiens*

In his compositions for the Office and Mass of Corpus Christi, Aquinas assigned this hymn to Lauds, a position it retains in the revised Breviary today. The final two stanzas are familiar to many as the first hymn sung at Benediction of the Blessed Sacrament.

1.1   *Verbum supernum prodiens:* Aquinas here exploits the exordium of a pre-Carolingian hymn, *Verbum supernum prodiens / a patre olim exiens* (on which, see Walpole, 302–4). In that hymn reference is to the procession of Son from the Father, and not to the descent of the Son in the Incarnation, as here.

2.1–4   *discipulo . . . tradendus . . . se tradidit discipulis:* Contrast between betrayal by Judas and Jesus's self-giving is accentuated by the repetition of the verb in *tradendus . . . se tradidit;* self-giving precedes *(prius)* betrayal.

3.3–4   *ut . . . totum cibaret hominem:* The theme of self-giving continues ("feeding them with his whole human person, consisting of the double substance"). This is the correct sense of *totum hominem,* not "the whole of mankind."

4.1   *socium:* That is, he "associated himself" with the human race.

4.4   *in praemium:* The reward is the conferment of the Eucharist.

5.1–2   *hostia, quae caeli pandis ostium:* Note the play *hostia . . . ostium.* In the tradition of the Latin Fathers, emphasis is laid on the Redemption as the expiation of sins through Christ's sacrificial death.

See further Raby, *CLP* 409–10.

98. *Pange, lingua*

This, the best known of Aquinas's Corpus Christi hymns, was and is appointed to be sung at First Vespers; but it is also the processional hymn on Holy Thursday, when, following celebration of the Eucharist, the consecrated hosts are borne to the Altar of Repose to be distributed on Good Friday. The final two stanzas are familiar to many as the second hymn in Benediction of the Blessed Sacrament.

1.1   *Pange, lingua, gloriosi:* The exordium echoes the opening words of the celebrated hymn of Fortunatus (hymn 20 above).

1.2   *mysterium:* The Greek word at Eph 5:32 is rendered in the Latin Vulgate as *sacramentum.* Aquinas deploys it here to indicate that the sacrament of the Eucharist contains the mysterious presence of Christ.

1.5   *fructus ventris generosi:* So Elizabeth at Lk 1:42: "Benedictus fructus ventris tui" (Blessed is the fruit of your womb). The word *generosi* may bear the double sense of "highborn" (following the genealogy at Mt 1:1–16) and "noble" in the moral sense.

2.6   *miro clausit ordine:* That is, the "wondrous ordering" of Last Supper, Passion, and Crucifixion.

3.2   *recumbens:* The ancients typically ate meals lying on their sides on couches.

3.3–4   *observata lege plene cibis in legalibus:* Jesus observed the Law fully by celebrating the Passover at the prescribed time, and by consuming the paschal lamb *(cibis in legalibus).*

3.5   *cibus:* The play in *cibis/cibus* reminds us that Christ is become the paschal lamb.

4.2   *verbo carnem efficit:* Referring to the biblical formula of the consecration (Mt 26:26–29).

4.5   *ad firmandum:* That is, to strengthen hearts in belief in the Real Presence.

5.3   *documentum:* An "example serving as precedent" (so *OLD*) of the Passover.

See further Raby, *CLP* 408–9.

[SAINT THOMAS AQUINAS]

99. *Adoro devote*

This hymn does not belong to the group composed by Aquinas for Corpus Christi, and the authorship remains uncertain, since there is no contemporary evidence to ascribe it to Aquinas. A. Wilmart's exhaustive study could declare only a *non liquet,* but Raby more positively argues for Aquinas as author.

1.1   *latens veritas:* The reading is preferable to *deitas,* because Christ's humanity as well as his divinity lies hidden; see 3.2 below.

2.3   *Credo quidquid dixit,* etc.: He thinks especially of the words of Christ (Mt 26:26–28) repeated at the Consecration of the Mass.

3.4   *quod petivit latro:* See Lk 23:42.

4.1   *sicut Thomas:* So John 20:26–29.

5.4   *dulce sapere:* Evoking Ps 33:9: "suavis est Dominus" (the Lord is sweet) and 1 Pet 2:3: "dulcis Dominus" (the Lord is sweet).

6.1   *Pie pellicane:* The verse at Ps 101:7, "Similis factus sum pelicano solitudinis" (I am become like to a pelican of the wilderness), could be interpreted as an image describing Christ's victory over Satan, for there was a tradition (see Paulinus of Nola, *Ep.* 40.6) that the bird batters snakes into submission and devours them. But more influential here is the medieval tradition that the mother bird draws off her own blood with which to feed her young; this is seen as symbolizing Christ's gift of his blood in the Eucharist. See Lampen, "Pie Pelicane, Iesu Domine," 68–92.

See further Raby, *CLP,* 410–11; A. Wilmart, *Recherches de théologie ancienne et médiévale* 1 (1929): 21–40, 149–76.

Anonymous

100. *Stabat mater*

The authorship of this celebrated hymn has long been debated. The authorship of Innocent III (Pope 1198–1216) has been widely canvassed, but rests on no contemporary witness. A more credible candidate is the Franciscan Jacopone da Todi (d. 1306), author of the vernacular *Donna del Paradiso,* for the hymn is ascribed to him in three codices of the fourteenth or fifteenth centuries. Though the ascription remains uncertain (see Raby's discussion), the poem is certainly characteristic of Franciscan spirituality, with its intense concentration on the sufferings of Christ and his mother.

1.1   *Stabat mater:* Her presence at the Crucifixion is not attested in the synoptic gospels, but at John 19:25 she stands near the cross and is entrusted to the beloved disciple.

1.6   *pertransivit gladius:* As prophesied by Simeon at the Circumcision. So Lk 2:35: "Tuam ipsius animam pertransiet gladius" (Thy own soul a sword shall pierce).

2.2   *benedicta:* So Gabriel at Lk 1:28: "Benedicta tu in mulieribus" (Blessed art thou among women), perhaps echoed here with a hint of irony.

4.1   *suae gentis:* The whole of mankind, not merely the Jewish race.

4.3   *flagellis subditum:* So Mt 27:26: "[Pilate,] having scourged Jesus *(Iesum . . . flagellatum),* delivered him to them to be crucified."

5.1   *fons amoris:* As the mother of Christ she is the source of love, for Christ is God (so 5.5 below), and "God is love" (1 John 4:8).

8.1   *Virgo virginum:* A title of Mary which appears in several twelfth-century litanies and devotional hymns, as in the later Litany of Loreto.

9.2   *cruce hac inebriari:* Compare Bonaventure's hymn *In passione Domini* (93.4.2 above): "May all these things [viz. the sufferings of Christ] gorge us and inspire sweet drunkenness *(inebrient)."*

See further Raby, *CLP* 436–43.

Bibliography

PREVIOUS EDITIONS, TRANSLATIONS, AND COMMENTARIES OF
THE HYMNS IN THIS VOLUME

Ambrose

Fontaine, Jacques, ed. *Hymnes/Ambroise de Milan.* Paris: Editions du Cerf, 1992.

Bede

Fraipont, Johannes, ed. *Bedae Venerabilis Liber Hymnorum.* Corpus Christianorum, Series Latina 122: 405–70. Turnhout: Brepols, 1955.

Columba of Iona

Bernard, John Henry, and Robert Atkinson. *The Irish Liber Hymnorum.* 2 vols. London: Henry Bradshaw Society, 1898.
Clancy, Thomas Owen, and Gilbert Markus. *Iona.* Edinburgh, 1995.

The New Hymnal

Milfull, Inge B. *The Hymns of the Anglo-Saxon Church.* New York: Cambridge University Press, 1996.
Wieland, Gernot R. *The Canterbury Hymnal.* Toronto: Pontifical Institute of Mediaeval Studies, 1982.

BIBLIOGRAPHY

Peter Abelard

Szövérffy, Joseph. *Peter Abelard's Hymnarius Paraclitensis.* 2 vols. Albany: Classical Folia, 1975.

Prudentius

Assendelft, Marion M. van. *Sol ecce surgit igneus: A Commentary on the Morning and Evening Hymns of Prudentius.* Groningen: Bouma's Boekhuis, 1976.

Bergman, J., ed. *Carmina.* Corpus Scriptorum Ecclesiasticorum Latinorum 61. Vienna: Academia Litterarum Caesarae Vindobonensis, 1926.

Dressel, Albert. *Aurelii Prudentii Clementis quae exstant carmina.* Leipzig: Hermann Mendelssohn, 1860.

Eagan, M. Clement, trans. *Poems of Prudentius.* Washington: Catholic University of American Press, 1962.

Hrabanus Maurus

Lausberg, H. *Der Hymnus Veni Creator Spiritus.* Opisden: Westdeutscher Verlag, 1979.

Theodulf of Orléans

Dümmler et al., eds. *Monumenta Germaniae Historica: Poetae Latini aevi Carolini.* 4 vols. Berlin: Weidmann, 1877.

Sirmond, Jacques. *Opera varia,* vol. 2. Venice?, 1728.

Various

Mone, Franz Joseph. *Lateinische hymnen des mittelalters.* 3 vols. Freiburg im Breisgau: Herder, 1853–1855.

Walpole, Arthur Sumner. *Early Latin Hymns.* Cambridge, 1922.

504

Secondary Works Cited

Boylan, Patrick. *The Psalms: A Study of the Vulgate Psalter in the Light of the Hebrew Text*, 2nd edn. 2 vols. Dublin: Gill, 1926.

Burn, Andrew Ewbank. *The Hymn* Te Deum *and Its Author.* London: Faith Press, 1926.

Davidson, Ivor J. *De officiis/Ambrose.* Oxford, 2011.

Devos, Paul. "La date du voyage d'Égérie." *Analecta Bollandiana* 85 (1967): 165–94.

Favez, Charles. *La consolation latine chrétienne.* Paris: Librairie philosophique J. Vrin, 1937.

Gough, Michael. *Ancient Peoples and Places.* Vol. 19, *The Early Christians.* London: Thames and Hudson, 1961.

Homes Dudden, Frederick. *The Life and Times of St. Ambrose.* 2 vols. Oxford, 1935.

Julian, John, ed. *A Dictionary of Hymnology,* rev. ed. London: J. Murray, 1915.

Kähler, Ernst. *Studien zum Te Deum und zur Geschichte des 24. Psalms in der Alten Kirche.* Göttingen: Vandenhoeck and Ruprecht, 1958.

Lampen, W. "Pie Pelicane, Iesu Domine," *Antonianum* 21 (1946): 68–92.

Mohrmann, Christine. *Études sur le latin des chrétiens.* 3 vols. Rome: Edizioni di storia e letteratura, 1958.

———. "A propos de deux mots controversés de la latinité chrétienne: tropaeum—nomen," *Vigiliae Christianae,* 8.3 (July 1954): 154–73

Nauroy, Gerard. "Le martyre de Laurent dans l'hymnodie et la prédication des IVe et Ve siècles, et l'authenticité ambrosienne de l'hymne 'Apostolorum supparem,'" *Revue des Études Augustiniennes* 35 (1989): 44–82.

Power, Eileen. *Medieval Women.* Cambridge, 1975.

Raby, Frederic James Edward. *A History of Christian-Latin Poetry from the Beginnings to the Close of the Middle Ages,* 2nd ed. Oxford, 1953.

Rahner, H. *Greek Myths and Christian Mystery.* London: Burns and Oates, 1963.

Rist, John M. *Stoic Philosophy.* Cambridge, 1969.

Roca-Puig, R. *Himne a la Verge Maria, "Psalmus Responsorius": papir llatí del segle IV.* Barcelona: Asociación de Bibliófilos de Barcelona, 1965.

Sandbach, F. H. *The Stoics.* Chatto and Windus: London, 1975.

Stevenson, J. "Altus Prosator," *Celtica* 23 (1999): 326–68.

von den Steinen, W. *Notker der Dichter und seine geistige Welt.* 2 vols. Bern, 1948.

Walsh, P. G. "Golias and Goliardic Poetry," *Medium Aevum* 52 (1983): 1–9.

Young, Karl. *The Drama of the Medieval Church.* Oxford, 1933.

GENERAL REFERENCE WORKS

Copleston, Frederick Charles. *A History of Philosophy.* 9 vols. Garden City, N.Y.: Image Books, 1962.

Woodcock, E. C. *A New Latin Syntax.* Cambridge, Mass.: Harvard University Press, 1959.

Index of Incipits

General Index

promised the Spirit, 56.1.3, 75.3.3
right hand of, 53.3.4, 54.2.1–2
Felix. *See* Nabor and Felix (martyrs)
"Fraud" (personified), 83.3

Gabriel, 63.2.2
insemination of Mary, 62.3.2
prediction of Christ, 19.5.2, 66.2.3
Galilee, 29.6.3, 29.8.2, 76.5.4
Gehenna, 64.13.9
Genesis, 64.15.4
Gentiles, Christ as redeemer of, 5.2.1
Gervasius and Protasius (martyrs), 11
God, 6.5, 9.1, 15.1.2, 28.6.2
arrival prefigured by dawn, 16.12
as creator, 1.1.1, 4.1.1, 6.6.1, 18.1, 18.33.2, 25.1.1, 26.1, 27.1.2, 30.2.1, 31.3.3, 35.1.1, 39.1.2, 43.1.1, 44.1–2, 45.1–2, 46.1–3, 47.1–2, 52.1.1, 64.1.1, 64.5–6, 68.1.1
as guide of martyrs, 12.2.4
as healer, 39.3.1–2
as judge, 64.18, 68.4.1
as light, 25.1.2–4, 27.1.1
as redeemer, 72.5.1
as ruler, 17.3.4, 18.2.1, 18.42, 21.4.4, 28.13.1, 36.1.1, 64.17.1–2
as ruler, of heaven, 4.1.2, 27.1, 46.1.1
as source of light, 34.1.1–2

birth of, 3.8
city of, 74.22
devotion of, 44.3.1
faith in, 32.1.1
glory of, 24.4.4, 30.1.3, 56.5.4
grace of, 34.4.3, 44.3.2
martyrs of, 59.1, 12.4.2
mercy of, 39.1.1, 51.6.2–4, 52.2.3–4
on high, 34.3.1
power of, 4.8.3, 36.1.1, 37.1.1, 39.1.3, 64.12.1
praise of, 15.1.1, 24.4.4, 25.3.2, 26.3, 28.1.3, 28.13.3–4, 33.1.1, 42.2.3, 52.3.3
prayer to, 24.1.2, 39.2.1–2, 59.4
removal of death by, 18.5–6
removal of sins by, 51.8.1, 57.6.3, 72.3
restoration of sight by, 18.20.3–4
restorative power of, 18.35.2, 18.38.1–2
right hand of, 3.8.4, 15.7.1
submission to, 17.22
unity of, 4.8.3, 97.6.1
word of, 6.3.2
Goliath, 85.1
Greek people, speaking in tongues, 56.6.2

Hebrew people, 74.7, 74.13–14, 84.1.3
hell, 64.13
Christ's journey to and back, 5.6.3, 16.17.4, 53.3.1–2, 88.1.3–4
Herod, 19.8.1, 19.10.3